T0402522

Performing the Greek Crisis

Studies in Dance: Theories and Practices

Series Editorial Board

TITLES IN THE SERIES:

Performing the Greek Crisis: Navigating National Identity in the Age of Austerity
by Natalie Zervou

Kinethic California: Dancing Funk and Disco Era Kinships by Naomi Macalalad Bragin

Inhabiting the Impossible: Dance and Experimentation in Puerto Rico,
edited by Susan Homar and Nibia Pastrana Santiago

The Body in Crisis: New Pathways and Short Circuits in Representation by Christine Greiner

Corporeal Politics: Dancing East Asia, edited by Katherine Mezur and Emily Wilcox

dance
studies
association

The Dance Studies Association (DSA) advances the field of dance studies through research, publication, performance, and outreach to audiences across the arts, humanities, and social sciences. As a constituent member of the American Council of Learned Societies, DSA holds annual conferences; publishes new scholarship through its book series, proceedings, and Conversations Across the Field of Dance Studies; collaborates regularly with peer institutions in the United States and abroad; and presents yearly awards for exemplary scholarship. A complete list of books in the series can be found on the University of Michigan website, www.press.umich.edu.

Performing the Greek Crisis

*Navigating National Identity
in the Age of Austerity*

Natalie Zervou

University of Michigan Press
Ann Arbor

For questions or permissions, please contact um.press.perms@umich.edu.

Published in the United States of America by the
University of Michigan Press
Manufactured in the United States of America
Printed on acid-free paper
First published May 2024

A CIP catalog record for this book is available from the British Library.

Library of Congress Cataloging-in-Publication data has been applied for.

ISBN: 978-0-472-07675-8 (hardcover : alk. paper)
ISBN: 978-0-472-05675-0 (paper : alk. paper)
ISBN: 978-0-472-90443-3 (open access ebook)

DOI: https://doi.org/10.3998/mpub.12473027

The University of Michigan Press's open access publishing program is made possible thanks to additional funding from the University of Michigan Office of the Provost and the generous support of contributing libraries.

*For Artemis—in awe of your inquisitiveness and curiosity.
For all the dancers and artists in Greece—this work would not
have a reason to exist if it were not for you.*

Contents

Digital materials related to this title can be found on the Fulcrum platform
via the following citable URL: https://doi.org/10.3998/mpub.12473027

Illustrations

A Note on Transliteration and Translation

All Greek terms referenced in this work are listed in the Greek alphabet and have been transcribed for English readers following the UN's system, adopted in 1987 and based on the ELOT 743 conversion system of the Greek Standardization Organization (UN Department of Technical Cooperation for Development 1988).

The original language of some of the works referenced is Greek and German. I have translated all passages into English and make it clear whenever it is my translation. All interviews are also translated by me unless the original language of the interview was in English.

Acknowledgments

When I first moved to the US to pursue graduate studies in 2010, I still considered Greece my "home." Even though I knew that I would likely not return anytime soon, I refused to let go of that attachment. In some ways, this research was born out of a personal need to understand my experience and contextualize my complicated and increasingly nostalgic relationship with the place I grew up in, which still holds all my childhood memories. As a reading of this book will render clear, the personal is woven with the scholarly as my attempts to contextualize the Greek crisis and to capture the fluctuating landscape of the arts coincided with a need to cultivate and maintain vibrant ties to the community I viewed as my home. Reflecting on the last ten years when this work flourished, I am overwhelmed with gratitude for everyone who helped bring *Performing the Greek Crisis* to fruition.

First and foremost, my appreciation is extended to the dancers, artists, and choreographers, without whose vision, creativity, and hard work there would not be a reason to write this book. I cannot thank you enough for your time, generosity, and your persistence. Although many of you did not know me, you generously opened your homes, invited me to your studios, shared your creative processes, and let me into your world. Your creativity and your works are what breathes life into this book. The performing arts, especially dance, are consistently undervalued in Greece, and artists often fight to legitimize their profession and ensure fundamental labor rights. More often than not, this labor goes unacknowledged. I hope that this book does justice to your persistent efforts.

The seed for this research was planted during my PhD in *critical dance studies* at UC Riverside. The inspiring scholarship of Marta Savigliano, my dissertation advisor and mentor, was the reason I decided to move halfway across the world to pursue doctoral studies. I am forever indebted to her for helping me shape this project in its early stages and for her critical guidance. I also extend my deep gratitude to my dissertation committee members, Anthea Kraut and Linda Tomko. Their scholarship, teaching, and mentorship inform my work and writing daily. Thank you also to Jens Giersdorf and Jacqueline Shea Murphy for their early feedback, which helped shape this research into what it has become. I owe special thanks to Susan Ossman, who created a welcoming space for experimentation, where I could critically contextualize and embody the nuance of a diasporic serial migratory identity. In Ossman's *Moving Matters Traveling Workshops,* I had a chance to collaborate with Priya Srinivasan and experiment with meaningful ways of bridging theory and practice. Our late-night chats during this workshop helped me solidify my voice as a scholar.

While these professors' mentorship was central to developing this book, countless other scholars I have crossed paths with have deeply impacted my work. Thank you to Susan Manning, Janice Ross, and Rebecca Schneider for facilitating the Mellon Workshops in *Dance Studies in/and the Humanities.* The feedback I received in these workshops and the community they fostered have been indispensable in my trajectory from graduate student to junior faculty member. Thank you also to all dance and theater colleagues who engaged with draft excerpts of this writing at the Mellon School of Theater and Performance Research at Harvard University. While colleagues and peers from US institutions offered significant feedback in the writing process, I am indebted to all the dance scholars, dance reviewers, and critics from Greece who contributed their thoughts and feedback on the content and the framing of this work. Thank you for opening your homes to me or spending time tucked in cozy coffee shops in Athens, patiently sifting through ideas. Betina Panagiotara, Anastasios Koukoutas, Natalia Koutsougera, Stergiani Tsintziloni, Katia Savrami, Vasso Barboussi, Maria Tsoukala, and Irene Loutzaki, thank you for your time and the conversations we have had.

Embarking on this long research journey would not have been possible without financial support from various institutions. I am indebted to the scholarship support I received from the Alexander S. Onassis Public Benefit Foundation for pursuing studies abroad. Without this scholarship, it would have never been possible for me to study in the USA. The Dissertation Year Fellowship from UC Riverside made it possible to embark on ethnographic fieldwork in the early stages of this project, and I am forever grateful for this opportunity. As junior faculty, the University of Wisconsin—Madison Office of the Vice Chancellor for Research and Graduate Education provided support for this research with funding from the Wisconsin Alumni Research Foundation.

The shaping of this research into a book manuscript and continuous field-work was completed after I joined UW Madison. I appreciate the support of all my colleagues at the Dance Department in this process and, in particular, the mentorship of Andrea Harris. At the dawn of the pandemic, I received the First Book Program award from the University of Wisconsin—Madison Center for the Humanities, which provides collegiate support for junior faculty revising their first book. The feedback I received from senior colleagues Andrea Harris, Laurie Beth Clark, Laura McClure, Chris Garlough, and Pam Potter was pivotal in getting the manuscript into publishable shape. I am so grateful for their time and considerate feedback, especially since our meeting took place in April 2020, when the world had just stopped.

To Studies in Dance series editor Clare Croft, thank you for shepherding me through the publishing process, believing in this work, and supporting it from its early stages. Thank you to the anonymous readers for their close reading of my work. Their constructive feedback transformed and strengthened this manuscript. I also extend my appreciation to Senior Editor LeAnn Fields for the guidance and to the whole production team at the University of Michigan Press.

I was fortunate to work with different research assistants in the near decade it took to shape this research into a book. Lauren Gerlowski spent a summer crafting the two maps in this book and generously responded to every request for additions and changes I forwarded her. Konstantinos Papakostas helped with the Greek transcriptions of interview recordings and data collection. Lauren Lynch assisted with formatting, source organization, and image acquisition. Finally, Caitriona Quirk assisted with many tasks in the manuscript's final push. Thank you all for your work. Your assistance has been indispensable.

Immense thanks also go to my close friend and writing buddy Meghan Quinlan, who was always ready to read drafts and encouraged me to keep going. Even though we are not in the same state anymore, it always felt like she was right there with me throughout the entire process. Gratitude is also extended to Liz Sexe for closely reading several iterations of various chapters and for approaching my writing with curiosity and generosity. Thank you both for always asking me the challenging questions that needed answering and pushing me to grow.

Writing a book is a curiously solitary process that, at the same time, takes a village to accomplish. Beyond all the scholars, colleagues, and writing buddies who contributed to this process, I could not have achieved such a feat without the support of my family and friends. Thank you to my family in

Greece for always providing a home and especially to my mother for always believing in me and supporting me unconditionally. To my friend Kostas, who has always been eager to help track any resource needed and trace legislations and governmental decrees, thank you for always being a phone call away despite the eight-hour time difference. To my friends in Madison, who are more like a chosen family, thank you for believing in me and cheering me on. To my partner, Paris, who has been with me throughout this lengthy journey, thank you for reading every draft, scrap of paper, and Post-it note I have ever written and for patiently helping me sift through ideas. This book would not have been possible without your unwavering support. I know it may not be customary to thank pets, but they do provide unquestionably loving support. So, with that said, Cassie, my little furry friend, who has been my sidekick since 2015 and has traveled across the Atlantic multiple times to accompany me on extended research trips, thank you for warming my lap during countless writing sessions. Lastly, to Artemis, my child, who is four years old as I write this, you have changed me and this work more than you will ever know. Even though you won't remember this, you were there when this work took its shape. I sat on a yoga ball, typing away with you wrapped to my chest. This book is for you and all the dancers and artists in Greece.

· · ·

Special thanks to those who granted permission to reproduce previously published material. Some performances discussed in chapters 2 and 3 were initially analyzed in *Futures of Dance Studies* (2020), edited by Susan Manning, Janice Ross, and Rebecca Schneider. Reprinted by permission of the University of Wisconsin Press. © 2020 by the Board of Regents of the University of Wisconsin System. All rights reserved. Arguments and ideas explored in chapter 5 originally appeared in my articles "Fragments of the European Refugee Crisis: Performing Displacement and the Re-Shaping of Greek Identity," *TDR (The Drama Review)* 234 (Summer 2017): 32–48; and in "Emerging Frameworks for Engaging Precarity and 'Otherness' in Greek Contemporary Dance Performances," *Dance Research Journal* 51, no. 1 (2019): 20–31 (special issue on precariousness).

Introduction

It was the last day of October 2015 when I attended Rootlessroot's (2015) performance *Europium* [*The end of the world will be better this year*][1] at the Onassis Stegi in Athens, Greece. Europium, the chemical element, is known for its volatile and unpredictable nature, much like the narratives circulating internationally about Greeks during the Greek financial crisis. Its abbreviation, Eu, is a reference to the European Union (EU) and the fragile balances between Greece, at the time considered the most volatile economy in the EU, and its lenders, the comparatively "healthier" economies.

Tall wooden pillars stand erect in a crescent shape at the back of the stage. The dancers have carefully positioned them there one by one. Sweat glistens on their exposed limbs, evidencing their hard work. A white light illuminates the center of the stage. The pillars in the background are barely visible through the shadows in a faint yellow hue. Two dancers lurk in the dark behind the large wooden poles giving them gentle nudges, so they tilt forward to be caught by one of the others right before they hit the ground. Dancer Paul Blackman walks onstage holding a microphone tripod stand and, standing under the center light, enthusiastically addresses the audience. "Oh my gosh! . . . Isn't it amazing what we're trying to do here?" he asks, looking around him as the other four performers (Linda Kapetanea, Jacob Ingram-Dodd, Konstantina Efthymiadou, and Manuel Ronda) are tearing down the remaining wooden pillars to construct the *raft of Medusa*.

According to the performance program, the *raft of Medusa* refers to the true story of the French frigate *Méduse*, which sank in 1810 because the captain, appointed in an act of political preferment, was unable to navigate it. "I know what you're looking for, though," Blackman continues, grasping the microphone stand firmly with both hands. "You're looking for this smooth, seamless, almost invisible transition, right? But unfortunately, we are all going through a very chaotic moment in history. And that is exactly why I wanted to thank you all for coming to see us." He looks straight at the audience with his hand resting on his chest in a gesture expressing genuine gratitude. "It's really hard to leave your home right now, so really, thank you for coming!" His monologue continues as the dancers behind him work tirelessly to build the wooden raft structure. A few pillars form the base, and a dozen others are resting on top of them perpendicularly at a slight incline. One piece protrudes vertically in their midst, serving as the raft's mast.

In his oration, Blackman advocates for the necessity of the raft, as "the borders have become blurred now more than ever, and it is now when we need to set sail to new lands." The uncanny irony is that after the *Méduse* ran aground, people boarded a hurriedly constructed raft to survive. Nearly everyone on that raft died. The few survivors who were found after thirteen days were dehydrated and starved. The parallelism between the *raft of Medusa* story and the countless boats of refugees escaping civil conflicts arriving daily on Greek shores is impossible to miss. Blackman introduces himself as the captain of the raft. He admits his excitement, even though this is his first time sailing a boat, and he barely knows how to swim. None of that matters, though, he says. Only the team's ambitious vision and participation in the European project matter.

At that point, Linda Kapetanea picks up his microphone stand and motions him onto the raft. Blackman's speech becomes even more vehement, his tone rising as he proudly explains why this raft will stand out amid the international competition. Around him, the construction intensifies. Manuel Ronda, drags Blackman's right leg slightly to the side to stabilize him in a firm stance. At the same time Kapetanea provides tall, thin branches, which Ronda carefully tapes on Blackman's calf. Soon they move on to his left leg, immobilizing him, as he continues his address uninterrupted, holding on to the microphone stand with both hands. Next, they move to other parts of his body, attaching wooden planks on his back with masking tape, fastening them around his neck and attaching his left hand to a sturdy upright plank resembling a thick crutch. Eventually, Blackman is wholly entombed in the wooden structure and becomes an indiscernible figure drowning in a sea of wood. Completely unfazed by his entrapment, his enthusiasm grows as his address focuses on how what they have built will serve future generations. He marvels at the teamwork it took to build the raft and attempts to rile up the audience in celebration of the team spirit, asking them to cheer and shout "Hoorah," which gets a few hesitant responses from some viewers. At this point, the raft's "captain" is hidden behind so much wood that it is almost impossible to discern a human figure anymore, making his words appear as a disembodied voice echoing in space. He tries again, prompting encouragingly: "How about a hoorah for this European culture?" This call is met with complete silence. "Yeah, that's what I thought," he says.

The silence does not discourage him, though, as he excitedly celebrates this project's greatness. This project, however, is something that he has never explicitly named. Even though he is already buried deep within the wooden structure the others have fastened on him, they continue to add pieces. The more built into the structure he becomes, the harder it gets to speak. Panting, he asks: "If you had one chance . . . Yeah, that's what they said to me. You got one chance. You can either agree or disagree. You can either say yes, or you can say goodbye. And in the end, I agree. I agree with all the strict rules. I agree with all the measures." The mention of "one chance" evoked the damp memory of the July 2015 public referendum. The popular majority had voted to reject the third round of austerity measures, yet they were still enforced, pushing people to their limit. Blackman seems to be nearing his limit too. He starts shouting, and the speakers echo him, making his last few sentences unintelligible.

Performers Linda Kapetanea and Jacob Ingram-Dodds step away from the raft and head to the side of the stage. Blackman struggles to continue his address. Percussive music gradually takes over and swallows his pleas as the raft construction slows. In response to the music, Kapetanea begins to shake. It is a full-body convulsion that Ingram-Dodds attempts to control by wrapping a black piece of fabric around her waist. The fabric momentarily constrains the convulsions but soon turns out to be ineffective. Kapetanea struggles to escape the cloth's hold. In this fight, it seems like her agency is slowly fading as the fabric holder becomes a puppet master controlling and constraining her movements until she succumbs.

She is hunched over, hanging by her waist from the cloth, as her feet and hands touch the floor. Ingram-Dodds drags her to the front of the stage. Her whole body starts to shake once more as she makes one last futile attempt to escape, yet she is firmly held in place. Having confirmed that she cannot move on a horizontal plane, she starts jumping, with her legs and arms flailing in the air, as she is momentarily flying parallel to the floor. This repetitive movement becomes a blur, and for a moment, the performers morph into a rider holding on to and trying to tame a wildly galloping horse. Despite the effort and exertion in their movement, neither the rider nor the horse go anywhere. An exercise in futility. They remain fixed on the same corner of the stage until the warm yellow glow illuminating them gives way to complete darkness.

The Body in/and the Greek Crisis

As the closing scenes of *Europium* suggest, the Greek crisis should be understood in the context of Greece's ambivalent relationship with the EU. The captain's entombment in the raft by his comrades during his efforts to excite them about the European project offers a glimpse into people's conflicting experience with austerity measures during the crisis. People felt immobilized and trapped by the measures. At the same time, the creditors' rhetoric promoted austerity as the only way for the country's economy to recover.

The Greek crisis decade (2009–2019) is a constructive time for examining the conflicting intersection between embodiment, austerity, narratives of national belonging, and national identity construction. During the crisis years, the tensions between externally imposed expectations (such as those of Greece's creditors) and the lived experience under austerity reignited Orientalist anxieties all too common in Greek history. The dancing body has historically been the vehicle for expressing and negotiating such contradictions.

The struggle to establish a sense of Greek national identity and belonging in the context of Europe has been present since Greece's establishment as an independent nation-state (1832) and has been revisited since its entry into the EU (1981). As someone who grew up in Greece, I can personally attest to the fact that the body and embodied engagement, either in the form of dance or as means of exercising one's democratic rights (such as through participation in a protest), are part of daily life and assist in cultivating a sense of identity and belonging. Dance and other types of embodied engagement (such as marching for instance) are central to any event of national or social significance. School parades, *panigyria* (πανηγύρια),[2] religious holiday celebrations, national holidays, and social gatherings all often revolve around dancing.

In the context of Greek society, the body's ability to interact with and influence the political sphere is an accepted paradigm. Popular protests, uprisings in response to governmental directives, and strikes in response to changes in labor laws have been very common occurrences dating back to the early twentieth century.[3] A plethora of successful popular protest examples throughout Greece's history demonstrate a deep-rooted belief in participatory democracy, where participation is embodied.[4] Embodied agency and acknowledging the body's ability to exercise pressure on the political sphere were revisited in the early years of the crisis, as people's need to express their opposition to governmental directives intensified. In the period between 2010 and 2012, the Indignant Citizens Movement (Kinima Aganaktismenon Politon; Κίνημα Αγανακτισμένων Πολιτών) was the most popular nonpartisan anti-austerity movement in Greece; it organized solidarity sit-ins and strikes across major cities regularly.

Beyond the social sphere, another notable shift in embodied engagement during the early years of the crisis was the substantial number of people who took up running or biking outdoors, which was documented through an increased number of organized races (Tzartzani 2014). Such heightened awareness of embodied agency attributed more visibility to the dance community, more broadly (captured through an anecdotal increase of people of all ages signing up for dance classes or engaging in dancing on their own), and to contemporary dance, more specifically, as an art form that can critically engage with the political sphere, as suggested by the description of *Europium*. At the height of the crisis decade, international media often reported on the flourishing artistic scene in Greece and glorified the crisis as the vehicle that made this change possible.

The framing of crises as opportunities (Klein 2007; Sutton 2010) is a common trope observed in both popular discourses and critical theory scholarship. When I started this research in 2013, I, too, fell into the trap of romanticizing the Greek crisis as an occurrence that created fertile ground for the dance field to blossom into new directions. Now, many years later, I recognize that crises serve as magnifying lenses exposing preexisting infrastructural shortcomings. The dance field in Greece and the labor of performance artists have been chronically undervalued, so what the crisis did was create even more dire circumstances for art workers. So much so that artists' only choice was to react by devising alternative modes of creation to retain their ability to make work. Thus, an approach that focuses on the boost of artistic activity and ignores its underpinnings in the context of the financial crisis would be incomplete.

Contrarily, an approach grounded on corporeality can more potently capture the complex layers of the crisis experience. It acknowledges the effort, the hyperextension—both literal of the limbs and metaphorical of one's capacity to commit—and ultimately the bodily exertion inherent in navigating unforeseen circumstances. Here, I am bringing into conversation the work of dance scholars Anusha Kedhar (2014, 2020) and Ann Cooper Albright (2019). Kedhar (2020) relates the concept of flexibility—a desired physical trait among dancers—to their ability to navigate and manage the demands of dance labor within a neoliberal framework. She asks how dancers may move against neoliberalism while still operating within and from it. I adapt this question to the context of the Greek crisis and borrow the concept of flexibility to consider how dancers both worked in line with and against the limitations imposed on them through the austerity measures enforced on Greece. I then extend Kedhar's notion of flexibility to encompass somatic skills akin to those identified by Ann Cooper Albright. Albright theorizes responses to crises (or what she identifies in her book title as "unstable ground") as an "experience of responsiveness" (2019, 4), redirecting attention to bodies as sites where politics and somatics converge. Since bodies are the means through which individuals experience and interact with the world, the physical practices one engages in cultivate skills that one can harness in moments that call for unprecedented adjustments. Such an approach, drawing on embodied knowledge and corporeality, is not only able to illuminate the previously undertheorized aspect of embodiment in the context of the Greek crisis, but it also grounds theoretical endeavors on the tangible plane of lived experience, avoiding potential fetishization or romanticizing of the Greek crisis.

In popular discourse, crises often attain an almost mythologized dimension. They oscillate in a duality between being measurable—through statistics or scientific evidence—and thus manageable with the guidance of experts, while at the same time, they can be elusive entities prone to fetishization or spectacularization. The fetishization of crises refers to a trend of approaching them as catastrophes and presenting their impact as a spectacle for mass consumption. For instance, the events that constituted the Greek crisis and the data that made the phenomenon measurable (such as the total debt amount, interest rates, unemployment rates,[5] numbers of business closures and layoffs, etc.) were repeatedly visualized and turned into charts that pervaded the media. The importance of documenting crises in measurable parameters is indisputable, yet at the same time, the intensive focus on quantifiable data detracts from the impact that crises have on individuals' lived experiences and can ultimately be dehumanizing.

Bodies and an acknowledgment of their materiality are central to a subject's experience and to political action. As dance scholar Christine Greiner posits: "Bodily presence *can*, and indeed *does*, organize itself as a political action" (2021, 76; emphasis added). It is precisely this recognition of the body and its materiality as both cultural construction and locus of political and social control that propels the research presented in this book. In moments of crisis, especially in the first years of the austerity measures, when the values and safeguards people had previously taken for granted (such as pensions, a minimum wage, or unemployment benefits) were suddenly upended, a wave of introspection ensued. As this book, based on my research among the dance community in Greece, shows most people's response to the shifting conditions imposed on them by austerity measures had been to turn "inward" and focus on themselves and their bodies. When everything is in flux in a moment of crisis, the only stable referent is one's own body.

In the contemporary dance field, which in Greece is commonly associated with leftist values, introspection materialized as a critical reconsideration of the past and led to increased engagement with previously marginalized aspects of Greek history. While it is impossible to capture in a few sentences the breadth and complexity of "leftist values" in the context of the arts community in Greece, the term is used to convey the political orientation of many performance artists. In my personal conversations with the dancers and choreographers throughout the years of conducting this research, it became apparent that most of them adhere to political ideologies that can be broadly classified as leftist or liberal. These include socialist beliefs of collectivization, syndicalism, collective organizing, communist ideals of ownership, or even anarchist skepticism of hegemonic hierarchies. Perhaps in response to the alarming rise of ethnocentrism and in efforts to counter it, a new thematic trend emerged in the arts that focused on rendering the significant differences and inconsistencies between the idealized classical past and the neoliberal present visible for critique. Dance productions were among the first sites where such negotiations of national identity and citizenship materialized. Amid the ethnocentric political turn in Greece and Europe more broadly during the 2010s, Greek choreographers and performers emerged as activists and advocates of human rights. They created works that either offered critical frameworks to theorize the moment of the crisis or worked to raise awareness of the impending political extremism.

It is precisely at the crux of such tensions that this project was born. The magnifying lens of the crisis made discursive anxieties around Greek identity construction hypervisible. Pairing this with the intensification of embodied engagement as a means of advocacy both locally and globally renders the Greek dance scene an ideal case study for theorizing the crisis's impact on bodies and proposing a framework for future scholars concerned with the intersections between embodiment and crises. Recognizing the pivotal role that choreographers and performers played in capturing the shifting landscape of the crisis and proposing alternative means to navigate these unprecedented circumstances puts emphasis on the Greek dance field as a critical agent. Aided by the popularization of numerous protests in response to austerity measures, the human body as a site of agency and advocacy became increasingly normalized in the decade of the Greek crisis.

Prelude to the Crisis

The roots of the Greek crisis are often discussed as reaching back to the 1980s, when Greece was experiencing unprecedented political stability. The military dictatorship (known as the *Regime of the Colonels*, or colloquially as the junta) had just been abolished in 1974, and a bipartisan parliamentary system of governance was established. The post-junta decade was marked by colossal spending and expenses in the public sector (Kitromilides 2013; Mazower 2013), which encouraged excessive foreign borrowing. In 1981, Greece entered the European Economic Community (EEC),[6] which heralded a new era in the country's economy marked by prosperity. The growth of Greece's economy was capped by its entry into the Eurozone in 2001,[7] when the country transitioned its currency from the drachma to the euro. In the early years of the twenty-first century, the Greek economy appeared stable. As political scientist Stathis Kalyvas (2015) remarks, in 2008, the country was in the exclusive club of the forty richest nations on earth and ranked twenty-sixth globally on the Human Development Index. Yet, as Kalyvas continues, unrest was brewing below this superficial stability as "the amazing expansion of the Greek economy ha[d] a very soft underbelly" (2015, 154). The Greek sovereign debt crisis in the aftermath of the 2007–2008 global financial crisis was triggered by structural weaknesses in the Greek economy and a lack of monetary flexibility due to Greece's Eurozone membership.

Delving deeper into the delicate balances and hierarchies between Greece and the EU, media and communications scholar Yiannis Mylonas (2020) proposes a framework that suggests a helpful analogy. Mylonas views the EU as an empire, both organizationally and in reference to its internal hierarchies. In this analogy, core EU members (such as Germany, France, Belgium, Luxemburg, and the Netherlands) are the *center*, while the countries that became members in later enlargements of the EU and the Eurozone are the *peripheral* economies. I find this comparison especially apt for conceptualizing the challenges Greece faced, not only in the integration process but more so during the crisis.

Simply put, all members of the EU commit to making policy adjustments to participate in the European integration process. Integration, one of the core pillars of the EU, advocates for industrial, political, economic, legal, social, and cultural consolidation of the policies and processes of member states. The desired outcome is economic and monetary stability. While every country faces considerable challenges in this overly ambitious task, some member states, such as the core EU founding members, already share common traits that make the integration process smoother. In turn, modeling the integration process in accordance with existing policies among core members makes it harder for peripheral members, such as Greece, to fully align their policies with the existing frameworks. After all, as Kalyvas remarks, even though Greece was an advanced economy, "it also displayed some institutional features resembling those of the emerging economies of the developing world" (2015, 154). Said features included clientelism, lack of transparency and nepotism in the public sector, dysfunctional institutions, and lack of a sophisticated and competitive business sector. All these elements starkly contrasted with the characteristics of the capitalist monopolies of the core EU members, who were already "healthy" economies and adjusted to the euro easier than their peripheral counterparts. An understanding of the EU through the center/periphery dichotomy thus allows for mapping the geopolitical tensions present within the EU space and prefaces the hegemonic imbalances informing the political tensions incited by the crisis.

The economic challenges and the tensions between the neoliberal and ordoliberal frameworks (the German variant of liberalism that emphasizes the role of the state in ensuring that the free market produces results close to its theoretical potential)[8] imposed on Greece planted some of the first seeds of social unrest and popular resistance to measures related to the European integration process. The hegemonic imbalance between the EU center and the Greek periphery, of which people became increasingly aware in the first decade of the twentieth century, awoke dormant memories of a wound that history had not yet healed, namely the Greek Civil War (1946–1949). In some ways, the clash of ideologies between the political left (who opposed European integration) and the right (who advocated for its necessity) reignited the political binary that had historically been deeply divisive. In her book detailing the history of the Greek left, Neni Panourgia reflects on 2008 as the year that marked a turning point:

> But there, unspoken, was the civil war—always, everywhere present, silently brought to mind though never spoken of, wounds that never really healed. And if anyone thought that they had, the December Events of 2008 would have proven him [sic] wrong. The uprising of the high-school students, sparked by the murder of one of them, fifteen-year-old Alexis Grigoropoulos, by a Special Forces policeman after yet another demonstration against the excess of the government, brought center stage the festering wounds of the modern Greek polity. (Panourgia 2009, xvi)

The student uprising that Panourgia is referencing first manifested as a protest against injustice and police brutality. The events spanned from December 6 (the day of the shooting) until Christmas. In the last week of demonstrations, there was no longer a clear agenda of demands. Initially, high school students and youth took to the streets across Greece, but as the protests persisted, more and more people from all walks of life joined. Gradually, within three weeks, the reasons for the protest had been broadened to include the interests of various groups such as university students, immigrants, anarchists, and "anti-establishmentarians."[9] The protests gradually morphed into other forms of expressing opposition, such as the occupation of university buildings across various campuses, strikes, and looting. Molotov cocktails were thrown at authorities, and fires were set in downtown Athens, with protests spreading to other urban areas. The protests seemed to capture general unrest and dissatisfaction that could not be pinned down to one thing. People from across Greek society used their bodies in public spaces to make their feelings known.

The December 2008 events were colloquially documented in the media as *Dekemvriana of (Δεκεμβριανά του)* 2008, or the "[events] of December 2008." *Dekemvriana* is a term that has historically been used to capture a conflict between the Greek left and right in December 1944, which set the stage for the civil war that followed in 1946. This rhetorical choice further attests to the memories and parallels awakened. The peculiarly broad agenda of the December 2008 protests triggered a wave of distrust against authorities and resistance to sovereign power. The 2008 popular uprisings are thus treated by theorists (Panourgia 2009; Douzinas 2013; Sagris, Schwartz and Void Network 2010) as the starting point of a social crisis, which prophesied the turmoil of the financial crisis in the following decade.

A Timeline of the Greek Crisis

The year 2008 also marked the start of the global financial crisis that erupted in the US. At first, there was no indication that the crisis would impact Greece, yet as 2009 rolled in, these estimations changed. The international financial rating agencies downgraded the Greek government bonds, and in turn, its sovereign debt was assessed as unsustainable (Mylonas 2020). The main trigger was Greece's inability to borrow to service its high public debt. The Greek economy was threatened with default and the possibility of exiting the Eurozone (the so-called Grexit), which would undoubtedly have dire consequences, not just for the Greek economy but for the stability of the euro and other Eurozone economies. If a default were to happen, it would significantly stall the European integration process.

To combat the crisis, Greece entered a series of bailout agreements, which were implemented in three rounds in 2010, 2012, and 2015 thus effectively turning Greece into a guinea pig for testing austerity measures. Each agreement, known as a memorandum of understanding (MOU), imposed a series of austerity measures and was signed between Greece, the European Commission, the European Central Bank, and the International Monetary Fund (IMF). The three creditors became colloquially known as the *Troika*. The purpose of each MOU was to provide financial assistance to Greece to finance its debt. Each agreement included a series of austerity measures and terms that the country had to adhere to, which encompassed policies to improve tax administration, reductions in pensions, alterations in public sector wages, and increases in value-added tax.

The first MOU in May 2010 granted financial assistance to Greece that would be disbursed over three years. The program optimistically projected a return to economic growth in 2012. By early 2011, however, it became clear that things were not developing as anticipated, and a second rescue package for Greece was announced and officially implemented in February 2012. One measure that stands out from this second package is the debt-restructuring deal known as private sector involvement (PSI). Dubbed a financial "haircut," this measure entailed restructuring the Greek debt held by private investors to lighten the country's overall debt (Kalyvas 2015; Xafa 2013; Skaperdas 2015). It was the most prominent sovereign default to date and the first within the Eurozone.

The second MOU coincided with a series of interrelated shocks that forced Greece into a downward spiral (Kalyvas 2015), causing the country's economy to effectively default under PSI restructuring (Skaperdas 2015). Personal incomes were reduced by a third, pension plans suffered losses of up to 65%, unemployment reached 27% (compared with the 15% projected by the IMF), and youth unemployment soared to 60%. Beyond these structural and fiscal challenges, political divisiveness made it even more difficult to reach consensus on reform decisions, especially as partisan polarization reached new extremes with a staggering 7% of votes cast in favor of the fascist party Golden Dawn (Chrysi Avgi; Χρυσή Αυγή) in the May 2012 elections. The most impactful manifestation of this political rivalry was the failure to elect a president of the republic[10] at the end of 2014, which led to early elections in 2015 and, in turn, to a new round of negotiations between Greece and its creditors (Stournaras 2019).

Under the newly elected party *SYRIZA* (Συνασπισμός Ριζοσπαστικής Αριστεράς abbreviated as ΣΥ.ΠΙΖ.Α.; translating as Coalition of the Radical Left), the negotiations took a different turn. Greece's prime minister, Alexis Tsipras, announced a public referendum to seemingly return some agency to voters. It gave them some chance to decide their fate and to voice whether they would be willing to accept the conditions of a third—even stricter—adjustment program. The voters overwhelmingly rejected the bailout conditions with a majority vote of no, amounting to 61%. Despite the referendum result, which became a mere bargaining chip in bailout negotiations, Greece entered the third MOU in July 2015. By that summer, the European refugee crisis was also in full force and significantly impacted Greece's economy as the country was one of the main entry points for refugees arriving in the EU. The bailout negotiations included funds to alleviate the refugee crisis, yet the signed three-year agreement enforced even harsher austerity conditions than those initially rejected by the voters. The most notable measures included capital controls and another bank recapitalization round. Greek banks closed for several days,[11] and a cash-withdrawal limit of 60 EUR per day was enforced immediately.

I was in Greece in the second half of 2015 and vividly recall the evening when the capital controls were announced. Hordes of people left their homes and queued up at their neighborhood ATMs to withdraw as much money as possible before the controls were enforced. It was close to midnight when I went to stand in one of those lines, and I remember gaping at the commotion in the residential neighborhood at such a late hour. The queues often spanned entire blocks as folks hastily parked, and double-parked, their cars to get a good spot in the line. I tuned in to the spontaneous conversations between neighbors offering tips about which ATM still had not run dry or expressing their indignation, anxiety, and uncertainty about how this new round of measures would further impact their lives. It goes without saying that mistrust of the government had just deepened even more. After their enforcement in 2015, capital controls were gradually modified and minimized until they were finally removed in September 2019.

Scholarship on the Greek financial crisis marks August 2018 as the date when Greece officially exited the third bailout program. Yet for the purpose of exploring the impact of the crisis on the Greek dance scene, *Performing the Greek Crisis* considers the decade between 2009 and 2019. The first year after the onset of the crisis that Greece sold ten-year bonds, which was viewed as a sign of recovery, was 2019. Thus, this year became the bookend for this research exploration.

Having introduced a few critical moments in the Greek crisis here, I revisit them in the following section and pair them with historical analysis to continue painting the picture of the delicate balances between Greece and the EU. I introduce dance practices as critical sites of the embodied negotiation of hegemonic hierarchies between the European center and the Greek periphery, thus further illustrating the significance of the Greek crisis as a case study.

"Where It All Began": Imagining and Choreographing the Greek Nation

The significance of Greece as a case study extends beyond its unfortunate position as a textbook example of economic decline in the context of the global financial crisis to a site for negotiating the challenges of national identity construction in the context of austerity. Paying attention to the tensions that emerged during the crisis, such as the blaming of external factors (i.e., German loan sharks, the *Troika*, or the EU) or the disbelief and mistrust in the government that intensified during the crisis decade, reveals imbalances that are deeply entrenched decades, if not centuries, in the past. These imbalances result from geopolitical tensions and power struggles due to Greece's romanticized historical importance for a broadly and loosely defined "West" and its strategic geographic position for trade and naval military influence. Greece's perceived historical significance and the inconsistencies between its glorified past and present lived experience permeate this book, as dance was one of the main sites where negotiations of Greek national identity construction manifested.

Classical Greece (between the fifth and fourth centuries BCE) is often positioned at the core of national narratives of contemporary Greek identity even to this day. Tourist campaigns hail Greece as "the place where it all began" (Shohat and Stam 2014), thus fabricating origin myths positioning the country at the center of Europe, and sometimes even the "West." The fetishized idea of Greece being the "cradle" of Western civilization is an all-too-common perception that is unabashedly reproduced. Indicatively, Greek education prioritizes notions of lineage and continuity from ancient Greece to the present (see Zervas 2012, 2017), presenting ancient Greek cultural heritage as the birthplace of democracy, theater, and civilization in the European geographic space. Tourist and product marketing campaigns also play into this trope, often centering ancient ruins as part of their visual reference and exalting the country's mythical cultural heritage. A spot from the Greek

National Tourism Organization released in 2005, which has since gone viral and is still used, prompts visitors to "Live your myth in Greece" and offers images of crystal-clear swimming waters alongside ancient ruins. The presumed centrality of Greek cultural heritage also circulates in racist platitudes casually brought up as a joke to highlight the long legacy of the country's history. A common one is the saying "When we [Greeks] had democracy, they [Northern Europeans] were still hanging from trees." This implies that people in other countries were still in an animalistic state and not yet civilized, thus flipping the hierarchical binary of center/periphery discourse and instead elevating Greece as superior. Such banalities circulated widely during the decade of the crisis and were fueled by the popularization of the dangerous ethnocentric rhetoric of the Golden Dawn extremist right wing party.

Treating classical Greece (understood here both as a geographic location and a historical period) as the main point of reference to construct the identity of a people who happen to reside in the same geographical space two and a half millennia later is absurd. It glosses over centuries of tumultuous history, which have actively shaped and molded Greek culture. Such pivotal moments indicatively include the Byzantine Empire (330–1453), Ottoman rule (1453–1821), the Balkan Wars (1912–1913), the two World Wars (1914–1918 and 1939–1945), the Greek Civil War, and the Greek junta (1967–1974). This is by no means an exhaustive list but rather an exercise in illustrating the absurdity of claims of cultural lineage from ancient Greece to modern Greece.

Greece was declared an independent nation-state in 1832, yet territorial disputes and cessations continued until 1947 (see Figure 1), which marks the date that Greece's borders were finally established as the geographic entity known now. This fact further illuminates how, despite the popular rhetoric of cultural lineage, the construction of a cohesive sense of national identity is a much more recent occurrence.

Once the independent Greek nation-state was founded, the leaders of the Greek Enlightenment and the Greek Orthodox Church took on the task of drafting a national narrative, and providing newly liberated peoples with a sense of unity through educational programming. Dance, and especially regional dances from the newly liberated areas of southern Greece, such as *kalamatianos (καλαματιανός)*, *tsamikos (τσάμικος)*, and *syrtos (συρτός)*, were incorporated into school curricula as part of this agenda. Every new territory that got liberated implemented the same curriculum. Thus, these three dances became "panhellenic" (Torp 1992), a status that contrasted with their strictly regional character and rendered them into embodied practices that were exercised throughout the entirety of the geographical area of Greece.

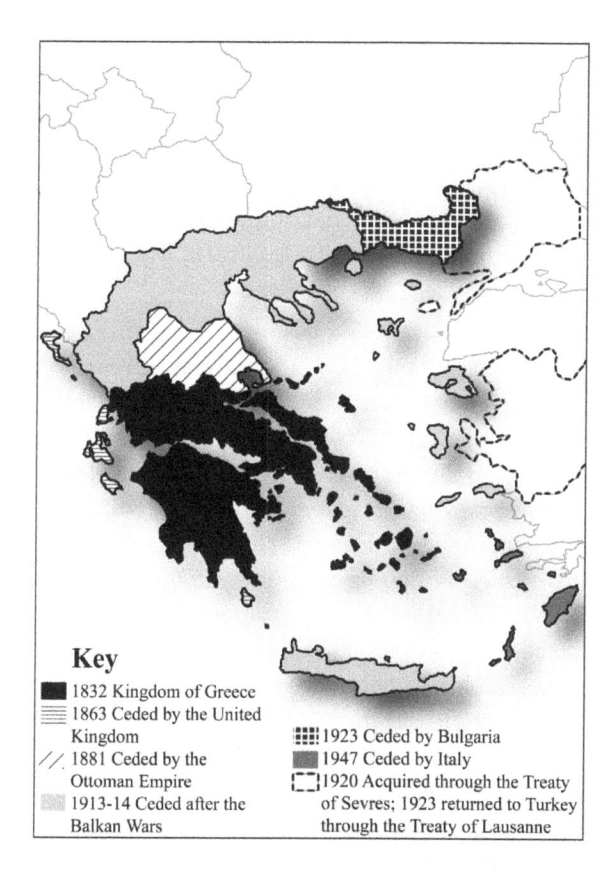

Figure 1. Map of territorial expansion of Greece, 1832–1947. Map data is adapted from Flemming (2010). Country boundaries shapefile data is from Natural Earth Dataset. Territory lines were drawn by Lauren Gerlowski. Projection is a Miller Cylindrical World Projection.

Key

- 1832 Kingdom of Greece
- 1863 Ceded by the United Kingdom
- 1881 Ceded by the Ottoman Empire
- 1913-14 Ceded after the Balkan Wars
- 1923 Ceded by Bulgaria
- 1947 Ceded by Italy
- 1920 Acquired through the Treaty of Sevres; 1923 returned to Turkey through the Treaty of Lausanne

Reflecting on the process of selecting folk dances to foster a sense of unity, dance scholar Stavros Stavrou Karayanni highlights the criteria that made these particular dances great vehicles for the emerging "imagined community" (Anderson [1983] 2006) of the Greek nation:

> These dances, with their communal character and their clearly defined gender parts, came to symbolise a newly freed Greek nation, while their austere veneer of principle and nationalist verbosity helped to gloss over Greek dependence on Western European powers. (Stavrou Karayanni 2006, 254)

The term *austere veneer* pointedly hints at the disconnect between the present experience and the tumultuous history that a performance of unity was attempting to mask. As Stavrou Karayanni (2006) further remarks, other dances, such as *tsifteteli (τσιφτετέλι)*, were purposefully omitted from public school syllabi because their 4/4 rhythm and movement vocabulary (consisting of improvisational shoulder shimmying and hip shaking) were reminiscent of belly dance and thus directly referenced Ottoman influences. While this topic is explored in more depth in chapter 1, I preface it here because this careful curation and erasure of embodied practices is in line with the purging narratives of lineage and cultural continuity from ancient Greece that to this day permeate national imaginings.

The modeling of the Greek nation according to romanticized European imaginings has been a popular topic among historians, cultural anthropologists, and modern Greek studies scholars (Clogg 2002; Faubion 1993; Gourgouris 1996; Hamilakis 2009; Herzfeld 1986; Yalouri 2001; Zervas 2012; and others), who have critically analyzed this process and treated it as a case study in historical constructivism. The pressures imposed on the newly founded Greek nation to conform to the mold of European imaginings provided through philhellenic[12] support (such as funding for military troops) are eerily similar—in terms of the hegemonic structures of operation at play—to the pressures to conform to EU austerity policies during the crisis.

Greece, then, was hailed as the locus of Eurocentric fantasies of cultural superiority while, at the same time, it was marginalized as an underdeveloped member of the European periphery. Despite philhellenic aspirations to restore post-Ottoman Greece to its "ancient glory," the reality was that the people residing in the Greek geographical space at the time had very little in common with their ancient antecedents. Literary studies scholar Álvaro García Marín perfectly captures this:

> The classical ideals of Western Philhellenism embraced by modern Greeks themselves gave birth to a nation compelled to fit an abstract model built by European enlightenment in its own image rather than the daily practice of the Greek community—Greek-speaking and Christian Orthodox, but most of all a *millet*[13] among others in the Ottoman Empire. (García Marín 2013, 54)

This "abstract model" was grounded on the erasure of ethnic minorities residing in the geographical area of Greece after its liberation and on the whitewashing of Greece's fetishized ancient past. The erasure of dances discussed earlier is another example of such exclusionary practices implemented to dissociate the residents of the newly liberated territories from any traits that were read as Ottoman and thus threatened to "orientalize" the newly constructed modern Greek subject. The urgency to purge Greekness of any Ottoman influences is rooted in Eurocentric anxiety to align Greece with racial and religious perceptions of Europeanness grounded in Whiteness and Christianity.

In 1987, Martin Bernal, a scholar of political history, published the highly controversial work *Black Athena,* where he proposed an alternative hypothesis for the roots of ancient Greek classical civilization, positing African and Semitic influences. Peer academic criticism discredited the work's validity at the time of publication and in subsequent decades. On the cusp of the 2020s, however, Bernal's thesis was revisited as some scholars regarded its initial dismissal as indicative of the systematic whitewashing of Greek antiquity. A dispute that broke out at the 2019 Society for Classical Studies conference on the future of classics documented this discursive shift. Some scholars pushed for an acknowledgment of the discipline's role in whitewashing antiquity, referencing the dismissal of *Black Athena* as proof (Poser 2021). Yet according to the established view, to accept Bernal's hypothesis, or even to begin to consider it, would threaten the very pillars upon which the constructed superiority of Whiteness and classicism is based and would irreparably shake the core of what is perceived as the cornerstone of "Western civilization."

One can only imagine how impactful such a revisionist approach to Greek history could be. An interesting exercise would be to revisit American modern dance history using this lens and reexamine the works of early modern dance pioneers who grounded aspects of their approach in classical Greek antiquity. References to ancient Greek ideals abound in the works of Isadora Duncan, Ruth St. Denis, Ted Shawn, Ruby Ginner, Eva Palmer-Sikelianos, and Martha Graham, to name a few. Yet, in many instances, the classical ideals that some of these pioneers referenced and reproduced as quintessentially Greek, and thus "Western," in their attempts to legitimize their nascent art practices were, in fact, romanticized constructions and reproductions of a phantasmic ideal that perhaps never even existed to begin with. Such an undertaking could be a whole other book, yet I am suggesting it here as an exercise to expose the holes not just in the process of Greek nation-building but also in what is considered quintessentially "Western."

In his book *Dream Nation* (1996), comparative literature scholar Stathis Gourgouris fuses psychoanalytical approaches with colonial theory to discuss the institution of the Greek nation as a process of imaginary signification (*Phantasiebildung*), which he defines as "the enacting of an implicit social fantasy within a specific historical realm . . . akin to what Freud called dreamwork" (Gourgouris 1996, 261). Following Gourgouris's line of thought, the

Phantasiebildung at play in the construction of "modern" Greece (the irony that one needs to specify that it is "modern" further attests to the totalizing assumption that Greece is the Hellas of the classical past) is an inherently Orientalist practice. Gourgouris is following Edward Said's definition of Orientalism as a framework depending on a hegemonic power structure that ensures the "flexible *positional* superiority" (Said 1979, 7) of Europe (or, more broadly, the West/Occident) over those that it constructs as its "Others." In the case of Greece, the act of freezing it in a premodern time and the geographical rendering of it as on the outskirts of Europe prove this point. Maria Koundoura (2012), a literature scholar who has also theorized the formation of Greek national identity, similarly points out how this freezing of Greece in an ancient past, and its construction as premodern, relegates it to the political, economic, and social margins of European modernity.

One thing that further complicates the position of Greece in the margins and thus contrasts it to the European center has been the financial dependence of Greece on European powers at pivotal historical moments. Anthropologist Michael Herzfeld (2002) captures this dependency under the term *crypto-colonialism*. As the name implies, crypto-colonialism is a covert form of political and economic dependence experienced by nominally independent countries such as Greece. This peculiar dependency is "articulated in the iconic guise of aggressively national culture fashioned to suit foreign models" (Herzfeld 2002, 900). Even after Greece became an independent nation-state, financial dependence and foreign borrowing persisted. Such crypto-colonial dynamics resurfaced in the delicate balances maintained between Greece and its international creditors during the Greek crisis. Herzfeld continues: "Crypto-colonialism is thus about the exclusion of certain countries from access to the globally dominant advantages of modernity" (2002, 921). This observation certainly holds true for Greece, not only because of the financial crutches and military support it has received after achieving independent nationhood but also because of the complex dynamic of simultaneously being a tributary state for European ideals and being fixed to the past. Such is the fixity on the past that the current living population is sometimes reduced to stereotypical perceptions that do not correspond to reality.

So, in this sense, crypto-colonialism is not only descriptive of the financial dependencies and hierarchies as they manifest within the fragile balances of the EU space, but it is also indicative of the epistemic hierarchies that fix discourses about Greece in the distant past and gloss over its present. As postcolonial theorist Homi Bhabha ([1994]2004) remarks, colonized subjects often strive to model themselves according to the colonizers' expectations.

Greece complicates the typical postcolonial model because it was colonized by a non-Western power, namely the Ottoman Empire (Kolokotroni and Mitsi 2008). As described earlier, Greek people felt the pressure to "purge" any Ottoman influences and to model themselves after the fossilized ideals of an ancient past to conform to the expectations of European modernity. Even though this process was initiated in the early years of Greek independence (the 1830s), some threads are still present in today's social fabric.

In the context of the Greek crisis, media studies scholar Yiannis Mylonas reconceptualized these hegemonic tensions as "debt." In Mylonas's metaphor:

> Greece is thus symbolically indebted to its ancestors (as defined by the West), whom it needs to deploy as benchmarks for it to reach their greatness and achieve a historical continuity in greatness. Simultaneously, Greece is also materially indebted to its (Western) creditors, whom it needs to pay off (through austerity, privatizations, and neoliberal deregulation). These two dimensions for debt collide. (2020, 28)

Indeed, cultural and fiscal responsibility narratives abounded during the crisis decade and were often utilized by the media to sensationalize the crisis (for more, see Mylonas 2020 and Douzinas 2013). Fusing the notion of debt with the theoretical framework of colonialism and crypto-colonialism, some scholars (such as Carastathis 2014) have considered the Greek crisis an example of debt colonialism, whereby the crediting bodies (IMF, European Central Bank, and the European Commission) act as the colonizer, and Greece, the colonized subject. Interestingly, notions of debt, or being indebted to ancestors, also permeate the mythology surrounding the establishment of modern dance in Greece. Early twentieth-century embodied experimentations emerged in line with practices of archeological reconstruction and statue-posing approaches, thus offering an embodied grounding for these theoretical frameworks.

This colonial framing further attests to the Orientalist structure of Greek debt and offers an alternative perspective for examining austerity politics. Political theorist Anna Carastathis observes that austerity discourse related to the Greek crisis "used racial logic to justify Greece's place on the European economic periphery" (2014, 10). This became particularly evident in the media's use of the acronym PIIGS to stand for Portugal, Italy, Ireland, Greece, and Spain, which were perceived to be the weakest economies within the Eurozone during the European debt crisis. The choice of this acronym purposefully evoked qualities associated with the animal with which the term is homonymous: laziness, lack of productivity, corruption, and wastefulness (implying that these countries wasted the European resources provided to them). The racial profiling of these five countries under such a derogatory acronym harkens back to antiquated anti-Irish and anti-Mediterranean racism of the British and Ottoman Empires. The second characteristic that Carastathis identifies as Orientalist is the fact that austerity policies exonerate powerful core states such as Germany and France and the financial or political institutions that they dominate by "concealing histories of military occupation; their support for dictatorships; and as host countries, their benefiting from exploitative labor migration" (2014, 10). Lastly, Carastathis claims that the Troika's MOUs paved the way for Greece's financial recolonization. This final point accords with criticism of the vision of European integration discussed earlier and the many policy inconsistencies or the tensions (cultural, fiscal, political, etc.) that such a process brought forth.

The Intersection of the financial crisis with the intensification of the European refugee crisis further complicated matters because it urged a reconsideration of the concept of citizenship in both transnational and national terms. Once Greece became a member of the EU in 1981, a negotiation of the balance between national and supranational[14] identity was set in motion. With each enlargement of the EU (the most significant was in 2004, when ten new members were added), both the borders of trade and of movement across countries broadened, and thus the concept of citizenship was in constant flux. Citizenship negotiations further intensified in the mid-2010s, as the European refugee crisis and a crisis of asylum presented Greece with unprecedented challenges.

Thus, to recap, the challenging of the racial construction of Whiteness as a pillar of national identity is not unique to the Greek case study. In fact, discourses of White supremacy and ethnocentrism have seen a resurgence in the US and in various EU nations since the early years of the twenty-first century. Yet what is unique about Greece is the symbolic significance that race (specifically Whiteness) holds in the Western cultural legacy. While many historians and modern Greek studies scholars (Gourgouris 1996; Hamilakis 2009) agree that the cultural lineage between modern Greece and classical Greece is a construct, rarely do they tackle race as a component of that construct. Openly accepting the multicultural influences and diverse racial roots of Greece, as a geographic space, and of its population, as the group of people that happened to reside on what has been recognized as Greek soil throughout history, would bring about a significant rift that would challenge core ideologies framing what is perceived as the West. Such an undertaking cannot possibly be completed in one book, yet by prioritizing the embodied experience and the pivotal role of bodies in shaping Greek identity, I hope to contribute to this dialogue.

A Brief History of the Dancing Body in Greece

There are at least two competing ways the Greek body is constructed through participation in dance. One is through embodied practices perceived as *"native."* A primary example is folk dance, which is understood as indisputably Greek and has repeatedly been employed as "living proof" (see Stratou 1966, 1978) of the lineage from ancient Greek embodied practices to the modern Greek experience. The other is through the "imported" genre of concert dance in line with early American modern dance, German *Ausdruckstanz* (Expressionist dance), and, later, contemporary dance approaches. Historically, in Greece, dance has been a way of socializing, preserving regional traditions and customs, and passing down oral histories through song lyrics and movements. As such, folk dance is often theorized as endemic and as the "authentic" form of Greek expression, compared with concert dance practices, which separate performers from audiences and propose a formalized structure that does not allow audiences to join in the performance.

Performing the Greek Crisis focuses primarily on the "imported" genre of concert dance, especially on the modern and contemporary dance lineage, rather than ballet. Ballet's roots are too clearly steeped in European court tradition and, therefore, cannot be woven into the narrative of Greek identity effectively. The rigidity of ballet's movement vocabulary and the close ties of its history to systems of monarchic rule render it foreign to Greek sociality. Even though Greece was under monarchic rule from 1832 until 1973 (barring interruptions due to foreign occupation), its system of governance, known as "crowned republic" (vasilevomeni dimokratia; βασιλευόμενη δημοκρατία), has mostly been democratic; the role of the monarchy was mostly ceremonial. Contrary to ballet, early modern dance, with its American lineage, and German *Ausdruckstanz*, with its mystical explorations, are more easily related to romanticized narratives of Hellenism, as investigations of "natural"[15] movement abounded, and aesthetic references to classical ideals of beauty prevailed. When these approaches were introduced to Greek practitioners and audiences through the travels of Duncan or through Palmer-Sikelianos's Delphic Festivals in the late 1920s, they were welcomed with fervor and glorified as a celebration of the "true essence" of Greece. Prominent figures of modern concert dance in Greece, such as Koula Pratsika, Rallou Manou, and Zouzou

Nikoloudi, further solidified these connotations in their works by fashioning the Greek dancing body per ancient imaginings. Examples include dressing dancers (performing both folk and modern) in Grecian tunics, thus refraining from embracing modern Greece's cultural complexity and diversity and staging the performances amid ancient ruins or in ancient outdoor theaters to solidify the classical aesthetic references.

Furthermore, this dichotomy between native and imported embodied practices is indicative of at least two more points of contestation. The first one regards *access* and *social class*. Studio dance classes and training in concert dance practices are expensive and have historically been afforded by affluent individuals. This was especially true for the early generation of modern dance pioneers in Greece, who largely came from wealthy families. Social class and financial access to dance training inevitably sketch out the second dichotomy between *urban centers* and *rural peripheries*. Concert dance practices are regularly presented in urban centers with the space and infrastructure to host them. Urban centers are also the main sites where training in these concert dance practices takes place. Folk dance, on the other hand, while present in urban areas, still thrives in the rural periphery. Customs and traditions that have faded in big cities still hold strong in some rural communities, and folk dance thrives there as part of social gatherings or regional celebrations. Of course, I am keenly aware that the above is a somewhat simplified mapping of the hierarchies at play and that the reality is much more complex. However, it is essential to preface these points of tension early on, as the center/periphery binary resurfaces within the country's borders and is mirrored in the ways that dance genres are valued and circulate within the confines of the nation-state.

Providing a clear and concise definition of contemporary concert dance, as it is understood in the 2020s and as it circulated in Greece during the crisis decade is a challenging endeavor. In an article published in *Dance Research Journal* in 2017, SanSan Kwan enumerated the challenges in undertaking such a task, highlighting the racial and ethnic dimensions and the dominance of Euro-American aesthetics in what is commonly identified as contemporary concert dance. In Greece, professional dance training in contemporary dance comprises anything from American modern dance techniques, such as those developed by Martha Graham, José Limón, or Merce Cunningham, to Release technique or more recent somatic approaches such as Gaga or Fighting Monkey. Similarly, the aesthetics of contemporary dance productions range from minimalist performances that highlight the body and its movement to elaborate and grandiose sets, such as those observed in the legacy of *Tanztheater* approaches.

During my training in contemporary dance at one of the private, professional dance conservatories in Greece, "contemporary" (sygchrono; σύγχρονο) was, I recall, an elusive entity. Everyone practicing it knew what it was and identified it when they saw it performed, but no one could accurately define it. When I moved to the US and attended performances advertised as "contemporary," I assumed that I would be able to easily relate to them and "read" them. They were "contemporary" after all. But it was only after at least half a decade, a few American dance history courses, and numerous discussions with peers that I finally felt I could relate to what I was watching. By contrast, attending performances by European ensembles on tour felt much more familiar and relatable. My individual experience is nothing more than an opinion, yet this anecdote hints at the impossibility of viewing "Euro-American aesthetics" as a cohesive and easily identifiable trait. On the contrary, the historical legacies and diverse genealogies of dance in the US (a country encompassing so many distinct approaches often varying by region) and Europe (an entire continent) should be teased apart and fleshed out. This is one of the undertakings of this book, to sketch out what "contemporary concert dance" is in the Greek context and which embodied lineages it is in conversation with. In tracing the embodied legacies that Greek contemporary dance engages with, I make evident that even though this form of dance may broadly fall under the "Euro-American aesthetics" umbrella, it is certainly not valued as their equivalent.

Greek dancers have had to argue for themselves as part of the European avant-garde because Greek contemporary concert dance has often had the same fate that Greece has relative to the EU: it has been relegated to the periphery. The esteemed place that "contemporary" holds in the canon of European dance renders it a tangible way for the Greek subject to approximate Europeanness. Fluency in contemporary concert dance recenters Greece in the European dance canon instead of being pushed to the artistic margins of the European avant-garde. The chronic lack of resources and infrastructure in support of all arts in Greece continues to be a hindrance to true equality in these conversations, but nevertheless, Greece is afforded a seat at the table. Especially during the crisis decade when Greece was the receptor of intense criticism, the plethora of artistic activity was a positive glimmer that subverted the negative stereotypes saturating the media.

In the pages of this book, the Greek dance scene emerges as a vibrant community brimming with creativity and resourcefulness. While these qualities do exist, they do not result from substantive institutional support. Instead, they are born from the artists' individual determination, personal investment, and commitment to their art form. The media celebration of the art scene's growth during the crisis often obscured the resiliency required to persevere and create work despite the budget cuts and the austerity measures. The media opted for a fetishized representation of Greece (and Athens in particular) as a new hotspot for the arts. Some sources even went so far as to claim that "Athens is the new Berlin." This bold comparison not only points to the political tensions between Germany (one of the main creditors) and Greece as the scolded child of the EU, but it also once more illustrates the deep-rooted desire to reclaim Athens (and by extension Greece) as a European center of artistic inspiration.

The hierarchies and tensions observed between the EU center and the Greek periphery are thus not only limited to the political sphere. The same hierarchies and power struggles inform the landscape of concert dance, where "contemporary" becomes the vehicle for elevating one's status and thus subverting Greece's marginal positionality within the EU hegemonic structure.

The Infrastructure for Dance in Greece

In the realm of dance production, 2011 marked a rupture from the established order. In preceding decades, the Greek Ministry of Culture[16] issued an annual call inviting dance and theater companies to apply for subsidies. Two separate committees (one for dance and one for theater) appointed by the Ministry had deliberated and allocated funds to selected applicants to create and present work in the upcoming season (September–May). With the austere budget cuts in response to the crisis, the subsidies ceased in 2011. The effect that this sudden break had on the creative work of performers was gradual. Productions slowly died down, and many choreographers refrained from creating works between 2011 and 2013. Adapting to the austere conditions, choreographers and performers began seeking alternative ways to produce performances. Collaborations between ensembles emerged; artists reclaimed abandoned spaces to present their work and sought alternative funding routes, such as subsidiary programs from the EU or festivals. Most performances examined in chapter 2 were produced during the period when subsidies had ceased, namely between 2013 and 2017.

Even before the funding challenges, the infrastructure in support of dance in Greece was significantly flawed. Professional dance education certificates were not acknowledged as equivalent to higher education degrees. Beyond the ongoing struggle to legitimize the performing arts in education, other examples attesting to the lacking infrastructure include the absence of designated theater and studio spaces for professional dance ensembles. A quote by dance historian and choreologist Katia Savrami sums it up perfectly: "Professional dance education in Greece always seems to be in a mode of austerity" (2019, 41). Austerity, in this context, is both literal, regarding the funding funneled toward arts education, and metaphorical, regarding the ministerial investment in the sector and the updating of pedagogical practices.

Notably, the curricular requirements mandated by the Ministry of Culture for professional dance schools have not been updated since 1983 (President of the Hellenic Republic 1983). Professional training in concert dance prioritizes ballet technique as a foundational practice in which students are required to train daily, followed by modern or contemporary dance approaches, which also constitute daily praxis. Secondary class offerings vary based on each school's budget. They include folk dance, improvisation and eurhythmics (akin to methods popularized by Émile Jaques-Dalcroze), dance history, anatomy, pedagogy, and introductory concepts in developmental psychology so that dance graduates will cultivate the skills required to teach dance to various age groups, starting from young children.

Such training priorities highlight a hierarchy that values technique and virtuosity over other skills, such as choreographic composition. This approach produces dancers with great technical prowess and cultivates an international reputation for Greek dancers, which allows them to pursue careers at renowned companies abroad. At the same time, the emphasis on embodiment and the comparative lack of theoretical classes akin to international dance studies approaches (except for dance history classes) evokes a Cartesian duality that hinders dance training from being recognized as analogous to university-level education.

Dance graduates in Greece are thus constantly struggling to legitimize their discipline. In the decade preceding the crisis, there were attempts to found an institution that would grant the equivalent of a university degree. The proposal regarded turning the Greek National School of Dance (Kratiki Scholi Orchistikis Technis; Κρατική Σχολή Ορχηστικής Τέχνης) into a higher learning institution.[17] This proposal was on the path to fruition, as the proposing committee comprising dance scholars and teachers had submitted the paperwork to the Ministry of Culture for consideration in October 2011 under the government of the Panhellenic Socialist Party (Panellinio Sosialistiko Kinima; Πανελλήνιο Σοσιαλιστικό Κίνημα), known by its acronym PASOK. According to an oral account of the event (Katia Savrami, interview, January 9, 2014), the ministerial committee had deemed the proposal ready to be approved. Yet in November 2011, Prime Minister Georgios Papandreou resigned, and a provisional government was appointed.[18] The plan thus fell through, and budgetary priorities shifted because of the crisis.

Discussions of the devaluation of dance degrees resurfaced in the last few years of the crisis. In 2017, after governmental subsidies were reinstated, many degrees were reevaluated, and changes were implemented across academic fields belonging to the so-called technological education sector. The renewed controversy around dance's value surrounded Article 79 Law 4481/2017, which equated arts degrees from privately owned dance schools licensed by the Ministry of Culture to degrees earned from technological educational institutions (TEIs).[19] TEI degrees, initially ranked below universities, became equivalent to university degrees as a consequence of the 2017 law. When the TEI degree upgrade happened, dancers once again requested the reevaluation of their degrees as equivalent to university-level education. The bill concerning dance did not pass. As I am writing these lines in early 2023, dancers have taken to the streets once again to protest the potential further devaluation of their degrees as equivalent to high school diplomas, per Presidential Decree 85/2022. Following repeated uprisings, demonstrations, and mobilization by artists asking for the inclusion of performing arts degrees (dance, theater, and music) in higher education curricula, discussions have resurfaced around the establishment of a higher education institution for the performing arts (Anotati Scholi Parastatikon Technon; Ανώτατη Σχολή Παραστατικών Τεχνών).

The Methodological Challenges of Documenting the Greek Crisis: Returning to the Body

Theorizing and simultaneously documenting events as they unfold has been one of the biggest challenges of this research. My positionality as both an insider in the Greek concert dance community and an outsider, because of my role as a researcher, further complicated this process.

Like many of the performers I interviewed for this book, I felt limited in my early twenties by the options in the dance field in Greece. I had just graduated from one of the professional dance schools and completed a degree in political science with a focus on international and European studies. I was eager to bridge the two disciplines, yet there were no programs or degrees at any Greek institution that offered an opportunity to embark on this exploration. In 2008, I went to the UK to pursue a master's in dance cultures, histories, and practices. Upon completing the program, I lived and traveled for research in Germany and returned to Greece in early 2010. I spent the first half of 2010 in Athens. At the time, even though the wheels of the crisis had been set in motion, its implications had not fully set in. The last few months of my stay were clouded by bureaucracy, hasty preparations, and US embassy visits to acquire a student visa to pursue a PhD in critical dance studies at the University of California, Riverside. I left Greece in early September 2010.

Tracking the developments of the Greek crisis from afar and being unable to vote remotely, I was deeply concerned with the alarming rise of extremist right-wing ideology represented by the Golden Dawn's election into the Greek parliament in 2012. As my research up to that point focused on the intersections of national identity and performance, the rise of extreme nationalism in my home country planted the initial seed for *Performing the Greek Crisis*.

In late 2013, I returned to Greece for an extended period (ten months) to conduct the first round of on-site fieldwork. I attended numerous performances, interviewed choreographers, dancers, and dance scholars, visited libraries and archives, and feverishly documented everything. Because of my professional dance training in Athens, I was, in some ways, an insider. At the same time, having been away during the first few years of the crisis, which were arguably the most intense in terms of how many new measures were imposed and how many changes people had to adapt to, I had landed in a place that I called home yet knew increasingly less about. My graduate classes, which had equipped me to critically analyze events and neatly organize them in theoretical frameworks, made me even more of an outsider, as I was working to capture and frame others' lived experiences.

As a researcher occupying the liminal space of both belonging in the Greek dance community yet not quite, I felt a feeling of excitement because the crisis was rife with theoretical possibilities. Simultaneously, for all the artists and scholars whom I met and spoke with for this research, the crisis incited feelings of frustration, despair, and, in some cases, persistence and resilience. I empathized and shared these sentiments during our encounters and even more so during the writing process. Still, as an outsider who was documenting these encounters to later scrutinize them under various critical lenses, I must admit my privilege. The reality I am attempting to capture in *Performing the Greek Crisis* has only ever fleetingly been my own. What you, the reader, will encounter is still inevitably filtered through my perspective.

The research methods utilized in *Performing the Greek Crisis* are an amalgam of my scholarly journey. I fuse ethnographic methods (such as participant observation and qualitative interviews) with critical dance studies approaches (such as critical theory–based analysis of performances), and quantitative data analysis. In this interdisciplinary mix, I sometimes harness tools and skills I have cultivated through years of dance training. Such skills include heightened spatial and embodied awareness, and readiness to respond to environmental stimuli, a skill cultivated primarily through the practice of improvisation.

In the context of navigating a crisis, when a rupture to the established order occurs, an instinctual reaction is required. This reaction cannot be rehearsed, as it responds to an unprecedented event. Yet that very moment of impromptu improvisation draws on deeply ingrained habits and skills one has acquired in the past. A dancer has learned how to fall without getting injured. They have practiced reorienting and continuing to perform after an error or misstep. Rehearsals and training have cultivated dancers' muscle memory and heightened their sense of responsiveness to others and their environment. As such, the adaptability nurtured through improvisational games in the studio or through experimentations during rehearsals turn into skills that allow them to readily engage and respond to ruptures in the established routine and to subsequent changes that a crisis might set in motion. These skills are at the crux of the Greek dance community's success, resilience, and perseverance in the crisis decade.

The value of embodied training is not only apparent in the readiness of the dance community to adapt to the precarity of the crisis; it is also latent in my methodology. Early in the fieldwork process, it became apparent that I could not rely on existing theoretical frameworks to capture the consistently fluctuating landscape of the crisis experience. The crisis had dismantled many preestablished systems, and none of the already limited infrastructures for dance functioned at full capacity. I soon realized that researching the crisis required a heightened sense of adaptability and improvisation. Instead of forcing events into predetermined theoretical frameworks, I shifted my attention to bodies and tuned in to the actions of responsiveness that performers and choreographers were practicing. The theoretical frameworks employed in *Performing the Greek Crisis* emerged through such close observations. The divisive binary of theory and practice dissolved as the artists' bodies were actively theorizing, and the theories were omnipresent in the performers' bodies.

As noted, the fieldwork for this book started in 2013 and continued intermittently both on-site and digitally (through virtual interviews) until 2019. The focal point for this work has been Athens, Greece's capital and the center for most contemporary concert dance activity. Most examples that appear in this book are works created and presented in Athens. Most professional dance schools are located in that city, and all entry and graduation exams for professional studies in dance occur there, even for students wishing to study in a different city. Dance ensembles meet and work in studios around Athens, and the majority of the country's theater spaces are also located there, making it a vibrant urban landscape offering a plethora of performance venues. Smaller cities and rural communities throughout Greece have comparatively limited exposure to the arts and performances.[20] In Athens, a regular performance season spans between September and May, and some of the most successful performances (more so theater productions than dance) then tour to regional venues over the summer months. Many international dance festivals are organized throughout regional communities in Greece also during the summer months, offering opportunities for restaging works that premiered in Athens.

A dance performance is the culmination of tedious rehearsals, long hours of effort, repeated trials and errors, and bodily exertion. What reaches audiences is a polished product, the pinnacle of months of work and research. All dance performances described in *Performing the Greek Crisis* were encountered at this final stage. I attended them as an audience member and spoke with most of the choreographers about their work afterward.[21] In my interviews with the artists, I delved into aspects of the rehearsal process, yet the *making* of the works was a process that I was not privy to. This was a deliberate choice because a performance is how audiences interact with the artists: through becoming immersed in their works. Beyond the traces of the rehearsal process contained in a performance, it is also the culmination of all the skills that dancers have meticulously cultivated in the months or years leading up to that moment. I want to zoom in on those skills and embodied training and propose, treating them as a methodological framework. For the purpose of theorizing crises, I would like to invite you, the reader, to consider the performances you encounter in this book, as well as the book itself, as a palimpsest that holds all the traces of past rehearsals, embodied knowledge, and physical effort.

Many of the performances I attended in my intermittent travels are recounted in this book through detailed descriptions either based on videos the choreographers generously shared with me or drawing on my meticulous field notes. Thus, even though I have made an effort to paint a picture of the performances and events I attended that is as objective as possible, my personal experience and peculiar positionality of being simultaneously an insider and an outsider to the Greek dance scene inevitably seep through. Therefore, whenever possible, the voices of all the artists and scholars I interviewed are foregrounded to paint a picture of the crisis experience through their perspectives. I honor the dancers' contributions and agency in the creative process by using their names when the size of the ensemble allows it (I have refrained from using names in large ensembles to avoid confusion).

Concert dance ensembles are constantly in flux in Greece, which is a peculiar condition. Ensembles and dance companies form and dissolve for each performance, although there are some exceptional long-term partners and recurring collaborations. Dancers are, quite literally, constantly on the move and tackling multiple work commitments simultaneously. Choreographers are the directors of their dance companies: they spearhead both the financial and creative planning and have all company-related operations run through them. They are the living archive of the company's work and a rare stable point of reference. Therefore, I have turned to the choreographers for their input in many instances where I offer a performance analysis. This choice is, by no means, meant to devalue the dancers' labor. On the contrary, dancers' voices are highlighted throughout the book as they are the ones who are actively shaping and moving the Greek concert dance field in new directions.

My focus on performances as the main "text" for analysis is a conscious choice to push back against the chronic devaluation of contemporary concert dance in Greece and to illustrate dance's role in discursively shaping, theorizing, and contextualizing the crisis experience and the ways that the Greek crisis has pushed for an embodied reframing of national identity construction. Dance scholars have repeatedly highlighted how bodies shape public discourse or discussed bodies as sites of communal and civic activism.[22] Yet scholarship addressing bodies' response to crises,[23] such as those experienced in the first two decades of the twenty-first century and the corporeal reality of navigating precarious conditions, was still in a nascent state when I first embarked on this research.[24]

The lack of scholarly attention to the intersection between crises and embodied experience was the most significant challenge I encountered in pursuing this work. The continuously fluctuating circumstances of the crisis and the lack of temporal distance from the events I was writing about made it difficult to adopt an existing theoretical framework. Instead, in an ironic mirroring of the experience of many of my research subjects, my only stable referent in this process was the body. Beyond *my* body, which interacted with the artists and moved through archives and performance spaces, the performers' bodies, their movements, and the theoretical concepts that materialized in the fleeting moments of their performance became the guideposts that shaped the theoretical framework for this book.

Overview of Chapters

The centrality of the body in nation-building throughout Greek history and the chronic devaluation of concert dance are at stark odds with one another. This antithesis permeates the chapters of this book, as I illustrate the combativeness of contemporary dancers and reveal the significance of dance in theorizing and proposing frameworks for contextualizing the experience of the Greek crisis decade.

Chapter 1, "Contested Bodies: Dance and Greek Nation-Building," is a historical dive into dance's role in Greek nation-building. Understanding the latent tensions between the past and the present and seeing how they materialized in dance performances is essential in contextualizing the historically latent anxieties that were reignited by the Greek crisis. Foregrounding milestone examples from the twentieth century, hailing from folk and concert dance practices, I problematize the construction of Greekness as an embodied lineage rooted in antiquity. Emphasis is drawn to the 1990s, hailed as the golden decade for dance in Greece; the decade is considered a landmark in Greek dance history and a prosperous time for contemporary dance performers and creators. Even so, the struggle for dance to be legitimized continued.

Chapter 2, "Fragments of a Precarious Landscape: The Crisis from Within," is a detailed look at the shifts in the contemporary dance scene in the early years of the crisis. It traces the waning institutional support for dance and describes artists' initial response to the 2011 budget cuts, which signaled the complete cessation of subsidies. I approach the crisis from the choreographers' perspective, mapping their efforts to continue producing work despite the funding challenges. Between 2011 and 2014, a heightened sense of collectivity emerged, fostering unprecedented collaborations between choreographers and ensembles, which led to a boost in creativity. Of course, this boost was tainted by meager wages and poor working conditions, which are addressed in parallel to emergent approaches for navigating the crisis. Homing in on the embodied research the dancers and choreographers conducted, I map out how they framed the crisis, and I capture the new narrative, methodological, and aesthetic directions they devised in response to the precarious conditions of early austerity measures.

Extending beyond the scope of the artistic response to budget cuts, chapter 3, "Choreographing the Periphery: Displacement and the 'Weird,'" expands the focus to consider displacement and its impact on the local dance scene. Displacement is first examined spatially through gentrification processes that reshaped the core of artistic activity in the three Athenian neighborhoods of

Gazi, Kerameikos, and Metaxourgeio, which lie at the heart of Athens' being hailed as the "new Berlin." The rebranding of the Athenian art scene made it appealing to international artists who relocated to that city. At the same time, however, many artists from Greece emigrated in search of better career prospects abroad. The mass exodus of young professionals, "the Greek brain drain," observed during the crisis decade received a lot of attention from the media, yet it was primarily focused on the departure of people working in the fields of tech or business. Continuing to explore facets of displacement, I bring attention to the artistic brain drain, which intensified in the second half of the crisis decade. Many of the dancers interviewed for this chapter were still in the early stages of navigating life abroad or had just returned to Athens in the last few years of the crisis (2017 onward). I offer some early hypotheses on how this international dialogue facilitated by the artists' displacement due to austerity conditions has contributed to the rise of the discipline of dramaturgy in Greece and a new aesthetic and methodological direction akin to the cinematic movement known as the Greek Weird Wave, popularized internationally in the 2010s.

As most artistic activity is centralized in Athens, the majority of *Performing the Greek Crisis* focuses on the dance scene in that city. Chapter 4, "The Rise of Regional Festivals," broadens this scope, however, and examines the popularization of regional festivals in the 2010s. The histories of two of the most prestigious festivals in Greece, the Athens and Epidaurus Festival, encompassing all performing arts (music, theater, and dance), and the Kalamata Dance Festival, focusing on Western contemporary concert dance, are introduced as they set the bar for similar endeavors. Following this examination of the festival canon, I then turn to three festivals established during the crisis: Dance Days Chania in Crete, one small step in Corfu, and Akropoditi DanceFest in Syros. I uncover the funding structures that made the festival coordinators' vision possible despite scarce resources, the culture of volunteerism that supports these regional initiatives, and the ways their international popularity is entangled in crisis branding, tourism, and cultural capital production, thus further complicating the center/periphery hierarchies already in place.

The Greek financial crisis coincided with what has come to be known as the European refugee crisis, roughly dated as dawning in 2015. Examining the Greek artistic scene during the crisis would be incomplete without considering the mass waves of migrants reaching Greek shores. The inward turn noted earlier, set in motion by the popularization of ethnocentric and xenophobic rhetoric, peaked when the European refugee crisis intensified. The overlap of the two crises initiated a reconsideration of the racial construction of Greek identity that, until the early 2000s, was theorized primarily on the grounds of Whiteness. Chapter 5, "Choreographies of the European Refugee Crisis," delineates how dance works were among the first sites to engage in the process of deconstructing notions of citizenship, refugee identity, and xenophobia. Through a close look at several works produced at the height of the refugee crisis, I trace the emergence of participatory methodological approaches for engaging with "Otherness" grounded in improvisation and question the ethics of staging such encounters.

Coda

The decade constituting the core of *Performing the Greek Crisis* (2009–2019) is bookended by the Greek financial crisis on one end and the COVID-19 health crisis on the other. The year 2019 was initially meant to signal a new beginning, as Greece had successfully exited the bailouts in 2018. Instead, 2019 bookmarked the beginning of a different type of crisis, the repercussions of which have only begun to be revealed. When I started writing this book, the experience of living through a crisis of national proportions was relatable only to limited audiences, more so ones in the perceived peripheries rather than the imagined center.

Now, as you are holding this book in your hands, the experience of a crisis is something that we likely all share. I ask you to take a moment and recall your embodied response during the early stages of the global COVID-19 crisis. What did it feel like when your daily routine was disrupted and all the little things you took for granted changed overnight? While the impending, invisible threat of a virus may, at first glance, be incomparable to the imposition of austerity measures, the sense of disorientation and imbalance that both incidents cause upon encountering them for the first time is similar. As you are reading, I invite you to meditate on the nature of crises and the subtle ways that our bodies, and we as people, adjust and adapt to change.

Notes

1. The description references the closing scenes of *Europium* and draws on a video recording of the live performance uploaded by the Onassis Stegi, as well as personal notes from attending the performance live (Kapetanea and Fruček 2015).

2. *Panigyria* are festivities usually organized to celebrate religious or national holidays. They often take place at a churchyard (for instance, when the festivity is

organized to honor the church's namesake saint) or in other public spaces, such as central squares (plateies; πλατείες) of a municipality or region.

3. Dr. Christos A. Ioannou, director of the Hellenic Institute for Occupational Health and Safety traces the history of the Greek labor movement to 1879 with the outbreak of strikes on the island of Syros. The General Confederation of Workers of Greece (GSEE; ΓΣΕΕ), the biggest trade union in Greece, was founded in 1918 and comprises more than eighty workers' unions and more than seventy confederations (Ioannou 1994, 1996).

4. A notable example of a protest that brought about political change was the uprising at the Athens Polytechnic, a mass student demonstration in 1973 rejecting the military junta that had started in 1967. The protests escalated into a revolt, and a tank crashed through the gates of the university (known also as the National Technical University of Athens, or NTUA) to subdue the resistance, causing many casualties. These events triggered the fall of the regime in 1974.

5. Indicatively, in the years leading up to the crisis (2006–2008), unemployment rates ranged between 7.9% and 9.2%. The curve started rising in 2010 with 11.9% unemployment and reached a peak in 2013 at 27.6%. The unemployment rates were consistently above 20% between 2012 and 2017 (National Statistical Service of Greece 2020).

6. The EEC was created through the signing of the Treaty of Rome in 1957 and was a regional organization targeting economic integration for its member states by creating a common market. In 1993, the EEC was renamed European Community and was integrated in the EU as one of its pillars. The other two were a common foreign and security policy, and judicial cooperation in criminal matters. The pillars were eventually eliminated, and the signing of the Treaty of Lisbon in 2009 signaled the streamlining of these policies and institutions into the current EU.

7. Data attesting to Greece's economic growth following its entry to the EEC include a steady increase of the country's GDP (in the decade 1980–1990, there was a 0.7% increase, followed by 2.36% in 1991–2000 and an average increase of 4.11% in 2001–2007) and a steady decrease of unemployment rates from the 1990s to the early 2000s (IMF 2021).

8. For more on ordoliberalism, see Dullien and Guérot (2012).

9. This term is borrowed by anthropologist Neni Panourgia, who coined it to describe the Greek term αντεξουσιαστές (*antexousiastes*), "where *exousia* stands for sovereign power" (2009, xvi).

10. The president of the republic (Proedros tis Dimokratias; Πρόεδρος της Δημοκρατίας, also referred to as president of Greece or president of the Hellenic Republic) is the head of the Greek state and has first place in the country's order of precedence. The chief executive of the government is the prime minister, whereas the president of the republic has a rather ceremonial role and is usually called upon in national emergencies. It is an elected role for a five-year term. March 2020 was the first time in Greece's history that a woman (Katerina Sakellaropoulou) was elected in this role.

11. Sources on the exact time frame of bank closures are contradicting and mention closures that lasted anywhere from one to three weeks. Capital controls were enforced on June 28 at midnight and were in effect for four years, two months, and three days (Varvitsioti 2019).

12. Philhellenism etymologically derives from the Greek terms φίλος (*philos*) meaning "friend" and Ἕλλην (*Hellene*), meaning "Greek." An intellectual movement that emerged in the 1800s, it advocated for Greek independence from the Ottoman Empire. For more, see Zacharia (2008) and Most (2008).

13. In the Ottoman Empire, subordinated peoples continued their religious and cultural practices and were organized in *millets*. As Richard Clogg observes, "Broadly speaking *millets* means a religious defined people" (Braude ed.2014, 65) and is mostly used in reference to Muslims, although occasionally the term also referred to Christians and Jews.

14. "Supranational" describes the structure of the EU, along with the term *intergovernmentalism*. Both terms refer to the mode of exercising national sovereignty. Neill Nugent defines these terms as follows:

> *Supranationalism* involves states working with one another in a manner that does not allow them to retain complete control over developments. That is, states may be obliged to do things against their preferences and their will because they do not have the power to stop decisions. Supranationalism thus takes inter-state relations beyond cooperation into integration and involves some loss of national sovereignty. . . . *Intergovernmentalism* refers to arrangements whereby nation-states, in situations and conditions they can control, cooperate on matters of common interest. The existence of control, which allows all participating states to decide the extent and nature of this cooperation means that national sovereignty is not directly undermined. (2006, 558)

15. For example, Fensham (2011), Dorf (2019), Macintosh (2012), Daly (1995), and Preston (2011) explore aspects of the intersections between "natural" movements and classical Greece.

16. Since its establishment in 1975 the Ministry of Culture has changed titles and designations numerous times, ranging from Ministry of Culture and Sciences (1971–1985) to Ministry of Education and Religious Affairs, Culture and Sports (2012–2013). In order to avoid confusion, I will be referring to it throughout the book as the *Ministry of Culture*.

17. The National School of Dance is a public institution for studying dance in Greece. Most other professional dance schools are privately owned and licensed by the Ministry of Culture. In Greek, the name of the institution translates to State School of Dance, yet on their website and social media, the English name appears as National School of Dance, which is what I have adopted in this book.

18. Loukas Papademos was appointed prime minister of Greece leading a coalition government uniting three parties: the socialist PASOK, the liberal conserva-

tive New Democracy (Nea Dimokratia; Νέα Δημοκρατία), and the radical right Popular Orthodox Rally (Laikos Orthodoxos Synagermos; Λαϊκός Ορθόδοξος Συναγερμός), known by the acronym LAOS.

19. This mandate regarded primarily degrees acquired until 2003.

20. Big cities such as Thessaloniki (in northern Greece) or Kalamata (in southern Greece) are exceptions, as they offer some opportunities throughout the year, yet they still do not compare to Athens and its vibrant arts scene, as many of the artists interviewed have attested.

21. During the fieldwork process I attended multiple performances in person and was also given access to digital recordings of past works by some choreographers. Many of these performances became the focus of this book, yet, inevitably, there are also many performances and artists whose work is not represented here. The works that are not captured in this book, still informed my argument, since my data collection process included reviews and dance criticisms of most works presented during the crisis decade and thus helped me identify the trends and aesthetics of the crisis decade.

22. Indicatively, see Albright (2013, 2019), Jackson (2004), Jackson and Shapiro-Phim (2008), and Martin (1998).

23. David Gere (2004) has theorized the intersection of dance and the AIDS epidemic in *How to Make Dances in an Epidemic: Tracking Choreography in the Age of AIDS*. Gere offers a valuable framework for considering the role of bodies in a moment of crisis. However, since the book is focused on a health crisis and is historically situated during the 1980s and 1990s, resonances with twenty-first-century crises are limited.

24. Following the 9/11 national security crisis and the subsequent xenophobia, scholarship on minority discrimination and xenophobia has flourished. Such works, however, are outside the geographical scope of this book, which is concerned primarily with the intersections between financial crises and embodiment. An early example of a scholar who bridges financial crises with the embodied agency of female bodies is gender and women's studies scholar Barbara Sutton. In her book *Bodies in Crisis: Culture, Violence, and Women's Resistance in Neoliberal Argentina* (2010), Sutton theorizes the intimate connections between women's bodies, women's rights, gender performance, and the Argentinian economy.

One

Contested Bodies

Dance and Greek Nation-Building

———

A folk dance ensemble of men dressed in traditional Cretan outfits performs by the glistening sea at the Heraklion port in Crete. They are holding on to one another by the shoulders, arms stretched wide as they execute intricate footwork to the sound of a Cretan lyra. The camera focuses on their knee-high boots as the man leading the circle singles himself out and embarks on a solo full of turns and virtuosic high jumps, bringing one foot high to touch the tip of his boot with his fingers as though he is attempting to dust it off before he falls back into the rhythm and joins the others. The camera then pans to Rallou Manou, one of the key figures of modern dance in Greece, who assumes the role of the narrator. Manou describes the erectness of the dancers' bodies as a sign of bravery and speculates that perhaps the elements of body percussion intrinsic to the performance are a remnant of the sword clangs of the ancient warriors known as *Kouretes* (Κουρήτες).

The reference to the *Kouretes* is an allusion to ancient Greek cosmology. According to Hesiod's poem *Theogony*, dating to the eighth century BCE, the world for the Greeks started with the tales of the Titans. Cronus, the king of all Titans, had a habit of eating his children. When his wife Rhea gave birth to Zeus, she decided to save him and hid Zeus in a cave in Crete. She swaddled a stone in place of the baby and fed that to Cronus. To conceal the baby's cries in his hiding spot, a group of armored male dancers known as *Kouretes* practiced a war dance in front of the cave's mouth and kept Zeus safe. This story is referenced in the second episode of the documentary series titled *Greek Dance Yesterday and Today* (O Ellinikos Choros Chtes kai Simera; Ο Ελληνικός Χορός Χθες και Σήμερα), produced by the state-owned Hellenic Broadcasting Operation (Elliniki Radiotileorasi; Ελληνική Ραδιοτηλεόραση, or EPT) in 1983 (Manou 1983). Episode 2 tracks the similarities between Minoan civilization (3500–2000 BCE) and "surviving" Cretan folk dance practices. In making a connection between the dance seen in the documentary and the myth of the *Kouretes*—who are, by definition, a mythological construct—the episode turns a fictitious event into an anchor that provides historical grounding for the well-known and broadly practiced war dance called *pyrricheios* (πυρρίχειος; translating as Pyrrhic dance).

Such blurring of fact and fiction is common in the cultivation of national identity through dance in Greece. It is especially true in the ways that dance has been incorporated into school curricula as a means of cultivating national pride. When I was in elementary school, we participated in annual school parades on March 25, the day of the national celebration marking the revolution against the Ottoman Empire. The week leading up to the parade was always rife with activities commemorating the heroes of the revolution and their resistance, perseverance, and bravery. We would craft Greek flags, color line drawings of famous resistance fighters, sing the Greek national anthem, and listen to stories from that time. One of the stories we were repeatedly told was about the *dance of Zaloggo*, a heartbreaking tale of defiance, self-sacrifice, and infanticide.

The story unfolds in 1803, when Ali Pasha, the Ottoman ruler of Epirus (a region in northern Greece), besieged the territory of Souli and ordered the village's evacuation. The villagers resisted, and some of them got trapped. Many women, children, and expecting mothers were among the trapped population. To avoid capture and potential enslavement, the women threw their children off a cliff and proceeded to hold hands, sing, and dance as they slowly jumped to death themselves. Until the mid-1990s, many schools enacted a theatrical version of the event in which girls dressed in traditional regalia and held swaddled baby dolls (Loutzaki 2006). Even though my school did not participate in these reenactments, we were taught the folk song tied to the event and would sing it proudly every year. Throughout my elementary and secondary education, the *dance of Zaloggo* was presented as a historical fact and an act of unwavering heroism. It was only when I embarked on this research that I realized that although eyewitness accounts of the mass suicide and infanticide abound and have been documented in multiple sources, the event's framing as a dance ritual has been questioned (Loutzaki 2006) and appears to be more in line with national imagination rather than historical fact.

Dance and the moving body have always been central to Greece's nation-building and national identity construction—so much so that the lines between fact and fiction are sometimes blurred. Mythological stories become romanticized and treated as historical occurrences weaving narratives of presumed lineage and continuity from Greek classicism. As noted in the introduction, there is an apparent tension between how Greece is imagined, romanticized, and valued as the "cradle" of Western civilization and the ways that its tumultuous history has actually shaped its present. The body, understood here as the living organism through which people engage and experience the world around them, has been at the core of this liminal experience between the opposing forces of the "West" and the "East."

This chapter inquires *how* the Greek nation is constructed through dance, how it is imagined and embodied, *by whom* and *for whom*. First, I draw on pivotal historical moments and performance examples that illustrate the staging of national narratives and imaginings. Then, I shift attention to the institutional support available for dance productions and trace the ways that budgetary priorities have historically aligned with national narratives of historical lineage. Chronologically, this chapter spans the twentieth century and is meant to briefly introduce the history of concert dance in Greece. Since summing up such a vast period is challenging, I am focusing on distinct milestones in the history of dance in Greece to highlight the significance of bodies as the contested sites where conflicting ideologies about national belonging were negotiated. Even though folk dance is not central to my investigation of the Greek crisis, it is prominent in the historical construction of the nationalist project and is therefore examined alongside contemporary dance in this chapter.

Imagining the Nation

The ties between folk dance and nation-building were first documented in the 1830s, after Greece was established as an independent nation-state, and continued into the mid-twentieth century, when the territorial reclamations concluded in 1947. Greece's long history of occupation by the Ottoman Empire spans from the fall of the Byzantine Empire in 1453 until roughly the start of the Greek revolution against the Ottomans in 1821. During these four centuries, Greeks were dispersed throughout various parts of the Ottoman Empire and were allowed to roam freely within its confines, which meant extensive cultural mixing. Greeks were also allowed to practice their religion, Orthodox Christianity (Brewer 2010; Braude 2014). When Greece gained independence, the nation-state comprised southern Greece—the areas now known as Central Greece and the Peloponnese.

Also following the declaration of independence, the Greek Orthodox Church undertook a mission to unite the populations in the newly established Kingdom of Greece. As some residents were non-Greek-speaking ethnic minorities, the process of nation-building started from establishing a common language and religion (Christian Orthodoxy), both of which Benedict Anderson ([1983] 2006) has identified as essential criteria for establishing the imagined community of a nation. The Orthodox Church held programs to teach the Greek language to everyone residing within the confines of the newly established Greek nation-state (Zervas 2012). Thus, education was at the core of fostering a shared sense of identity.

Folk dance was incorporated into school curricula to cultivate a sense of community and offer a shared movement vocabulary. However, folk dance movements were intensely policed to ensure that they did not in any way reproduce qualities that could be perceived as "Oriental." As dance scholar Stavros Stavrou Karayanni notes, "Nationalist ideology prescribed the parameters of acceptable kinesthetic expression and in the process defined its alluring other" (2004, 253). In other words, the governing bodies chose a few dances from the liberated territories, namely *kalamatianos*, *syrtos*, and *tsamikos*, and incorporated them into the physical education curricula at schools. Deemed "panhellenic," these three dances were taught to the population of each of the territories liberated in the years to come. The chosen dances shared a clearly defined and contained movement vocabulary. Everyone was taught the steps and performed them in unison to highlight the communal character of the dances. Other regional dances practiced at the time, which were open to improvisation, were excluded from educational curricula. The improvisational freedom of movement that such dances allowed was frowned upon and associated with inadvertent displays of sexuality or promiscuity, which were considered "Oriental" traits. Greek physicality—highly choreographed and controlled—was thus carefully dissociated from presumed "Oriental excess."

The pressure to dissociate Greek physicality from the "Orient" and erase four centuries of cultural mixing, as opposed to accepting them as part of Greek identity, was consistent with colonial ideals of the era. Having lost a shared national narrative during the Ottoman occupation, the newly independent Greeks turned to their European counterparts to assist them in defining what a modern Greek identity could look like. A Eurocentric movement of support for the Greeks, known as *philhellenism*, was ignited at the dawn of the nineteenth century and spanned various interests and activities. Philhellenism can be observed in literature in the writings of Lord Byron, one of the most renowned philhellenes; it also manifested as men volunteering internationally to join the armed forces and fight for Greece's liberation. In its intellectual manifestation, philhellenism was focused primarily on reviving aspects of the classical Greek tradition. It relied on a fantasy of modern[1] (i.e., post–Ottoman occupation) Greece as the continuation of ancient Greece and modern Greeks as the descendants of ancient Greeks.

Modern Greek identity was constructed on the romanticized desire of European supporters to recenter Greece as the cradle of Western civilization. Such a task required the systematic erasure of centuries of Ottoman cultural influence on the people residing in the territory that became the Kingdom of Greece. In the process of weaving the modern Greek national narrative, fiction was often conflated with fact, as exemplified by the opening anecdotes, so much so that, as Maria Koundoura remarks, "Greece's reality is dependent on its fictionality" (2007, 12). Modern Greek culture sought to conform to a Hellenic ideal that was unattainable (because of its fictionality). That ideal was based on the sheer fact that, geographically, Athens—the city where Plato and Aristotle once roamed in the ancient market—happened to be located in the territories gradually liberated from the Ottoman Empire.[2] Education was the driving force in establishing a national identity narrative. Educational curricula were modeled on philhellenic fantasies and desires and adapted European narratives about modern Greek identity, engaging in a faulty project of historical constructivism.[3] The dream of reviving a lost golden age and living up to European aspirations of what modern Greece should be and should represent was later adopted by the leading intellectuals of the Greek Enlightenment, who in the early twentieth century set forth a bold irredentist movement to restore the pre-Ottoman borders of the Greek nation-state.

Introduced by Ioannis Koletis in 1844, the Great Idea (Megali Idea; Μεγάλη Ιδέα) advocated for the reclamation of all the lands of classical and Byzantine Greece. Although irredentism was the core directive of the Great Idea, it also encompassed philosophical and ideological aspects, such as an emphasis on national unity and homogeneity. Although intriguing, the intricacies of the Great Idea are not pertinent to the scope of this book, so I will first draw brief attention to one of its tenets: the purging of Ottoman influences from the language, which mirrors a similar purging with respect to Greek physicality, pursued through the systematic teaching of the three panhellenic dances.

Adamantios Korais, another prominent figure of the Greek Enlightenment, established a new form of language called *katharevousa* (καθαρεύουσα, literally translating as "cleansed"). *Katharevousa* was an amalgamation of demotic (modern) Greek and ancient Greek, virtually an artificial dialect. It was considered Greece's official language until 1976. *Katharevousa*'s distinctive feature was that it was a polytonic writing system that followed slightly different syntax rules than demotic Greek, which is monotonic.[4] Demotic Greek was declared the official language in 1976, yet it was not until 1982 that the polytonic writing system was abolished. People used demotic syntax to speak after 1976, yet they still used *katharevousa* to read and write. To this day, residues of *katharevousa*, such as its sentence structure and sometimes even the polytonic system, exist in official documents issued either by the Green Orthodox Church or the state, thus reinforcing the continued formal concern with cleansing Greek politics and sociality of all references to its Ottoman past.

Another important tenet in the process of constructing a national narrative is religion (Anderson [1983] 2006). The predominant religion in Greece following the establishment of the independent nation-state was Orthodox Christianity. At first sight, Christianity may appear disconnected from ancient Greek ideals (or discourses of Hellenism), which are more closely aligned with paganism or polytheism. Upon a more careful look, however, traces of Hellenism, such as the ideal Greek body, are at the core of Christian thought.[5] Athena Leoussi, in her treatise on nationalism and classicism and the Greek body in Christian thought, remarks that the body of the Greek athlete (as captured in statues, for instance) has been identified by human anatomists as the biologically perfect physique (1998, 91). She argues that Christ's body has been modeled after the Greek athlete, presenting the ideal of a perfect man. Along the same lines, Richard Dyer remarks how the "European feeling for self and the world has been shaped by Christianity, a religion whose sensibility is focused on the body" (1997, 15). The Christian body is thus in alignment with the ancient Greek body. Given such a line of reasoning, it starts to become apparent how there was even more pressure on the modern Greek body to conform to European expectations. Refusal to do so would cause a symbolic rift with Europe. Folk dance was quickly associated with the Church because, regionally, folk dances were performed at *panigyria* celebrations organized in honor of religious holidays or name days.

Staging the Nation

Throughout the twentieth century, folk dance existed and circulated primarily as a means of socialization within regional communities. It was also a way of codifying and staging cultural heritage. There is extensive Greek scholarship that documents and theorizes folk practices, including music, lyrics, and dance. Mention of Greek folk embodied practices also appears in English-language scholarship in anthropological studies, such as the work of Jane Cowan (1990), and in dance studies, such as the work of Anthony Shay (2002, 2008) and the translation of Alkis Raftis's (1987) book. In most of these examples of English-language scholarship that circulate internationally, Greek folk dance is approached as a social phenomenon upholding and perpetuating communal and familial values and as a continuation of tradition. In comparison, concert dance practices in Greece have not been analyzed to the same level of detail, which is why I examine both folk and concert dance side by side here.

The Lyceum of Greek Women (Lykeio Ellinidon; Λύκειο Ελληνίδων) was the first institution in Greece to offer folk dance classes and to train women to become dance teachers. The Lyceum was established in 1911 by Kalirroi Parren, a teacher and journalist credited as one of the first feminists in Greece. It was the first organized women's association in the country, and it is active to this day, with many branches across regions of Greece. Here, I focus on one of the first folk dance performances organized by the Lyceum as indicative of early twentieth-century approaches concerned with staging the modern Greek body as a reincarnation of the classical Greek body.

In its early years, the Lyceum organized festivals known as *Anthestiria*.[6] *Anthestiria* had roots in classical Athens. It was an annual festival honoring Dionysus, the God of wine and entertainment. The first *Anthestiria* organized by the Lyceum occurred in 1911. In the 1911 publication *Logodosia* (Λογοδοσία) the Lyceum's founder, Kalirroi Parren, reminisced on this first festival:

> The Hellenic *Anthestiria* is the first genuinely Hellenic fest. A festivity on the first of May with Hellenic dances, Hellenic songs, Hellenic music, and Hellenic clothing. Our old and our new life join beautifully in a very graphic and poetic brotherhood. Our dancers, young girls from the best of families, performed the Hellenic dances with their beautiful archaic clothing, and through the grace of their movements and the nobility of their poses, they established that the dances that have been preserved are indeed the circular ones performed by the ancients around the altars. (quoted in Antzaka-Vei 2010, 233; my translation)

Despite its succinctness, this quote accurately mirrors the priorities of the irredentist political agenda of the era. In the archival images from the event, the all-female cast of performers are dressed in long tunics in direct reference to the classical past. The festival's name, taken from an ancient Greek celebration, is another symbolic gesture weaving in the thread of historical lineage. Most jarring, however, is the quote's concluding sentence, which makes a claim for the embodied archive preserved across millennia. The dances presented at *Anthestiria* are one of the first examples of the practice that has been undertaken by Greek subjects of modeling the Greek self according to European expectations. Next, I consider another instance of staging Greek subjects, one directed by an American artist.

Nearly two decades after the first *Anthestiria* festival, the ambition to restore aspects of the Hellenic past manifested in another festival with philosophical grounding and intended global appeal. The first Delphic Festival was organized in 1927. It relied on the vision of Greek poet Angelos Sikelianos[7] and was choreographed by his wife, the American philhellenist, archaeologist, and artist Eva Palmer-Sikelianos. The first Delphic Festival consisted of a staging of *Prometheus Bound*, an ancient Greek tragedy attributed to Aeschylus; a presentation of athletic games; and an exhibition of handicrafts. Eva Palmer-Sikelianos choreographed and directed the tragedy after conducting extensive archaeological and ethnographic research in Greece. Some of the chorus performers were dancers from the Lyceum of Greek Women. The organization of the first Delphic Festival is almost elevated to mythical status in Greek dance scholarship (Fessa-Emmanouil 2004; Savrami 2014) as it is considered the event that led to the birth of modern dance in Greece. Isadora Duncan is also often hailed for her contributions to the establishment of modern concert dance in Greece. However, Duncan's work was not in direct dialogue with locals in the ways that Palmer-Sikelianos's was, and I therefore refrain from delving into Duncan's impact in the examples discussed in this chapter.

Palmer-Sikelianos initially encountered ancient Greek culture and ideas in the Parisian suburb of Neuilly and in Bar Harbor, Maine (Dorf 2019). Later, she moved to Greece, where she conducted extensive research fusing archaeology and art, attempting to reconstruct ancient Greek performance. Palmer-Sikelianos viewed modern Greece as inextricably linked to ancient Greece and believed that any performance reconstruction would make sense only if presented in the space where the culture originated. Her study of ancient Greek music was thorough and was conducted in collaboration with esteemed music scholars of the time to claim her productions' "authenticity." The same holds true for her approach to creating the performance costumes, which she wove herself following ancient Greek weaving practices to create historically accurate fabrics. As Samuel Dorf (2019) remarks, the Greek government supported Palmer-Sikelianos's efforts because it realized that the performances would draw tourists. Some of her contemporaries, such as fellow archaeologists, admired her work as authentic, even though Palmer-Sikelianos in her autobiography *Upward Panic* acknowledged that "the performance was bristling with archaeological mistakes" (1993, 113). The sentiment of the time was that Palmer-Sikelianos was able to revive a lost sense of Greekness and "return Greece back to the Greeks," as her childhood friend Natalie Clifford Barney stated in a letter to the artist (Dorf 2019, 111). The notion of needing to "return" a lost sense of self back to a group of people is dismissive of the reality of modern Greece and has colonial undertones with its assumption that modern Greeks needed to be educated about their past.

Such colonial undertones are indicative of philhellenism more broadly and create a conundrum as they elevate the Westerner in the role of a well-intending savior and a figure to look up to. Yet, in doing so, they fix the Greek subject in a subjugate position that is nearly impossible to escape. Even though it is not colonization in territorial terms, the dynamics observed in such relationships are analogous to what Homi Bhabha ([1994] 2004) defines as the colonized subject's "process of identification." Echoing Frantz Fanon's (2008) concept of the colonial subject being always "overdetermined from without," Bhabha notes that it is "through image and fantasy—those orders that figure transgressively on the borders of history and the unconscious" ([1994] 2004, 61) that the colonial condition is defined. In line with Bhabha's observation, the modern Greek subject is defined in relation to an imagined ideal that is never truly attainable yet forever remains the desired standard. As such, the "alternative archaeology" (Leontis 2015) approach describing Palmer Sikelianos's reconstruction efforts was not a postcolonial approach, as Dorf (2019) suggests, but a highly curated performance of the Western gaze imposed on modern Greece.

The staging of the Western gaze is captured in the archival images documenting the first Delphic Festival (Figures 2–4), which capture the statuesque poses and handwoven garb of the—primarily female—performers. What fascinates me most about these images is how they flip the notion of the gaze. Figures 2 and 3 document the audience—all dressed in 1920s outfits—gazing at the performers and capture the temporal chasm between the imagined statuesque Greek ideal and the contemporary reality, at least as far as fashion and bodily comportment are concerned.

Not surprisingly, the performers who participated in the Delphic Festivals at the time accepted the imposition of a narrative that imagined modern

Figure 2. The audience watches *Prometheus Bound* presented at the 1927 Delphic Festival. Photograph by Elli Sougioultzoglou-Seraidaris (Nelly's). Benaki Museum/ Photographic Archives N.1886a.

Figure 3. The chorus of female dancers in *Prometheus Bound* perform at the center of the stage in the circular ancient theater of Delphi. Photograph by Elli Sougioultzoglou-Seraidaris (Nelly's). Benaki Museum/Photographic Archives N.1888.

Figure 4. The chorus of female dancers pose at the edge of the stage with the ancient site of Delphi as their backdrop. Photograph by Elli Sougioultzoglou-Seraidaris (Nelly's). Benaki Museum/Photographic Archives N.1912.

Greeks as descendants of classical civilization as an enlightening truth about their cultural legacy. The writings of Koula Pratsika, the leading performer at the Delphic Festivals, fervently reflect this newfound appreciation:

> 1926. DELPHI. . . . Eva accepts me. I know not what awaits me; I know nothing of what I will experience or what will weigh on me for the rest of my life. The rehearsals in Palaio Faliro. In Delphi, I am swamped with a light. I accept it like God's blessing. *An unknown side of Greece is revealed to me, one unbeknownst to us Greeks.* Not one of mere spirit, of study, of rhythm, of Plato, of the ancient texts and the writings. But a vivid presence, eternal, ageless, always youthful! Despite the centuries of slavery, the Greeks are still reverently holding on to their traditions, their language, their religion, their idioms, their music, traditional instruments, their Byzantine music, their traditional dances, their art of weaving, embroidery, outfits, clay pottery, wood carvings, jewelry. . . . My soul fills with light: to work, to study, and to return home so that I too can contribute and pay the small price of my existence to the country that I had the fortune to be born in. (Pratsika 1991, 16–17; my translation; emphasis added)

Pratsika's enthusiasm for discovering a "different kind of Greece"—albeit one in line with romanticized philhellenist imaginings—shaped her artistic agenda for years to come. Considered one of the founding figures of modern concert dance in Greece, Pratsika was the first to establish a professional school for dance in Athens in 1937. She bestowed the school to the state in 1973, when it was renamed the Kratiki Scholi Orchistikis Technis (Κρατική Σχολή Ορχηστικής Τέχνης; known as the Greek National School of Dance).

Another notable instance of tying the national narrative to embodied practice came a decade after Pratsika's performance at the Delphic Festival when she was invited to choreograph the invented tradition of the lighting of the Olympic flame in Archaia Olympia. There is no archaeological evidence to suggest that the lighting of the Olympic flame was a practice in ancient Greece. Instead, it is a tradition invented in the era of modernism. The choreographed ritual of the flame-lighting ceremony involved a group of women dressed in togas representing ancient priestesses and was first introduced in 1936. The 1936 Berlin Summer Olympics occurred under Hitler's National Socialist regime and was the first time in modern history when a torch relay was organized to bring the flame of Archaia Olympia to Berlin. The symbolism of the torch relay in the context of narratives about Aryanism, and the entanglement of such narratives with discourses of Whiteness and Hellenism, should not be overlooked here.

The second half of the 1930s signified a rather dark period marked by the rise of extreme nationalism in several European countries and the establishment of the dictatorial Metaxas regime in Greece (1936–1941). During the Metaxas dictatorship, the aesthetic reconstructions and reenactments of classical antiquity intensified and were regime-driven, which resulted in associating the extensive employment of Hellenistic rhetoric with the ethnocentrism of the far right. Folk dance was central to this mission as Metaxas styled himself as the First Peasant (Loutzaki 2001), thus fashioning an alternative lineage between "peasant" or "rural" folk dance practices and classical Hellenism. Grandiose celebrations with movement choirs were organized to commemorate the regime in annual festivities known as the *4th of August Festivities*, where folk dance was staged as a metaphor for the nation's supposed unity. Steeped in totalitarian propaganda and xenophobic rhetoric, the slogans circulating within these performances advocated for a "return to the genuine roots" and the "eschewing of foreign ideas" (Loutzaki 2001, 129). The performers who participated in the folk celebrations were laborers, farmers, and villagers from around Greece. As Pratsika (1991) notes in her autobiography, her school organized the festivities and directed the varying groups of participants in the four years when they took place between 1937 and 1940.

While Greek dance history scholarship does not include extensive mention of Pratsika's involvement in politics, scholars have pointed out her willingness to collaborate with the governing power and describe her educational mission as consistent with narratives of lineage similar to those adopted by totalitarian regimes (Barboussi 2015; Fessa-Emmanouil 2004; Tsintziloni 2015). The inaugural performance of Pratsika's school took place in 1938 at the Herodes Atticus Odeon (Ωδείο Ηρώδου Αττικού) and opened with folk dances performed to live music. This inclusion of folk dance in early concert dance performances indicates a need to frame concert dance as another locus of cultural lineage.

Archival sources documenting modern dance in Greece up until the midtwentieth century show female dancers, dressed as priestesses in tunics and performing in restored or preserved ancient Greek theaters and other archaeological ruins. Dancers in archaic outfits engage in practices reminiscent of Genevieve Stebbins's rendition of Delsartian statue posing,[8] restage mythological narratives and reconstruct images of the chorus from ancient Greek tragedies. A notable example is Rallou Manou, who started as Pratsika's student in 1933 and then studied dance in New York at the Hanya Holm School of Dance and with Martha Graham. She was the first to bring the Graham technique to Greece. Manou founded Hellenic Choreodrama (Ελληνικό Χορόδραμα) in 1951, an artistic union that fostered high-brow collaborations between esteemed musicians (such as Manos Hatzidakis), dancers, and visual artists (such as Yannis Tsarouchis). The same year, she established the professional dance school Rallou Manou, which offered classes in ballet and modern dance (Graham) technique. The productions of the Hellenic Choreodrama drew on Greek themes, both ancient and contemporary. In the early years of its operation, productions predominantly revolved around classical aesthetics and drew on mythological themes, whereas later, the focus shifted to post-Ottoman traditions and customs, which better reflected people's contemporary experience (Stamatopoulou-Vasilakou 2005).

Another notable pioneer of concert dance in Greece is Zouzou Nikoloudi, who was also one of Pratsika's early students and collaborators. Nikoloudi's most notable legacy was the founding of the dance company Chorika (Χορικά; translating as "of the chorus"), which focused on researching the chorus in the context of ancient Greek tragedies. The role of the chorus had been to act—usually commenting on the plot or the protagonist's choices—to sing, and to dance. The company's works revolved around explorations of these three elements in tandem. Chorika was founded in 1966 and performed intermittently until 2003.[9]

Folk Dance as a "Living Link with Antiquity"

A significant departure from staging folk dance in alignment with classical aesthetics occurred when Dora Stratou, a former student at the Lyceum of Greek Women, founded her own folk dance company, the Dora Stratou Dance Theater, in 1952. Stratou is considered one of the most prominent folklorists in Greece as she organized numerous trips throughout the country to research and document regional traditions. She completed twenty-five tours between 1952 and 1959, in which she documented the music, the lyrics, the dance steps, and the traditional regalia of each place she visited. As observed by critics of Stratou's work, such as Stavros Stavrou Karayanni (2004), she was driven by anxiety to de-orientalize Greece and purge it from any remaining Ottoman influences. This effort manifested as a resistance to documenting dances with movement vocabulary that could be interpreted as "Oriental" and an omission of music with "Eastern" rhythms or non-Greek dialects in the lyrics.

Still, evidently preoccupied with upholding narratives of cultural continuity with antiquity, Stratou embraced each region's traditional garb and regalia as surviving traces of a long cultural lineage. Contrary to her predecessors, who focused on dressing the dancing body in archaic clothing to revive lost links to classical antiquity, Stratou turned to comparative research to argue for a direct correlation between dance movements or motifs embroidered on traditional fabrics and similar patterns documented in ancient urns. Her approach honored folk traditions and dances as living and breathing evidence of a direct lineage, implying that traces of classical culture need not be revived, as they had never truly been lost. In Stratou's view, they were ever present, as long as one knew where and how to look for them.

Stratou published two books, *Greek Dances: Our Living Link with Antiquity* (1966) and *Greek Traditional Dances* (1978). The first was published by her company. The second was published by Organismos Ekdoseos Didaktikon Vivlion (Οργανισμός Εκδόσεως Διδακτικών Βιβλίων known as ΟΕΔΒ; translating as the Organization for Publishing Educational Books), and was incorporated into elementary school curricula in 1979, thus proving the continued emphasis on embodiment in Greek nation-building through education. In both books, Stratou puts forth the same argument, namely that the folk dances practiced in rural Greece were directly rooted in ancient Greek practices.

To prove her point, in the back matter of her second book, she includes pictures of ancient Greek urns, vases, and statues and juxtaposes them with images of dancers captured during a folk dance performance. Comparing the two images, she focuses on the similarities observed in the spatial patterns and the shapes created by dancers' bodies (such as how they are holding on to one another), claiming these as proof of a surviving embodied archive preserved in folk dance. For instance, one image captures a statue from the ancient Mycenaean civilization (1750–1050 BCE), which depicts three figures forming a semicircle and holding on to one other by the shoulders; a fourth figure stands in the middle of the shape playing a Cretan lyra. Right below, in a still image from a dance called *kotsaris* from Pontus, six female dancers dressed in traditional regalia hold on to each other by the shoulders, with a male performer standing beside their circle playing the lyra. The implication is that the similarity between these two images is indisputable proof of the survival of ancient traditions in modern folk practices. This approach to structuring an argument is questionable as it is easy to stage a scene to mirror archaeological findings.

Stratou develops a similar argument about the shapes created by the dancers in space. She links the circular shape characteristic of most folk dances with the fact that dances were performed in a circle around an altar in ancient times. She also provides evidence for traditional regalia's resonances with antiquity by including photographs of patterns drawn on urns and vases, such as spirals or flowers, and tying those to the embroidery found on many rural regalia.

In documenting dances and music, Stratou refrained from studying any dances perceived as having Ottoman references. In her view, such references included hip shaking, shoulder shimmying, or other movements that were perceived as sexual or promiscuous, qualities associated with stereotypical perceptions of the "Orient" at that time. In her writing, the anxiety to conform to European standards of cultural refinement and to prove Greekness as worthy of being considered "Western" was overtly present. In the closing chapter of her first book, she remarks:

> I came to the conclusion that when Greece was liberated, following the war of independence in 1821, the primary concern, coming out of four centuries of enslavement from the Turks, and as such from the East, was to get rid of this burden; similar to taking off a piece of clothing that reminds you of an uncomfortable situation that you experienced while wearing it. [They wanted] to get closer to the West . . . The West

that we are connected to in so many tangible ways ever since Sicily and South Italy were called "Great Greece" (Stratou 1966, 54; my translation; ellipsis in original)

As this quote demonstrates, her documenting of folk songs and dance was driven by her personal bias. She deliberately excluded Eastern-sounding melodies and non-Greek lyrics from her documentation. This exclusionary approach led to the invisibilization of the emerging genre of urban folk music, called *rempetika (ρεμπέτικα)*, which rose to popularity during the period she was conducting her research.

In the 1950s and early 1960s, *rempetika* became a way to affirm a shift in national identity and consciousness and to capture the critical sociopolitical changes that marked the postwar constitution of Greekness. The dances performed to *rempetika* music were furthermore marketed as a renewed national image for internal and external mass consumption. In 1964, the movie *Zorba the Greek* became an international box office hit, and this caused a rise in tourism to Greece. This popular movie coincided with a renewed national image that no longer emphasized the rural character of folk dances but had a more urban focus. Images of Greeks holding on to each other's shoulders, dressed in blue pants and white T-shirts, emerged in the aftermath of *Zorba the Greek* and soon became a trademark of the new international image of modern Greekness. *Rempetika*[10] started as a marginal and transgressive practice, as most of the early songs discussed delinquency and drug use, but the genre gradually became the "authentic" song and dance of the city. As a modern tradition, *rempetika*'s roots can be found in the practices of the populations hailing from Asia Minor, as evidenced in the rhythmic patterns typical of the genre and the movement vocabulary (such as hip gyrations for women). The traces of Eastern movement vocabulary, the oft delinquent narratives, and the hybrid rhythms of *rempetika* dances challenged Stratou's argument of an "untainted" lineage.

Stratou's research coincided with large population movements from rural areas to urban centers, thus giving rise to distinctions between centers and peripheries. *Rempetika* was gaining ground in urban centers as a hybrid genre encompassing a plethora of regional influences, while the distinct regional rhythms and movement vocabularies of folk dances were preserved in the rural periphery. Focusing mainly on the periphery, one of Stratou's most significant contributions was the reclamation of the rural subject as a "noble peasant." Contrasting popular stereotypes about rural subjects as unrefined, uneducated, and uncivilized, Stratou's mission aggressively westernized "peasants" through manufactured ties to classicism. To put these shifts into context, in the decade of the 1940s, Greece was still recuperating from the Second World War, when it was under tripartite occupation (by Germany, Bulgaria, and Italy), and the civil war that immediately followed. Although mass arrests of communists continued into the early 1950s, the country had momentarily returned to democratic governance under Prime Minister Konstantinos Karamanlis. The mid-1950s, when Stratou completed her ethnographic documentation journeys and began touring with her company, introduced a sense of relative stability. The intense political turmoil of the time cultivated a space for considering what it meant to be Greek in the mid-twentieth century. This, in turn, led to a shift in the arts, coming to terms with some aspects of Greek identity that people had not been open to seeing before. Such elements included the richness of rural communities, the significance of Turkish elements in the Greek culture (such as culinary influences), or the cross-cultural rhythm medleys in traditional music, as captured in *rempetika*.

Mid-century modern dance practices also demonstrated a disengagement from the classical aesthetic (notwithstanding exceptions), while some of the most prominent modern dance choreographers, such as Rallou Manou, started embracing aspects of contemporary Greekness. These experimentations sometimes included references to concepts that had roots in Greece's Ottoman occupation. One such example is the tale of Karagiozis, who is the main character of a folklore form of shadow theater descending from the Turkish shadow puppet play *Karagöz and Hacivat*, and the use of *rempetika* music in concert dance performances.

Dance in the Junta

The relative stability of the 1950s and early 1960s was short-lived, as 1967 marked the beginning of a military dictatorship that lasted until 1974. During that period, art production was strictly regulated. For example, some theater revivals of ancient Greek tragedies with political content were banned because they opposed the regime's principles (Loutzaki 2001). Dance during the junta was put on display at the service of the regime and was rife with Hellenistic references aiming to celebrate the assumed grandeur of the country and of its dictatorial regime. The work of some ensembles, such as Zouzou Nikoloudi's Chorika—which had just been founded in 1966—continued uninterrupted (Savrami 2015), and the same was true for Pratsika, who had close relationships with the colonels in power, just as she had two decades earlier with officials of the Metaxas regime (Barbousi 2014).

The junta officials extensively used mass media such as radio and television and associated the regime with folk music to create a link to national identity and shared cultural heritage. *Tsamikos* (one of the three panhellenic dances) became most overtly associated with the regime. Its connotation with bravery and masculinity—that of the revolutionaries who fought against the Ottomans—was coopted by the regime, which saturated the media with portrayals of the dance. As Papaeti (2015) argues, the colonels never missed a chance to lead performative displays of folk dance in the media. They "actively and publicly performed their virility, as well as their claimed roles as the carriers of tradition and the redeemers of the nation" (57).

A documentary titled *Dances and Regalia of Our Country* (Oi Choroi kai oi Foresies tou Topou mas; Οι Χοροί και Φορεσιές του Τόπου μας), which aired on Greek national television in 1969, further highlights the centrality of folk dance in the national narrative during the junta. The documentary compares archaeological artifacts with present-day dances and traditional regalia, which according to the narrator (Yannis Fertis), offer a "testimony of the sacred continuity [of Hellenes] that nothing was able to break" (Matsas 1969, 3:35–3:38). The argument presented in this thirty-minute broadcast mirrors Stratou's approach and ushers pseudoarchaeological narratives of lineage into the 1970s.

Even though dance was televised and presented as a site for celebrating the regime, song and dance were also used as methods of torture (Papaeti 2013, 2015) for individuals arrested and held in detention camps for their opposing political beliefs. Based on oral accounts of detainees collected by Papaeti (2013), individuals were often asked to perform either one of the panhellenic dances or *rempetika* for the guards' entertainment. Refusing to do so or dancing without the expected vigor was perceived as a lack of patriotism and could lead to further torture or physical punishment. The dual role of folk dance (as both a site of pride and a torture method) is a testament to the centrality of embodiment in constructing a sense of Greek national identity.

Cultural Policies for Dance and Structures of Organization

It was in the early 1980s, several years after the restitution of democracy, that concert dance started flourishing. For the first time, there was a move away from an intensive association with national identity narratives as artists began exploring individual aesthetics and experimenting with new approaches. In modern and contemporary dance practices, attention to individuality manifested as the popularization of new techniques and choreographic methods and an openness to experimentation based on individual performers' skill-sets and movement languages. These experimentations were in line with the postmodern movement in the US that had flourished two decades earlier. The eagerness to prove eloquence in Western contemporary dance trends at the time fostered an atmosphere of creative competition. The heightening of artistic individualism—understood as both a structure that elevates choreographers to the status of "creative genius" and as a system promoting competition between company directors for subsidies—ushered concert dance into neoliberal economic frameworks.

A look at the institutional history of the subsidization system for dance productions illuminates the ongoing struggle of concert dance artists to prove the legitimacy of their art form in the political realm. The government body tasked with supporting dance performances and other forms of cultural expression was the Greek Ministry of Culture, founded during the junta. The aim of the Ministry during the military dictatorship had been to create and manipulate the public image of Greek cultural production for local and international purposes (Konsola 2006). After the restoration of the democratic system of governance in 1974, which signaled the start of a period known as *metapolitefsi* (μεταπολίτευση; roughly translating as "political changeover"), cultural policies were revisited as an obligation of the state.

Article 16 of the Constitution of Greece, which was originally adopted in 1986, states: "Art and science, research and teaching shall be free, and their development and promotion shall be an obligation of the state." Contrary to the dictatorial regime's propagandistic priorities, Article 16 sought to ensure democratic access to the arts and prioritize freedom of expression. Even though democratization would ideally be expressed as all-encompassing cultural inclusion, in practice, this was not always the case. A divide emerged between intellectuals, considered the artistic avant-garde, and pop culture artists, whose work was produced for mass consumption and entertainment. The creative vision of the former group received more support than art produced for broad audiences since the latter was criticized as inconsistent with the ideals of the Greek Enlightenment.

Metapolitefsi was a period of intense democratic and civil rights reforms, which included changes in many sectors of civil life, such as welfare and education. The end of *metapolitefsi* is roughly situated in the mid-1980s, when a new era of realist liberalism and narcissistic consumerism began (Voulgaris 2008), marked by a shift toward neoliberal attitudes, neoconservative values, and economic growth for the upper-middle class. In terms of the ruling parties, these shifts were reflected as follows: Nea Dimokratia (Νέα Δημοκρατία;

New Democracy), a center-right party, was in power during the first years of the *metapolitefsi*, in 1974–1981 and then again in 1989–1993, while the center-left PASOK was in power 1981–1989 and then again in 1993–2004.

The 1980s marked a pivotal time for cultural policy developments as Melina Merkouri, an internationally renowned actress and activist, was appointed minister of culture in 1981. Under the PASOK government, the goal of democratizing the arts was revisited, and diverse cultural expression flourished. According to political scientist Myrsini Zorba, the increased diversity in cultural expression was spearheaded by leftist artists "as well as the social movements of the time (feminist, youth, and homosexual) which imparted their own hue and demands for the legitimation of diversity and the plurality of identities in cultural life" (2009, 250). Under Merkouri, the popular element of culture (encompassing folk music and dance) was an esteemed form of cultural expression.

These changes were all part of a broader framework of modernization continuing all the way to the 1990s. In Greece, modernization was often equated with adhering to or catching up with European standards. The focus on catching up perhaps intensified following Greece's 1981 entry into the EU (then known as the European Economic Union), which equated modernization with Europeanization. The inclusion of Greece in the EU brought further shifts in cultural policies, as they now fell under EU Community Support Frameworks (CSFs). Operating in line with European integration efforts, CSFs were multiannual funding programs aimed at leveling economic disparities in European regions. Even though cultural development was given priority, the CSFs still supported a traditionalist political view of culture. For instance, in the 2nd Operational Program for Culture (1994–2000), 90% of the budget was spent on protecting and displaying Greece's ancient cultural heritage, and only 10% was allocated to contemporary culture. In the 3rd Operational Program for Culture (2000–2006), the scale still tipped in favor of classical heritage with roughly 65% of the budget being allocated to classical culture (Zorba 2009). The most striking example of this preoccupation with the past as the central reference point for defining the present was Minister of Culture Melina Merkouri's campaign for the return of the Parthenon marbles, which were (and still are at the moment of writing) in the collection of the British Museum.

Concerning how these funding allocations applied to contemporary concert dance, the funds were distributed primarily to major cultural venues and conference centers and did not support alternative or independent cultural scenes. Contemporary concert dance, a genre concerned with developing new ideas and experimentations, was mostly excluded from this support framework. As a consequence, the established cultural hegemony of the classical past remained undisputed.

Greece's entry into the EU heightened the ever-present clash between the primacy of the glorious past and the fragmented present as the introduction of a supranational system of governance further troubled the understanding of national identity and sovereignty. In dance, this rupture in the conception of national identity coincided with an increase in the number of venues supporting cultural production (shortcomings notwithstanding) and manifested as a departure from past practices. As a result, the contemporary concert dance landscape invited more international influences, which reflected the new ideal of an open and borderless EU as solidified in the 1992 Maastricht Treaty. Greek dance historian Stergiani Tsintziloni (2012) proposes that the "dance explosion" of the 1990s is directly related to the EU's open borders, as they made new techniques and practices more easily accessible to Greek dance artists and broadened their scope of inspiration.

At the same time, a substantial number of contemporary dance works produced in the 1990s, potentially tailored to the funding priorities of the state, still played with concepts and aesthetics from Greek antiquity. Yet what distinguished that decade was a break from established practices, such as those of influential Greek modern dance pioneers (i.e., Pratsika and Nikoloudi), whose works were focused on reviving aspects of classical Greek culture. Instead, contemporary concert dance productions of the 1990s were inspired retellings of ancient narratives rather than attempted reconstructions. A factor that significantly contributed to this departure from past practices was the increase in people studying abroad (with the support of the State Scholarship Foundation; Idryma Kratikon Ypotrofion; Ίδρυμα Κρατικών Υποτροφιών), who upon returning to Greece disseminated the techniques and influences they had learned elsewhere. As noted earlier, some of the most influential currents circulating among ensembles in the 1990s were American postmodern dance approaches, contact improvisation, release technique approaches, and experimentations with aesthetics akin to Northern European *Tanztheater*.

Another aspect that facilitated the broadening of creative experimentation and provided the means for staging more complex productions was the state subsidies allocated for dance production, managed by the Ministry of Culture, in 1993. There was a significant departure from prior subsidization practices under Thanos Mikroutsikos's tenure as minister of culture. Mikroutsikos was a well-known composer who was prosecuted for his leftist ideals during the junta. Under his leadership, the funding budget for independent dance was significantly raised in 1994. In 1995, he proposed a new model: a few select companies were chosen for a three-year funding plan, a change from the annual programs that had been available until then. This year is a landmark in the history of contemporary dance in Greece as it signaled the founding of the Kalamata International Dance Festival (abbreviated as KDF), with support from the CSFs. KDF contributed to the increased visibility and dissemination of contemporary concert dance in the 1990s. Mikroutsikos was, however, replaced in 1996. Thus the "institutionalization of dance funding," a term used in the Ministry of Culture's 1995 press release to refer to a scheme creating "stable and secure conditions for artistic creation" (as quoted in Tsintziloni 2012, 133), was not realized.

Nevertheless, the establishment of annual funding structures—even though they were a rather uncertain source of income as they required artists to apply each year and be granted approval by the appointed committee—did contribute to a perceived sense of prosperity for dance in the 1990s. Indeed, for the most successful companies, subsidies were enough to sustain the artists. As choreographer and director of the dance company Lathos Kinisi (Λάθος Κίνηση, which translates to "Wrong Movement"), Konstantinos Michos noted in our interview, "When we still had state sponsorship . . . you could actually make a living out of being sponsored" (Konstantinos Michos, interview, March 5, 2014). At the same time, it should be emphasized that these funding opportunities contributed to the prioritization of dance production, as opposed to research or experimentation, other areas that could have been supported.

The ministerial subsidies allocated each year, were a significant source of income for choreographers and covered the expenses for one production per season. A call for applicants was published each year, and interested parties submitted their proposals, which were voted upon by a ministry-appointed committee. As committees shifted, so did the allocation of funds, which made the financial landscape for artists quite uncertain. In my casual discussions with choreographers, many admitted an awareness of potential bias and favoritism based on the committee formation each year and the governing party (which in turn defined the configuration of each committee).

The structure of ministerial subsidies for dance production contributed to a heightening of individuality, as choreographers competed with one another and were thus less likely to form collaborations across ensembles. Dance scholar Betina Panagiotara attributes the rise of individualism to the political landscape following the *metapolitefsi*. She notes how "artists had been liberated from political pursuits since democracy had been restored, but at the same time they had the option to work individually and express themselves after a long period of oppression" (2017, 231). Consequently, collective structures on the level of artistic production were not a very common occurrence in Greece. Most companies and ensembles were run primarily by one (rarely two) choreographers, with two notable exceptions: SineQuaNon[11] and Prosxima[12] (Πρόσχημα, read as Proschima), which were artistic collectives. Besides these exceptions, for the most part, the Greek dance scene comprised individual choreographers. The scarcity of collectivities in the 1990s could be understood as consistent with neoliberal trends at the time, which suggests that concerns with issues of authorship and equality may have prevented many artists from engaging in collective practices.

The Golden Decade

It is unclear how or when the phrase *golden decade* was coined to describe the blooming of the Greek contemporary dance scene in the 1990s, yet it is a common term used anecdotally in discussions with Greek dancers, choreographers, and scholars. Most artists involved in the Greek contemporary dance scene would indeed agree that it was an era of growth for contemporary dance. Beyond the arts, the 1990s have been documented as a time of unforeseen prosperity tied to lifestyle discourses, which circulated as a media idiom, promising upward social mobility and associations with cultural Westernization and sexual liberation.[13] In the dance field, prosperity was evidenced in the number of ensembles creating and presenting work, which grew exponentially in the 1990s; the stabilization of Ministry of Culture subsidies for dance productions; and the funding support for dance students pursuing degrees abroad, provided by the State Scholarship Foundation. Of course, the perception of what constitutes growth is relative. Haris Mandafounis, a prominent Greek choreographer particularly active in the 1980s, pointedly observed, "After nothing or almost nothing, there can only be blooming, one can only move upwards" (Mandafounis interviewed in Hassiotis 2001b, 3:18–3:23; my translation). Nevertheless, the dance field's growth in the 1990s was not without significant challenges and constant battles for the legitimation of the practice of contemporary dance.

One of the most comprehensive sources that paint an image of the decade of the 1990s is a six-part documentary series titled *Contemporary Dance in Greece* (O Sygchronos Choros stin Ellada; Ο Σύγχρονος Χορός στην Ελλάδα), which premiered on the public TV channel NET in 2001. The research and presentation were curated by dance critic and historian Anastasia Hassiotis.

Each episode focuses on a different aspect of the Greek contemporary dance scene and includes interviews with various generations of choreographers, dance critics, and performers. Notably, in the first episodes, Zouzou Nikoloudi and Maria Hors, a renowned teacher and member of Pratsika's ensemble between 1938 and 1955, are among those interviewed. Other choreographers participating and appearing in interviews include artists who shaped the field in the decades leading to the 1990s, such as Haris Mandafounis, and trendsetters such as Dimitris Papaioannou (who choreographed and directed the Athens Olympic Games ceremonies in 2004), and many others who continue to hold prominent roles in the field to this day.

Even though the series' goal is to contextualize contemporary dance in the present and to make it accessible to audiences, the introductory episode titled ". . . in the shadow of Greek myths" (". . . sti skia ton Ellinikon mython"; ". . . στη σκιά των Ελληνικών μύθων") offers a history of the genre of contemporary dance in Greece by discussing its roots in the influence of Isadora Duncan and Eva Palmer-Sikelianos; this narrative is akin to that introduced earlier in this chapter. The need to anchor Greek contemporary concert dance in the glorious ancient past and in the work of famous pioneers who were inspired by this mythology illustrates once more the desire to ground the imported practice of contemporary concert dance in narratives of lineage and to present it in a way that lay audiences can immediately recognize its cultural resonance and value. A striking quote from the narrator of the documentary captures this sentiment:

> One could say that Greekness, through which dance would be able to prove its utility, was a sum of elements which functioned as a model for verifying the characteristics of this art form as national. (Hassiotis 2001a, 8:16–8:26; my translation)

This quote reveals a persistent urgency, even at the beginning of the twenty-first century, to legitimize the value of contemporary concert dance and to claim its quintessentially Greek roots.

The documentary captures a fascinating generational clash in perceptions of Greekness. Some of the older-generation Greek choreographers interviewed (such as Pratsika's students) perceive Greekness in a manner consistent with the prevalent narratives of Greek dance history, rooting Greek modern dance in the approaches of Isadora Duncan and Eva Palmer-Sikelianos. The younger generations of choreographers interviewed conceptualize it differently. They relate Greekness to one's relationship to the surrounding environment, which they translate into spatial relations between dancers onstage. They claim that Greekness is not something that can be measured or named; rather it is a mindset, something that everyone carries, just by living and working in Greece. This attitude may attest to the fact that the stakes were different for later generations, who entered the field after contemporary dance practice had been accepted as an avant-garde form of expression. Their focus was no longer on solidifying the value of a new practice unfamiliar to audiences but rather being in dialogue with other contemporary scenes internationally. For the choreographers of the 1990s, ethnic affinity was not critical. Instead, they cared about participating in an international artistic dialogue, which was facilitated by Greece's entry into the EU. Even so, the need of the documentary narrator and director to explore the question of nationalism through dance in the first place is indicative of the latent anxiety to secure alignment with European ideals and to situate Greece at the European core.

In the 1990s, the Greek contemporary concert dance scene evolved in line with internationally prevalent movements. For instance, release technique was a widespread influence, as were *Tanztheater* approaches. Release techniques were incorporated into teaching practices and were later evidenced in the aesthetics of performances, whereas *Tanztheater* influences and attempts to fuse dance with theatrical elements were the most pervasive types of experimentation amid Greek dance ensembles. A significant trend in the 1990s was a break from linear narration in favor of fragmented narratives and explorations of concepts rather than stories. Along the same lines, improvisation became more popular and gave rise to experimental approaches to performance akin to those associated with American postmodern dance.

A condition that certainly contributed to these shifts was an increased accessibility to the works of international ensembles, through video recordings, at first, on VHS and, later, on DVD, or in person at two of the most prestigious Greek festivals (the Athens and Epidaurus Festival, which invited renowned international dance ensembles since the mid-1950s, and KDF, established in 1995).

While these changes in Greek contemporary dance were undoubtedly part of its perceived growth, at the same time, they have been the focus of critiques, which note a surface-level engagement with international aesthetics and methodologies, resulting in works of subpar quality. One of the main critiques was that while works may have aimed to achieve the visual results of *Tanztheater*, they lacked the methodological foundation to do so. This shortcoming is directly related to the structure of dance education in

Greece, which focuses primarily on technical training and pedagogy rather than compositional strategies or dance production.

Another critique of 1990s contemporary dance concerns how the notable boost of creativity affected the quality of the works presented. As Hassiotis notes in the sixth episode of the documentary series: in 2001, there were fifty contemporary dance ensembles, half of which received state subsidies. This quantitative growth certainly contributed to a broadening of audiences, yet there were still many challenges that artists were confronted with. Mirka Psaropoulou, a dance critic interviewed for the *Contemporary Dance Today* documentary, noted that not everyone can be a choreographer. She explained that in other countries, out of 500 dancers, perhaps only one choreographer will stand out. In contrast, everyone in Greece did both: choreographed and performed. Another dance critic interviewed for the series, Andreas Rikakis, echoed this sentiment and commented on the lack of artistic exposure of the younger generation of choreographers and performers.

While the fact that there was such a boost of interest in contemporary dance can be considered a sign of the field's growth, as noted, it also brought more challenges for creators. Ioanna Portolou, one of the artists interviewed for the documentary and the director of Griffón dance company, commented on some of the challenges: "There are so few [choreographers] who can present their work as they want to. Putting up a dance production with a thousand restrictions is not an accurate sample of one's work. You need to be able to create it as you have imagined it" (Hassiotis 2001b, 6:18-6:30). This statement highlights how the exponential increase of contemporary ensembles also strained the available financial resources. Another challenge was that with the increased number of ensembles, each group was responsible for every facet of production (rehearsals, finances, running tech, choreographing, and performing), which inevitably impacted the quality. This cycle saturated the opportunities for performing and choreographing as many companies were closed circuits, which limited dancers' mobility between ensembles.

Unionizing for Dancers' Rights

Even as competitive individualism was the trend in artistic production, collectivities in the form of unions and rights-advocacy groups prevailed during the 1990s. These entities organized artists' demands in hopes of countering the challenges inherent for dance professionals in Greece and changed the unstable landscape of cultural policy. In the seven years between 1989 and

1996, eight different ministers of culture were appointed, which presented many challenges for artists and jeopardized continuity and stability in cultural policy. Up until the late 1990s, the only union in place for dance professionals was the Union for Dance and Eurhythmics (Somateio Chorou kai Rythmikis; Σωματείο Χορού και Ρυθμικής), which was established in 1975. Listed as its primary aims were the promotion of the art of dance, which they strived for through the publication of *Choros*+ (Χορός+, *or* "Dance+"), the only Greek magazine reporting exclusively on dance (which ceased publication in 2009); the organization of dance competitions; and philanthropic initiatives. In 1998, the Union for Private Schools for Dance in Greece (Somateio Idioktiton Scholon Chorou Ellados; Σωματείο Ιδιόκτητων Σχολών Χορού Ελλάδος) was founded to create a forum for private dance school owners to advocate for their rights and to legitimize the profession of dance teacher. The group encompasses both professional dance schools and schools offering leisure curricula. A year later, in 1999, the Union of Greek Choreographers (Somateio Ellinon Chorografon; Σωματείο Ελλήνων Χορογράφων) was founded to promote and disseminate dance and related artistic activities, as well as to provide a forum for gathering information pertinent to members. The majority of choreographers in Greece are members of this union.

While these unions certainly opened the door for collective rights advocacy, it was not until 2008 that a union was finally founded with the specific aim of advocating for the labor rights of performers and artists working in the field of dance. The founding of the Union for the Workers in the Field of Dance (UWFD - Somateio Ergazomenon sto Choro tou Chorou; Σωματείο Εργαζομένων στο Χώρο του Χορού), close to a decade after the so-called golden era for dance in Greece is indicative of the continuing struggles that dancers faced. According to choreographer Maria Koliopoulou, who was one of the founding members of UWFD:

> The founding [of the union] was born out of a need to deal with foundational issues, such as how we work, how we work for other choreographers, how the dancers are working, how hires work at various institutions (such as the state theater or various festivals). Core issues that have not been resolved. There are no collective agreements; they have been abolished in the last few years. . . . UWFD is not a syndicate. The need to manage our labor conditions led us, the core group of UWFD, to found a union that would not only focus on the rights of dancers or the rights of choreographers or dance teachers [but of everyone in

the field of dance] since the majority of us in Greece are constantly negotiating all these different roles throughout various stages of our lives. (Maria Koliopoulou, Skype interview, December 18, 2019)

The UWFD's demands more than a decade after its establishment remain almost unchanged from the list of initial core demands,[14] thus demonstrating a lack of progress. Some of the core demands include a request for dance to be categorized as a seasonal profession (seeking a pension plan at age forty-eight for dancers and fifty-eight for others working in the field, compared with sixty-seven, which is the retirement age in Greece); for dance degrees acquired from professional dance schools to be considered equivalent to university degrees; for a university for dance to be created; and for a stage dedicated to dance performances to be constructed. Most dancers and choreographers cannot sustain themselves financially through their involvement in dance productions, and either work as dance teachers on the side, or take on jobs unrelated to the performance field. The UWFD demands become especially pertinent given the multiple work commitments that workers in the field of dance are often called to navigate.

Before the Crisis

In the first decade of the twenty-first century, dance production had fallen into to a somewhat steady rhythm. Subsidies, albeit frequently limited, were available and open to application by both individual choreographers and registered dance companies. Dance as a discipline was still not elevated to academic status, nor were the diplomas granted by professional dance schools equivalent to university degrees. Despite these challenges, there was a sense of progress and creativity, as many new works were created and new companies constituted.

Especially in the years following the 2004 Olympic Games in Athens, contemporary dance in Greece enjoyed a short-lived boost in popularity. I recall a performance by Dimitris Papaioannou, the contemporary dance choreographer who directed the opening and closing ceremonies of the Olympics. His first concert dance work following this, titled *2* (2006), was an unprecedented commercial success: it was extended twice and was performed seventy-three times in total, translating to an estimated 100,000 tickets (Papaioannou 2006, 2007). Papaioannou may be an exception due to his reputation following the Olympics, but this moment should still be celebrated as indicative of a growing interest in contemporary dance. Such a high number of performances is remarkable, as most works presented by an ensemble in a regular season are limited to a dozen performances on average. The concept of repertory common among contemporary dance companies internationally is not prevalent in Greece as it is very rare that a work is revisited and presented again.

A sense of uncertainty frequently tarnished the creative surge and increased interest in contemporary concert dance. Dancers newly graduated from dance schools experimented with choreography by creating their own dance companies. But after producing one or two shows, they later dissolved as the participants either found employment at other dance companies or switched their focus to teaching or other jobs providing regular income.

Unfortunately, the increased attention that contemporary dance received from audiences did not translate into improved financial support for choreographers across the board. The total amount of subsidies allocated to dance in 2004–2010 was an average of 500,000 EUR each year, and this amount was disseminated to anywhere between twenty and thirty ensembles. The fluctuating amounts allocated to each dance production and the annual selection process, along with the uncertain working conditions of contemporary concert dance more broadly, required a constant sense of readiness and willingness to start over. Reflecting on the conditions of dance production in Greece, choreographer Maria Koliopoulou remarked:

> You cannot settle, nor take anything for granted. You cannot think that the same will be true tomorrow because you are employed today. I have been working in the field for twenty-five years, and some of my colleagues have been in it for much longer, and you are in a constant state of vigilance. *The body carries that.* Especially if you have worked as a dancer, even when you become a choreographer, you carry that inside you. . . . *There is a sense of combativeness,* and I am not mentioning this as something positive or negative, but rather as a fact: *there is a different vibration in the body.* (Maria Koliopoulou, Skype interview, December 18, 2019; emphasis added)

What Koliopoulou captures as a sense of combativeness (machitikotita; μαχητικότητα) and as a distinct characteristic that the bodies of Greek performers carry because of the conditions surrounding their art manifests onstage as heightened physicality. Choreographically, it translates into demanding sequences and abrupt weight and level changes that—although controlled—seem to push the body to its limits highlighting its materiality.

On Athenian stages, bodies are often turned into spectacles, their technical training and prowess celebrated, as many artists I interviewed explained. As the following chapters unpack, these qualities become the defining feature of performances and choreographies of the Greek crisis.

Concluding Thoughts

As the selected examples from the twentieth century and the first years of the twenty-first century discussed in this chapter have indicated, the dancing body in Greece is in a constant state of contestation, with opposing ideals of national identity projected onto it. Classical aesthetics of beauty formed the core of early twentieth-century concert dance approaches, adhering to philhellenic imaginings and Eurocentric expectations of what Greece—and the "Greek body"—should symbolize. In the beginning, both folk and early modern dance embraced classicism, which was woven through with narratives of historical lineage. While some such narratives may have contained grains of truth, many imaginings veered into the realm of pseudoarchaeology. The ephemeral nature of dance challenges the validity of any claims of embodied lineage. If there is one thing that claims of lineage *do* prove, however, it is the central place that dance holds in the construction of Greek national identity.

The revivalist argument and the pressure to selectively seek evidence in support of this argument led movement researchers, choreographers, and folklorists to take exclusionary approaches that deliberately invisibilized the practices of certain ethnic groups or the cultural mixing that took place over centuries. Motivated by a pressure to conform to externally imposed (European or Western) romanticized perceptions of what modern Greece *should* represent, the early history of dance in Greece was shaped by ethnocentric narratives that propagated Hellenic cultural superiority. As such, the imagined community of the Greek nation constructed through dance practices was first and foremost concerned with racially and religiously purifying modern Greek physicality in line with Eurocentric ideals. The body created through dance was a White, Christian Orthodox, refined body. The last point on refinement is meant to capture the highly choreographed and curated nature of most productions until the 1980s, when individuality and improvisation emerged as desired qualities. Refinement is also an allusion to social class since most leading figures in concert dance were affluent women. Last, refinement hints at the exclusion of folk practices from discussions of what constitutes "high art" since folk was relegated to the rural periphery and devalued for a while. As the example of Dora Stratou's work illustrates, the value of folk dance had to be reclaimed and the folk body rebranded as "noble" to fit into Eurocentric narratives of Greekness.

During the *metapolitefsi* era, when democracy was restored and Greece experienced unprecedented economic prosperity and relative political stability, individual exploration in the performing arts flourished. Improvisation became a core tenet for both folk and concert dance. In folk dance, improvisatory movement explorations coincided with the popularization of *rempetika*, primarily concerned with individual expression. In contemporary concert dance practices, the shift to improvisation followed the popularity of postmodern dance approaches in the US. Quite a few dancers from Greece traveled to the US to study with the pioneers of postmodernism and, upon their return, introduced similar improvisatory practices in Greece. The changes to the Greek constitution implemented in the 1980s (such as Article 16 in 1986), which officially mandated the democratization of the arts and protected the freedom of artistic expression, further contributed to the turn toward individuality.

During the crisis decade, as the next chapter illustrates, the individualistic model of the choreographer as the "creative genius" dissolved and gave way to collaborative approaches and collectivities. The crisis seemingly also caused a rift in long-standing approaches to constructing a narrative of national belonging through embodied practices. Choreographers and dancers consciously criticized associations with ethnocentric or Hellenistic national narratives and critically inquired about what it meant to be Greek during the crisis by bringing to the fore the multiple layers of contestation that such a peripheral identity encompasses. Drawing on the history of the modern Greek nation-state, choreographies produced during the crisis decade contextualized Greekness in relation to recent periods of Greek history (such as the civil war) or tackled the marginal position of Greece relative to the EU. Choreographers thus framed national belonging as an activity concerned with the present or the very recent past and began dissociating Greek embodiment from its centuries-long linkage with classics.

Notes

1. In Europe, modernism was associated with cosmopolitanism and a crisis of representation (Lewis 2011), as well as with universal capitalism and cultural imperialism. In Greece, however, according to modern Greek studies scholar Dimitris Tziovas, modernism was experienced as an identity problem and "can be seen as

introverted, ethnocentric and anti-colonial" (1997, 2). I would add one more thing to Tziovas's list: de-orientalizing.

2. See also Faubion (1993), Gourgouris (1996), Hamilakis (2009), and Herzfeld (1986).

3. The concept of historical constructivism is borrowed by James Faubion, In his 1993 book, *Modern Greek Lessons: A Primer in Historical Constructivism*, he defines it as follows:

> Historical constructivism is . . . a practice of *significative* reform or reformation, though a practice whose reforms can and often have had immediate and direct repercussions on institutions and behavior. Its methodology consequently cannot be reduced to the sheer logic of means and ends, the logic of the rational decision, and rational action. Its methodology and its teleology both demand powers of judgment quite different from, quite beyond those that would enable its practitioners merely to determine the relations among causes and effects. Historical constructivism requires of those who would practice it the further power to judge and to maintain semantic and connotative coherence from one reformative step to the next. (Faubion 1993, xx)

4. Polytonic, translating as "many accents," refers to a system of writing in the Greek language that involves multiple diacritics. It was used in the writing of *katharevousa* and ancient Greek and contrasted with the demotic way of writing that is monotonic (only one accent per word).

5. See also Makrides (2009).

6. *Anthestiria* (plural) was one of four celebrations that took place every year in classical Athens in honor of Dionysus. The festival was celebrated during the month called *Anthestirion* (singular), which meant that the wines from the previous fall had been ready. The celebrations lasted for three days. They started in a happy and festive mood and ended in a bittersweet and often sorrowful way. The melancholic ending was based on the belief that during the second day, the souls of the dead rose from Hades (the underworld) and wandered among the living, while on the third day, they entered their houses and dined with them.

7. According to Georgios Kounoupis (1960), who discusses the historical roots of Sikelianos's Delphic Idea, it is centered around a "universal" principle because it signifies the harmonious equilibrium between matriarchy and patriarchy as the two primitive systems of rule, which first occurred in the geographical area now known as Delphi. Sikelianos believed in racial and ethnic equality, and according to Kounoupis, this was one additional reason that Delphi was of significance since it shared etymological roots with *adelphoi* (αδελφοί), meaning "brothers." Delphi thus implied a global sense of brotherhood and blood relations among humankind. Beyond racial equality, Sikelianos also believed in gender equality, which he understood as stemming from the collaboration between the social systems of matriarchy and patriarchy. He did not view women as inferior or sexualized subjects but

rather recognized and honored them as equal to men, if not superior (because of their reproductive value). Part of Sikelianos's and Palmer-Sikelianos's vision was the internationalization of the Greek language because they believed that it was the most valuable factor that could unite all nations. This belief stemmed from the rich history of ancient Greece and its cultural milestones, such as democracy and philosophy. The significance of the place of Delphi for the Greek national narrative should also be considered: according to Greek mythology, Zeus deemed it the center of the earth (*the omphalos of Gaia;* ομφαλός της Γής *or "navel of Mother Earth"*). Delphi was also the site of the most important oracle in the classical Greek world and the site of the Pythian Games, one of a series of very important athletic contests that is considered the precursor of the Olympics. Delphi is still often believed to have sacred properties and is a primary tourist site, since the ruins of the ancient Delphic theater, stadium, and oracle have survived and are still preserved and open to the public.

8. Stebbins, a devoted disciple of François Delsarte, brought his theories closer to dance by displaying them through a practice known as "statue-posing." Stebbins' Delsartism was developed in response to classical Greek aesthetics. See also Zervou ([2014] 2019).

9. The company's continuous operation was interrupted because of political turmoil and financial instability. According to Savrami (2014), the company spanned across the following three periods: 1966–1975, 1988–1990, and, finally, 1995–2003.

10. See also Kotaridis (2007).

11. SineQuaNon was founded in 1992 by five Greek graduates of the National School of Dance: Kiki Baka, Anna Sofia Kallinikou, Apostolia Papadamaki, Popi Sfika, and Dimitris Sotiriou. Many of the founding members subsequently studied modern and postmodern dance techniques in the US, such as Cunningham, contact improvisation, and release technique, and offered workshops in Greece upon their return.

12. Prosxima Dance Company was founded in 1996 by a group of Greek graduates who had just returned to Greece after completing their studies in London. In its first years, it comprised many international collaborations operating as a collective in which everyone was cocreating, coperforming, and coproducing.

13. See also Zestanakis (2017, 2020) for an in-depth analysis of lifestyle discourses in the 1990s and during the first half of the Greek crisis.

14. See also Zervou (2020) for an extended discussion of UWFD's activities during the crisis decade.

Two

Fragments of a Precarious Landscape

The Crisis from Within

————

In the early days of May 2010, the streets around the Greek Parliament filled with peaceful protesters. Known as the Indignant (Aganaktismenoi; Αγανακτισμένοι) movement, hundreds of people flooded Syntagma Square and the surrounding streets to protest the austerity measures imposed on the population of Greece. Indignant movement sit-ins and occupation protests signified an unprecedented phenomenon as they invited everyone to join and were not driven by a union or political party. The Greek Indignant movement was a gesture of solidarity with the *Indignados* in Spain, and united protesters responding to austerity measures internationally. This alignment with international movements already hints at a new direction facilitated by the crisis: an increased sense of solidarity and a feeling of togetherness that overrides partisan affiliations or ideological differences.

The choice to demonstrate solidarity through embodied engagement with the public sphere speaks to an attempt to reclaim embodied agency at a time when the body was increasingly devalued and overlooked. In my 2014 interview with dance historian Stergiani Tsintziloni, in which she reflected on the early years of the crisis, she noted:

> One of the characteristics of the period of the crisis is that the body is invisible. There is constant talk about the crisis, the economy, the austerity measures, the memoranda, about institutionalized issues and actions of a political and economic nature that are decided at a very high level. This impacts and affects the everyday life of all of us. In this day-to-day situation, *I feel that the body has no value.* The body is being abused, abased, and for real! I mean [take, for instance] all the things we hear

about the Golden Dawn. . . . *I feel that people are being pressured and enter a work process and a way of life where the last thing they care about is their body.* . . . All we hear about bodies has to do with their abuse. There certainly is a passivity. I think [the body] is immaterial in terms of a political ideology that completely disregards [the body's] material dimension and oppresses it in real and symbolic ways. Thus, anyone concerned with corporeality and the materiality of bodies is disregarded as nonexistent and is not heard. We are reentering an era of discourses. (StergianiTsintziloni, interview, January 20, 2014; emphasis added)

Here, Tsintziloni captures the complexity of the embodied experience in the early years of the crisis decade, when political rhetoric was highly disembodied yet people's bodies bore the immediate impact of the crisis. The austerity measures and the labor precarity they introduced (such as mass layoffs) made many people turn to manual labor or multiple part-time work commitments. Simultaneously, bodies were foregrounded as prime sites of political agency (as seen in the protests) and thus introduced a paradox in constructing, understanding, and framing Greek national identity in the early crisis years.

As bodies and embodied forms of expression have historically been at the core of Greek national identity construction, the onset of the crisis initiated a scrutinizing of established practices of collective nation-building. The problem magnified the existing deficits and shortcomings in various aspects of the social sphere. It mobilized an intensive process of reconsideration that encompassed institutional restructuring, a reconceptualization of the national narrative, and an overall reevaluation of the modus operandi. For the public, embodied forms of protest, such as the *Indignant* sit-ins or other anti-austerity marches, were the primary means of engaging in political activism. In private, the reclamation of embodied agency likewise shifted, taking on the form of participating in training regimens, signing up for dance classes, or exercising. Many interviewees observed an anecdotal rise in enrollment in dance classes or participation in dance as a recreational activity. In an article published in 2014, dance scholar Ioanna Tzartzani captured the rise of embodied engagement during the early years of the crisis:

On the individual level, more and more people are taking a personal interest in dancing and, while the traditional ballet conservatories for children may be suffering, adult classes are widely popular, and the number of students participating in the entry exams for the professional dance schools is also high. (2014, 43–44)

For professional dancers and choreographers, who were already versed in the primacy of embodied agency, the increased attention to the body presented an opportunity to reassert the significance of contemporary concert dance as a potent site for critical engagement with the sociopolitical sphere. The crisis's continually fluctuating sociopolitical and financial landscape affirmed the importance of bodies as the sole stable referents people had at a time when everything else around them was unstable.

Following the prosperity of the golden decade, the years after the 2004 Olympic Games in Athens are considered the prelude to the country's economic downfall. Beyond the Olympics, 2004 was a milestone year of celebration as the Greek national team won the UEFA (Union of European Football Associations) European Soccer Championship, thus fueling sentiments of national pride. I treat this year as the starting point for tracing the trends observed in government funding for performances till the 2009–2010 season, when the Ministry of Culture last approved subsidies for choreographers. After that, there was a seven-year pause until subsidies were finally reinstated for the 2017–2018 period. This pause forms the core of this chapter. This was a period when choreographers and performers gradually learned to adapt to the unprecedentedly precarious conditions of production and devised new approaches to creating work and finding new spaces to host performances. After painting a picture of these new work conditions, I turn to an analysis of specific performances to track the emergent narrative trends in the early years of the crisis. First, there was a clear departure from cliché narratives of a glorified past. Choreographers critically reframed historical memory and problematized dominant narratives of national identity in works that unearthed previously underexplored aspects of Greece's modern history. The second trend was a systematic engagement with the psychosomatic impact of the crisis and the strain it imposed on relationships. Themes of alienation and disorientation were commonly at the core of choreographies produced, as were explorations of political theories of precarity, austerity, and critiques of neoliberalism, all woven together to contextualize a subject's experience of crisis. The last trend regards new choreographic and staging approaches that emerged in response to navigating the frugality of the crisis condition.

Waning Institutional Support for Dance

The performing arts were one of the first disciplines impacted by the extensive budget cuts. During the first two years of the crisis, 2009–2010, no significant changes were observed in the dance scene regarding the funding structures

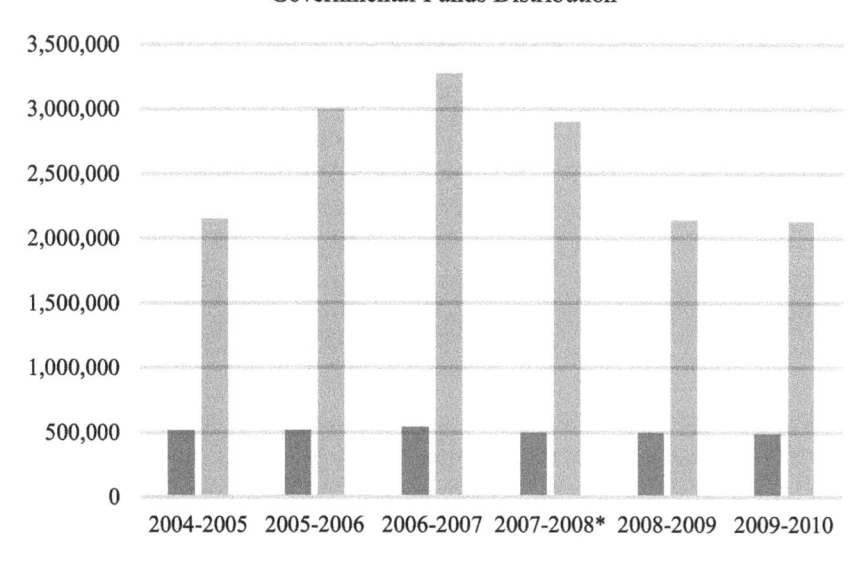

Figure 5. Ministry of Culture funding disparities between dance and theater productions. The data is based on the approved budget. All amounts are exact except for the approximate amounts shown for theater companies in 2007–2008 (marked with an asterisk), as exact data was unavailable for that year. Graph created by the author.

that supported choreographic creation. As had been the case for the preceding few decades, there was a call to apply for governmental subsidies each year. Between 2010 and 2012, the Ministry approved subsidies for educational programs but not for performances. Here, it is essential to note the word choice: I use "approved" rather than "disbursed" because available data on the sponsoring of companies and programs document discrepancies between the approved budget amount and the amount that was eventually disbursed. The same is true for the above chart (Figure 5), which illustrates the funding allocated to the performing arts in the years leading up to the crisis.

The approved budget for the 2006–2007 season was the highest, and I have therefore chosen it as an example to offer an indicative breakdown of the amounts awarded to ensembles. The highest subsidy approved that year to a single dance company was 50,000 EUR to Dimitris Papaioannou for his work 2. In contrast, the lowest amount given in the same period was 4,000 EUR to a company named Fygein Adynaton (Φυγείν Αδύνατον; Impossible to Leave). A comparison with theater company subsidies shows a sizable funding disparity: the largest amount given to a theater company during the same period was 295,000 EUR, while the smallest amount granted was 10,000 EUR. The total amount of subsidies approved for dance was 544,000 EUR, shared between thirty-one companies (all based in Athens), whereas sixty-six theater companies shared 3,275,000 EUR (fifty-one of which were based in Athens). The gaping disparities captured in the chart attest to two things: first, they confirm the devaluation of dance as an art form and a discipline of study, and second, they illustrate the plethora of theater companies and professional theater groups that exist in Greece.

Following the funding peak in 2006–2007, the next three years captured in the chart demonstrate a gradual drop in the approved amounts. Financially, this meant that even for the dance companies ranking first or second in received funding, the maximum awarded subsidy averaged 30,000–35,000 EUR. Even with this gradual drop in the funding budget, nothing prepared artists for a complete lack of funds. After the announcement that there would be no subsidies for 2010–2011, dance production slowed significantly. Choreologist and dance scholar Katia Savrami commented on this to me in an interview a few years after the cessation of ministerial subsidies: "The period that we have entered now is one of suspension. Complete suspension" (Katia Savrami, interview, January 9, 2014). Opportunities for dancers to find paid work were scarce or confined to the private sector, such as works subsidized by the Onassis Stegi. Even when production started picking up again after 2013, few works were created outside the support of private institutions during that period. These were either self-funded or relied on alternate funding sources, such as the European Strategic Investment Funds (ESIFs) distributed by the EU.

A notable funding scandal brought attention to the ESIFs and popularized them after 2013. In May of that year, Nikos Xydakis, a journalist and left-wing politician, wrote an acerbic article questioning the decision of the secretary-general of the Greek Ministry of Culture to approve an astronomical ESIF subsidy of 329,000 EUR to a single dance company called Echodrama (Ηχόδραμα). In the article, Xydakis (2013) claims that "none of the people questioned from the dance field knew anything about this artistic company," thus challenging the validity of the decision. Compared with the subsidies from preceding years, this grant was equivalent to two-thirds of the Ministry's budget, allocated to thirty companies, during a regular year. A representative of *Echodrama* (Yannis Pisimisis) provided a written response to Xydakis, highlighting that the only reason they received such an amount was that *theirs* was the only company to apply for the grant and had no competition. Following this controversy, more and more artists turned to ESIF grants and gained support from the EU. While it is unclear whether this event marked a change in direction, 2013 certainly was a turning point for artistic production.

Alternative Modes of Collaboration

After two years of adapting to the lack of subsidies and navigating the landscape of austerity, more artists turned to external funding, applied to festivals organized by private institutions, or sought alternative ways to fund their creative work. In search of low-cost options, many choreographers turned to site-specific or street performances. They became involved in initiatives and venues that were partaking in nonmonetary forms of exchange between the production staff, performers, and audiences, such as volunteering. Such a "tit-for-tat" barter economy is relatively common in the precarious landscape of contemporary dance, even in European art centers such as Berlin (Van Assche 2020). At the dawn of the Greek crisis, the barter system was utilized widely for navigating labor demands in performance production. Dance classes were offered on a pay-what-you-want/-can basis or with a suggested donation.

The most notable self-organized artistic venue that emerged in the crisis decade is the theater called EMPROS (ΕΜΠΡΟΣ; which translates as "Onwards Theater"). EMPROS was an abandoned theater building that closed in 2007. In November 2011, a group of artists known as Kinima Mavili (Κίνημα Μαβίλη; the Mavili Movement) occupied the building. Kinima Mavili took its name from a famous square in Athens's center known for its nightlife and street food. It comprised a group of artists (actors, directors, and theater scholars) who wanted to bring attention to cultural policy issues and the lack of spaces and support for newly founded theater groups and experimental ensembles. Until the moment of writing, the theater has been operating under occupation despite numerous government attempts to shut it down. Since its initial occupation, it has become established as a site of radical-left artistic endeavors and regular workshops, performances, talks, and classes, while there are also occasionally public demonstrations initiated by some of the participating collectives and artists. Most events hosted at EMPROS are free, open to the public, or offered on a barter system to make art accessible to broad audiences.

In the summer of 2015, a group of artists and volunteers from various arts backgrounds came together to reinstate another abandoned theater space in a different central spot in Athens known as Green Park. First occupied in June 2015, the space hosted a ten-day series of arts events designed as a "political and cultural intervention" (Green Park Manifesto 2015). According to the Green Park Manifesto:

> This activation refuses a particular temporal horizon and understands itself outside of the logics of ownership. The occupation is not defined by a particular ideology or interest but rather comes about as a result of the encounters born out [of] the experiments and struggles of the last few years. Thus, we look to rebuild modes of collectivity and solidarity and reclaim friendship for its political importance. We propose friendship as a model for organizational formations and autonomous instituting that exceeds neoliberal calls to order. (Green Park Manifesto 2015; original in English)

Collectivity and solidarity, thus, emerge as core values driving artistic initiatives during the crisis. Another instance of a reclaimed space is the Kypseli (Κυψέλη) Market, a building that used to host a local market and was similarly turned into a social hub hosting concerts, exhibitions, workshops, and seminars between 2006 and 2012.

The rise of volunteering initiatives and artistic collectives in the first half of the crisis indicates a new direction for the Greek performing arts landscape. Compared with the previously established competitive and individualistic model, collaborations between and across ensembles flourished once subsidies were no longer available. The most striking example was a collective of choreographers called Syndesmos Chorou (Σύνδεσμος Χορού, roughly translating as "Dance Link"), which was established in 2009 by the directors of five Athenian dance companies. According to their website description:

> *Syndesmos Chorou* is a network of dance companies that joined forces in 2009 in order to exchange ideas and resources and experiment with a collective mode of practice, within the specific context of contemporary dance in Greece. Their aim was to create a sense of community within the field of dance, to lead collective actions, and to offer opportunities for dialogue. Originally the network was founded by five companies: *Amorphy, Lemurius, Φora, Dalika,* and *Prosxima,* which were very recently joined by two more: *YELP* and *Zeta.* (Syndesmos Chorou n.d.; original in English; italics in original)

Choreographers Tzeni Argyriou (Amorphy), Katerina Skiada (Lemurius), Medie Mega (Φora), Vaso Giannakopoulou (*Dalika*), and Maria Koliopoulou (Prosxima) were the founders and directors of the first five companies. In 2013, the new members that joined were Mariella Nestora (YELP) and Iris Karayan (Zeta). All choreographers involved in this initiative are well-established in the Greek contemporary concert dance scene.

Prior to the establishment of Syndesmos Chorou, collaborations between multiple dance companies were atypical. The lack of dialogue between choreographers and companies repeatedly came up as a point of critique of the Greek dance scene in the many interviews I conducted for this research. Even though choreographers and performers frequently attended each other's productions, there were rarely opportunities for in-depth engagement with one another's works. Syndesmos Chorou actively sought to change that (at least between the participating members).

Exploring Syndesmos Chorou as a case study, dance scholar Betina Panagiotara (2017) notes that despite the generational gap between the members, they shared commonalities in their educational backgrounds. They had acquired degrees from professional dance schools in Athens, and all but one of them subsequently continued their studies abroad, thus "becoming familiar with the critical theoretical discourse on dance, diverse dance techniques, and choreographic approaches, as well as collaborative working modes" (Panagiotara 2017, 235). The mention of collaborative working modes is of particular significance here because most choreographers in the collective formed dance companies in partnership with other artists (such as authors or light designers), deviating from the predominant insular model in which a dance company is directed by one person. Syndesmos Chorou was born out of the need to share resources and create a forum for dialogue and discursive exchange during a time when financial resources were scarce.

In a interview with me in 2019, one of the collective's founding members, Maria Koliopoulou (the director of Prosxima), remarked how one of Syndesmos Chorou's priorities was to explore ways to engage audiences differently and open up dance to community members. To that effect, they fostered an initiative titled *x+1*, where *x* is a variable denoting the number of rehearsals that preceded the performance (e.g., 7+1 or 8+1). This initiative focused on involving people without prior dance exposure. Participants were invited to the creative process and actively shaped the final performance. Open forum discussions followed each iteration of *x+1*, where choreographers, participants, and audiences discussed their experience participating in the initiative.

According to Koliopoulou, the central questions underlying this initiative were the following:

> How can we bring dance closer to the people? In Greece, this is a relationship that is constantly in the process of being built, and its results are not always visible, even though there has been a continuity in the activities of companies and artists, and choreographers during at least the last twenty years. So that was one of the questions: How do we build this relationship, and how do we make dance accessible to broader audiences? So one of the laboratories that brought many people closer [to dance and to each other] was one we did in the dance community. We had professional dancers, amateurs, children, and a group of sixty-five-plus [years old]. . . . The most important was meeting different people in the context of dance. . . . The varying age groups and their different levels of dance engagement—professionals, amateurs, people who had never performed before—were our main target, and that was what people responded to the most. (Maria Koliopoulou, Skype interview, December 18, 2019)

The initiative's launch event, titled *7+1*, happened at the 17th KDF in 2011, where it ended with a performance at the regional stadium involving professionals and amateurs. Each participating member rehearsed seven times with different groups of performers, culminating in an evening performance combining everyone's work. A lengthy talk-back with audiences followed the show, which provided valuable feedback to Syndesmos Chorou members concerning the efficacy and impact of their outreach endeavor.

The collective's other initiatives included *Elxeis;* (Ελξεις, or "Attractions"), targeting dance students with the intent to introduce them to the work of Syndesmos Chorou and offer a chance for the members to get to know them as well. The plan was for the *Elxeis* initiative to be organized in conjunction with the directors of professional dance schools, yet only one meeting materialized with students of the Rallou Manou school, which centered on their needs in the field. Syndesmos Chorou also organized *feedback sessions* and *meetings* that targeted the involvement of other companies aiming to build structures for opinion exchanges between artists in the dance field in Greece. *Syndesmos Chorou* also participated in the reactivation of EMPROS through an initiative called *Chrisi #3* (Χρήση #3; or Use #3) in 2012, which encompassed a series of events, such as meetings, exhibits, workshops, presentations, and interdisciplinary performance collaborations between dancers, students, scholars, journalists, and dramaturgs. Overall, Syndesmos Chorou opened the door for fostering dialogue between artists in ways that had not been available before. In doing so, it permitted a reflection on past practices, exposing some of the inadequacies of the previously established individualistic model.

Backstage in the Dance Field

The noted shifts toward increased engagement in volunteerism and collaboration during the early years of the crisis were signs of growth for Greek contemporary concert dance. The circumstances created by the Greek crisis forced artists to devise alternative ways to make work and inspired aesthetic, narrative, and methodological shifts, as the following sections address. Indulging in discourses that celebrate crises as an opportunity for restructuring prevents adequate engagement with the dire consequences of crises for individuals' lives. While the Greek financial crisis did indeed inspire significant infrastructural reconfigurations in the sociopolitical sphere, the artists' individual experiences and their everyday working conditions were marred by a disregard for the art of dance and a devaluation of bodily labor, which was sometimes also demonstrated by employers within the field, such as the studio or school directors.

The conditions of employment for laborers in the field of dance in Greece have chronically been characterized by low wages and professional precarity. During the crisis, however, the situation worsened incomparably. A choreographer and teacher of contemporary dance who holds an MFA degree in dance from an international institution and has worked as a dance teacher in both professional dance schools and public high schools spoke with me in confidence about her experience. She was employed in a high school, yet she could not be appointed as regular faculty because her degree in dance was not recognized as a higher education degree, so she was asked to reapply for the job every year. In 2013, when she reapplied for the coming academic year, the school informed her that the hourly rate had changed because of budgetary cuts and would now be 3 EUR per hour. The school offered no additional compensation, such as reimbursement for transportation expenses. Needless to say, this rate was well below a living wage.

At the height of the crisis, dance studios and professional dance schools experienced similar budgetary challenges that caused them to lower their wages even more. Wages for dance teachers had always been relatively low, averaging about 10–15 EUR per hour, but during the crisis, they dropped even lower or were rendered conditional to the studios' monthly income and enrollment rosters. The budget cuts also impacted the Ministry of Culture's exam committees. The lack of funds threatened the cancellation of entry and graduation exams, which further jeopardized hundreds of young dancers' already precarious career paths.

Conditional pay had long been a reality for many dancers working as performers. As another dancer confided to me, some choreographers did not pay their dancers, nor did they cover insurance for them, yet they still expected them to be available around the clock to attend rehearsals. Said choreographers were intolerant of the fact that to survive, dancers had other job commitments on the side. Although the need for additional jobs has always been the case in the Greek dance scene (most dancers and choreographers are also dance teachers), the meager wages during the crisis pushed dancers to additional jobs, often not related to their profession, which resulted in more strain on their bodies and made them prone to injuries.

These hardships and the limited opportunities mobilized artists—by necessity—to respond to this devaluation of the dance field, gradually giving rise to more politicized performances. This new creative wave comprised works concerned with various aspects of the crisis experience. Such works were so trendy that crisis narratives were not always engaged with critically, but sometimes just superficially, to partake in the hype and be marketable. One of the most prolific dancers in Greece, Ioanna Paraskevopoulou, who was fortunately able to work uninterrupted during the early crisis years, remarked on this new direction:

> There was an observed rise in works produced by Greek choreographers that bordered being a fad, as many festivals were being organized [abroad] dedicated to the Greek crisis. Choreographers engaged with the crisis as a theme and created many political pieces. For me, the most significant thing was how the necessity born out of the hardships motivated people in the art field to create works in collaboration with each other and come up with new artistic proposals. Personally, I believe in works that are political because those who create them are experiencing a challenging reality, and not because the crisis is a trendy topic to engage. (Ioanna Paraskevopoulou, email interview, March 1, 2019)

Indeed, many works produced after 2013 exemplify what Paraskevopoulou critiques as only thematically engaging with the crisis. Yet plenty of works created at the same time belonged to the other category she identified: pieces that were political because their creators critically engaged with everyday aspects of the crisis. As it was a period when subsidies had already stopped, it also meant that artists no longer felt compelled to fit into a mold. Although there was never any official governmental direction or formal censorship of topics that were, or were not, allowed, as some choreographers I interviewed hinted to me, artists seeking funding often catered to the tastes and expectations of the committee reviewing the proposals. Thus, the lack of governmental support can be directly linked to the shift toward more political and politicized performances that critically engaged with the precarity conditions. Such a shift of focus is not unique to Greece but is characteristic of the precarity experienced by many contemporary dance artists across other European centers (such as Germany and Belgium). According to Van Assche (2020), for subjects working under precarious conditions, the future continually lapses into the background, and the focus is on the present, as artists struggle to cope in the moment. While in other European dance scenes, this resulted in works critiquing the artistic "precariat" (Standing 2010), in Greece, the engagement with the present moment often manifested as a critique of contemporary Greekness and Greece's peripheral position in the EU, as exemplified by the works analyzed in the next section.

Reframing the Dominant Narratives of Greekness

In the industrial setting of Building E of the Athens and Epidaurus festival, a crowd is lined up to enter the performance space. Building E is a large, empty warehouse that used to house a furniture factory and has been repurposed as a performance space. Its concrete floors have been preserved and are used as the stage. A staggered seat structure has been placed in the middle, leaving a pathway for audiences on either side. I step through the door, and my eyes take a moment to adjust to the darkness. An audiovisual installation of nine screens playing simultaneously greets audiences upon entry. Each screen projects an interview with a different person, such as poets, painters, journalists, or philosophers, who express their views on issues of memory, history, the present moment, the crisis, and familial roots. Audiences cluster around different screens to listen to the themes discussed, which sets the tone for Tzeni Argyriou's *Memorandum—A Mechanism of Reminder* (Memorandum—Enas Michanismos Enthymisis; Memorandum—Ένας Μηχανισμός Ενθύμησης 2014).

A large-scale multimedia installation by Vassilis Gerodimos dominates the stage. Long metal pipes connect to strings, and large pieces of paper tightly attached to the lines simulate scaffolding. Instead of supporting some sort of monument, the scaffolding onstage supports the void. As I make my way to my seat, a performer (Miguel Pereira) is already on the stage, moving through a series of gestures. Curving his fingers, he places his hands in front of his eyes as if trying to look at the audience through a pair of binoculars and then rests his chin on the back of his fist, seemingly contemplating. His contemplation is interrupted when he raises his hand as if wanting to ask a question in a classroom. He moves through a series of similar gestures, with the pace accelerating as time progresses. Once everyone has made their way to their seats, the lights turn off momentarily, and a loud buzzing sound fills the space. The performer's body casts a gigantic shadow on the back wall. Gradually, the shadow's movements take on a life of their own, no longer corresponding to the gestures Pereira performs.

"Miguel, would you like to restart?" A female voice becomes audible over the loudspeakers. The lights dim to blackness, and the performer disappears. Holograms of people wearing a headlight, similar to the one used by mine workers, fill in the absence left by the performer. Black-and-white images of people engaging in manual labor crowd the walls around the stage, showing people from a different era. Their haunting presence is eventually interrupted by the entry of a second dancer (Soledad Zarka). Dressed in all black, with a black headscarf covering her hair, she walks in slowly, hunched over and holding a flashlight. Her demeanor evokes women in rural villages, stereotypically associated with grandmotherly figures, who tend to be the gatekeepers of a place's oral histories. As Zarka makes her way around the perimeter of the stage, more images appear on the back wall. Some depict derelict construction sites, ruins, or bricks. One of them bears the phrase, "Fellow patriot, what did you contribute to the fight today?" (Τι έκανες σήμερα πατριώτη για τον αγώνα;).

A door opens in the back wall, and Simon Rummel, the third member of the ensemble, walks onstage. He is holding a violin bow, which he uses to interact with the wires comprising the scaffolding structure, playing them like musical strings and producing a live soundscape. Interacting with the scaffolding structure becomes a theme as all performers climb it, bang on it, and even reposition parts of it, making the installation a kinetic sculpture and a site for multiple projections. Zarka unfolds paper rolls reminiscent of papyrus scrolls, which she then fixes on the structure, turning them into projection screens (Figure 6). She changes into white clothes, turning her body into another site for projections. Pereira is at the front of the stage, getting undressed in the darkness. Wearing only a pair of boxers, he uses the flash-

Figure 6. Promotional video for Tzeni Argyriou's *Memorandum—A Mechanism of Reminder* (2014). Screenshot from video (Argyriou 2015, 2:44).

light to illuminate and simultaneously fragment parts of his body with the light. Soon his entire body becomes a canvas for the projection of a multitude of faces from the past.

Elements such as the play with shadows or the overlap of ghostly holograms with the physical presence of performers permeate the piece and create a striking visual that conveys the layering of past and present. The convergence of multiple timelines is further exacerbated by the voice-over directing attendees to reflect on their sense of recollection, thereby turning them into active participants in this scaffolding of memory. Each audience member has a piece of white paper on their seat (placed there before their arrival), and based on our seat rows, the voice directs us to hold it over our heads. When we do, a sepia-colored projection of a face from an old photograph materializes against the white backdrop. This conveys the active role that each of us has in keeping other people's legacy alive and in shaping history.

Performers also invite audience members to participate by directing questions at us in multiple languages. The female voice over the speakers declares the questions in Greek; Miguel Pereira translates them into English, Soledad Zarka, into French, and Simon Rummel, into German.

How many of you have a good memory?
How many of you have good knowledge of recent history?

How many of you will remember tomorrow what you did today?
Do you have a relative that has been a war victim?
How many of you believe in Europe?

If the answer is yes, the dancers direct us to respond by embodying a specific gesture, such as the ones Pereira performed at the beginning: raise a hand, cover our eyes with our elbow, or hold on to imaginary binoculars. Participating in this informal polling exercise is enlightening and evokes many questions about each person's role in remembering, documenting, and narrating history. The environment created by the performance encompasses multiple layers of memory projected on the bodies of both performers and audiences. The questions directed at audiences, such as "How many of you will remember tomorrow what you did today?" offers commentary on the fallacy of memory.

Argyriou described her intentions for the piece:

> The work starts with my concerns about the problematic present moment. I mean the current era we are experiencing, but also how uncomfortable it makes me feel when I realize that the "roots of the evil" are back in time. That is why I chose this title, which also has a sense of irony: the Latin term "memorandum" means to remember; as such, it refers to every medium that assists memory in highlighting certain elements that should not be forgotten. (Argyriou 2014; my translation)

The choice to use the term *memorandum* holds a double signification that bridges the definition of the term as a written message made for future use with the crisis connotation that the term held for Greeks (referring to austerity measures imposed). The performance invited audiences to consider how their crisis experience might shape the future, akin to how the memories of the past that were enlivened through projections shaped the present.

This newfound engagement with aspects of history previously unseen in performance practices is a direct consequence of the wave of introspection initiated by the crisis. The state of shock in response to the austerity measures and memoranda heightened the chronically latent anxiety to contextualize Greekness. In response to this malleable moment of collective unmooring, after the early 2010s, there was a wave of works that critically reexamined history (Tsintziloni and Panagiotara 2015) and worked at the intersection of personal and collective memory.

Uncovering previously obscured aspects of the past and juxtaposing them with the present through the interplay of shadows, live bodies, and projections is an accurate visualization of the reconsiderations set in motion during the crisis. *Memorandum—A Mechanism of Reminder* is a lucid example of the emergent trend of renarrativizing Greekness observed in the first half of the crisis. It indicates that the glorified classical past was no longer relevant in contextualizing the present. Artists turned to aspects of Greek history that previously had been obscured from artistic productions. For instance, the images projected on the scaffolding evoked the 1922 Asia Minor Destruction and the Greek Civil War. Additionally, Argyriou challenged audiences to consider Greece's status as a member of the EU amid the turmoil of the austerity measures. The question "How many of you believe in Europe?" and the hesitancy to respond that I observed among fellow audience members were indicative of the lack of trust in Europe—as an ideal—and the peripheral position of Greece within the EU.

Another example of a work concerned with memory is also by Tzeni Argyriou, titled *Memoria Obscura* (Afanis Mnimi; Αφανής Μνήμη, 2012), which focused on the rural community of Grevena and was a performance presentation of a photographic album titled *Grevena 80 Years of Photographs 1895–1975* by Vaggelis Nikolopoulos. The performance encompassed significant historical events such as Greek independence (Grevena was liberated in 1912), the Second World War, the Greek Civil War, and moments from the locals' personal lives.

In a similar vein of exploring historical milestones in the collective imagination and juxtaposing them to personal histories, Maria Gorgia, choreographer and director of Amalgama Dance Company, released a trilogy of works between 2012 and 2014, concerned with the intersections between national identity and gender identity. The first work in the trilogy, titled *The Mattress* (To Stroma; Το Στρώμα, 2012), explored masculinity in parallel with the history of the Greek state from its establishment in the mid-1800s to 2012, when the piece premiered. It was a solo for a man performed with a mattress that symbolized the spatial confines of the nation-state and the notion of home. The second piece, titled *Hidden in the Olive Groves* (Krymmeni stous Elaiones; Κρυμμένη στους Ελαιώνες), premiered in 2012 and restaged in 2014, was a solo for a woman. The work uncovered the history of the enfranchisement of Greek women. Both performances were a collage of oral testimonies from significant historical figures and archival sources framed by the critical lens of the choreographer. The third piece, *On the Seesaw* (Sti Trampala; Στη Τραμπάλα, 2014), was a duet focusing on the present and addressing the Greek financial crisis. I examine this piece in more detail in the following section.

Mono (Μόνο; or Only, 2014) by Konstantinos Michos, a solo for the choreographer in conversation with musician Antonis Stavrinos, is another work that I would classify as belonging to this wave of revisionist history. Initially premiering at EMPROS, the piece was marketed as a performance exploring embodied memory and the question of what can be achieved with *only* one dancing body, *only* one musician, and in *only* this moment. In its minimalist approach to the present, the piece unearthed aspects of collective history under the guise of individual embodied memory.

All the works discussed were created between 2011 and 2014 and are indicative of a critical engagement with historical narratives, initiated by the crisis. Most of the performances mentioned sought to contextualize the experience of Greek subjects at that historical moment by framing the present as an aftermath of the modernist past. The choreographers thus offered frameworks for grounding contemporary Greekness as shaped by the legacy of events that occurred during the twentieth century. Such a turn to narratives from recent history suggests a break from previously established practices that relied on romanticized narratives of classical Hellenism.

Alienation and the Disoriented Subject

In response to observing people's everyday interactions and their reactions and to the crisis, choreographers often explored the concepts of alienation and disorientation in performances produced in the years after subsidies ended. Two performances I witnessed in 2014 stand out in this regard as they each took a different approach to the topic.

Fragile Nothing (2014)

In March 2014, Syndram Dance Company and choreographer Chrysiis Liatziviry, in collaboration with the dancers, premiered the work *Fragile Nothing* (Efthrafsto Tipota; Εὐθραυστο Τίποτα). In the work, the stage is set up like a house on the move, with carton boxes and white file boxes rising like a wall at the back of the stage. In one corner, there is a tall table. At the center of the stage is a box with mirrors glued to its surfaces. There are four performers isolated in different parts of the stage. Not looking, not wanting to be seen, they are hiding—hiding behind a stack of boxes, curling beside them, and crawling around them until they slowly emerge into the light.

A red-haired woman (Sofia Kyriazidou) laughs in a corner. A man (Yannis Polyzos) raises his fists, fighting with an invisible opponent. Another dancer (Eleni Lagadinou) drops to the floor with an audible thud, while the last member of the ensemble (Christina Sagou) is at the back pushing some boxes – pushing and going nowhere. They all pause, yet the laughter persists. They are each lost in their own sphere of reality. Not facing each other, they battle their demons. Kyriazidou's laughter turns maniacal and borders on crying. The others stare into the void, speechless. They repeatedly engage in the same routines, like four shadows of Sisyphus. Their mouths move, and they appear to be speaking, yet no sound is heard. Sagou mumbles soundlessly until she suddenly yells: "STOP!" The laughter ceases in response, and Polyzos surrenders to his invisible opponent, sinking to the floor. In the momentary silence, a slapping sound becomes audible. Lagadinou, at the other end of the stage, is hitting her palm with her other hand, her breath echoing loudly from the exhaustion of countless repetitions.

Then the tension and the struggle that all dancers have been embodying momentarily eases. Their movements become softer. The music accelerates, and their calmness gives way to frantic energy manifesting as dizzying turns. Invisible bonds drag the dancers to the wall, where they form a line facing the audience. The line morphs into a human chain inscribing patterns into the space, creating momentary links and partnering relations between varying pairs of dancers. The links created between two dancers are constantly reset. There is a sense of disconnection even though the dancers interact with one another by forming points of contact or bearing each other's weight. They appear empty, like vessels void of character, pawns being manipulated by an invisible hand. In a jarring moment of realization that they are not alone, they lock eyes with one another, and that causes a visceral reaction of spasms in some while it drives others to a frantic circular run. Connections between dancers continue to form and dissolve as they couple up in tight embraces, only to be pulled apart again.

"STOP!" yells one of them, and with the command, the room is engulfed in darkness. When the lights turn on again, the dancers are isolated in different parts of the stage, performing their old routines. Lagadinou stands out as she uses one of her arms—which appear boneless—to flagellate herself. The grotesqueness of the act is interrupted by moments of stillness—a stillness so piercing and torturing that it is almost palpable. In these moments of pause, the dancers open their mouths in silent screams (Figure 7). Their facial features convey a deep-rooted sense of agony, yet the fact that there is no sound to the scream is disturbing.

Figure 7. *Fragile Nothing* (2014). Dancers depicted from left to right: Sophia Kyriazidou, Eleni Lagadinou, and Yannis Polyzos. © Elpida Tempou.

Realization comes after this sudden, soundless outburst, and the performers gather themselves and reset. They fix their clothes and their hair and look at the audience, almost ashamed of what they have just let them witness. Upon regrouping, they start experimenting with different ways to create connections. Touch and withdraw. Hug and be separated. Gain a leader and lose her. Be thrown down and fall, sometimes with help, while other times just pushed aside like worthless obstacles. No relationships that form between the dancers are solid. Everything is in a constant state of flux.

As the piece nears its conclusion, the dancers have slowly developed a new routine, a ritual of oscillating back and forth. It is a lulling sensation that gives off a deceptive sense of security. The music has changed to a soothing—almost hypnotizing—sound. The dancers exit the stage through a narrow door that had barely been discernible up to that point. A faint light comes off the door, giving shape to a diagonal line that cuts the stage in half. All dancers but one drift offstage, and the one left behind hesitantly proceeds toward the light. Her hair covers her face, and she is hunched over and limping. Her arm is extended as if she is reaching out to something. The limping continues, and she starts to laugh. Her cackling is barely a whisper, the sound of a person on the edge of madness. She has become a shadow of her former self, reduced to the essence of hopelessness. The lights dim, and she collapses as her suppressed laughter continues.

One by one, the others rejoin her. They are crawling, running, and sliding. The laughter faintly persists as the scene turns into frantic chaos. Bodies are being carried, pushed, shoved, directed, pulled, abused, and dropped. The frenetic energy reduces them to an animalistic state. Sometimes, the neuroses that each dancer developed earlier resurface. Any sense of direction, security, trust, and composure is lost. The lights fade to darkness. The door at the side of the stage cracks open again, illuminating the now familiar diagonal. The dancers reenter, and a faint light is discernible under their clothes. Almost forming an arc with their bodies, as one visibly bears the weight of the other, they slowly cross the diagonal. The door closes, and thin strips of light attached to the dancers' skin are now the only visible traces left to indicate their trajectory in the darkness.

In *Fragile Nothing*, alienation is paired with isolation, as the piece focuses on the lack of meaningful relationships during the crisis. Created for four performers (three women and a man), the performance has no set characters or identifiable relationships between the dancers. The scenes appear deliberately fragmentary to obscure the possibility of working out a linear narrative from the performance's beginning to end. Pervasive throughout the piece is a sense of individual struggle and the motif of performers engaging in repetitive and compulsive behaviors.

The choreographic strategy employed in *Fragile Nothing* presents the dancers' bodily tension and indignation as volatile suppressed energy. As a viewer, I constantly expected that energy to blow up, yet it never did. I saw the performers contorting their faces into screams, yet I heard no sound. I found this to be an extremely effective, albeit frustrating, strategy, as I felt the tension continually building without any satisfactory release. In a 2014 interview with Liatziviry, I shared how the piece created a chaotic environment that highlighted a state of constant nonarrival. She confirmed that this was indeed a deliberate choice: "We decided to frame the performance as a house on the move not because we are moving out but to indicate this state of being in flux" (Chrysiis Liatziviry, interview, March 5, 2014). She remarked that people who experience this sense of flux either seclude themselves or react soundlessly, which was captured in the performance. The silent aggression, agony, self-harm, and depression present in the choreography were the results of observational research conducted by Liatziviry and the performers in public spaces and offices. Thus, the performance was an embodied culmination of their research findings, which produced a framework for contextualizing the sociopolitical landscape of the crisis. Speaking to the point of alienation and how she perceives it as a direct outcome of the crisis, Liatziviry remarked:

> We were interested in investigating the crisis, as it manifests and is represented by contemporary Greeks. While we were working on it through improvisation many times, it led to several relationships between the dancers. However, I did not want that at all because I believe that contemporary humans no longer have meaningful relationships. They are not actively nurturing them; thus, it is easy for relationships to fade. Every time a relationship started to form, we were cutting it down. I did not want to allow the audience to attribute familiar labels to any situation. It would have been an unambiguous statement within a very fragile nothingness, and this would have functioned in a self-negating way. (Chrysiis Liatziviry, interview, March 5, 2014)

Tuning in to the relationships that were forming between the performers in the piece and deliberately configuring them, Liatziviry captured the elusive reality of the crisis. Beyond human relationships, *Fragile Nothing* also tackled the mental state of people experiencing a traumatic unmooring, such as the Greek crisis, by creating haunting images of silent suffering that resonated deeply for many audience members.

On the Seesaw (2014)

Extending the exploration of alienation beyond the impact of the crisis on human relations, Maria Gorgia's *On the Seesaw* was presented first and foremost as an embodied exploration of political theory and discourses of precarity and devaluation, thus proposing a theoretical framework for contextualizing the crisis. The program notes situate the performance within influential political theory and precarity discourses:

> A man and a woman act and coexist in a space where the protagonists are a series of computer hardware equipment. They are "precariats." Insecurity, anxiety, fear, anger, resentment, short-term thinking, information overload, and online addiction have taken over them completely. . . . Even though the primary web [of the work] stems from the book *Declaration* by [Michael] Hardt and [Antonio] Negri [2012], and the second sources are *The Precariat: The New Dangerous Class* by

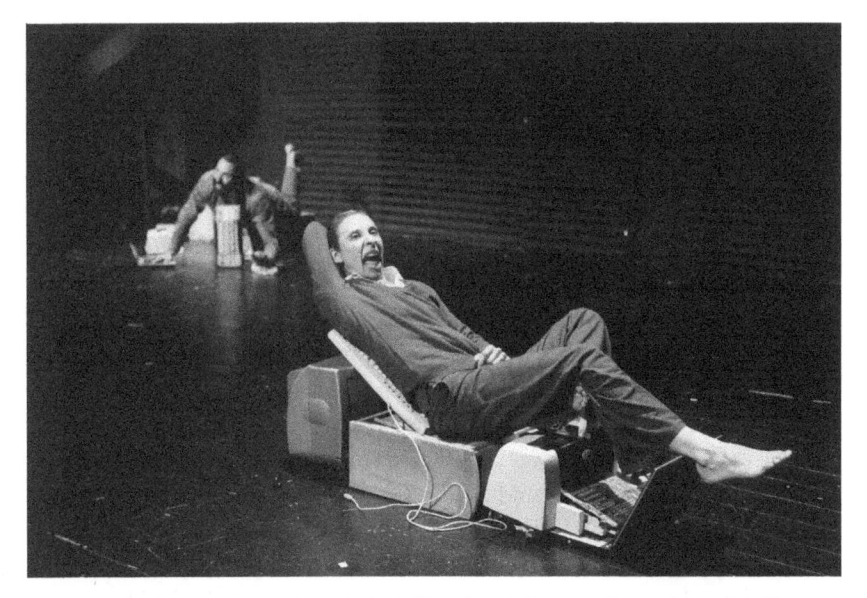

Figure 8. Performers Sania Strimbakou (front) and Stavros Apostolatos (back) leaning on makeshift furniture made from computer hardware in *On the Seesaw* (2014) © Angela Svoronou.

> Guy Standing [2011] and *Precarious Life* by Judith Butler [2004], the new work *On the Seesaw* focuses primarily on highlighting the issues and leaving open a window for suggestions on how to resolve them. (Gorgia 2014; my translation)

The four types of subjectivities introduced in *Declaration*—the mediatized, the indebted, the securitized, and the represented[1]—are personified in Gorgia's *On the Seesaw*. Each becomes an embodied character, and the defining characteristics of each are danced in exaggerated form to make these subjectivities legible and open to critical interpretation. The performance is rich in symbolism, so in what follows, I have selectively highlighted a few moments for analysis.

When audience members walk into Rabbithole theater in the Metaxourgeio neighborhood for *On the Seesaw*, the stage is full of old computer hardware equipment. The dancers Sania Strimbakou and Stavros Apostolatos are already onstage, reclining on the equipment, treating it like comfortable furniture (Figure 8). They take turns criticizing and reviling people in authority, the bureaucratic system, public administration, unemployment, and the dysfunctions of the state. Whenever one dancer's turn is over, that dancer continues to silently mouth their indignation and complaints as they rearrange their hardware to create new settings to inhabit. Most of their verbal commentary attests to frustration caused by austerity measures, work conditions, taxation, and deteriorating human relations. At first, they do not seem aware of each other's presence, but as their indignation grows, they turn against one another. Directing insults at each other, they slowly build pedestals with their computer monitors, which they climb as they continue to swear and turn the scene into an escalating verbal fight. Their confrontation grows more vulgar when the man finally gets off his pedestal to confront the woman face-to-face. As soon as they face each other on the same level, they freeze in defensive postures.

"Have you seen my hard disk?" the man (Apostolatos) asks while the woman (Strimbakou) remains frozen. He locates it in the debris and runs to the back of the stage to build a fortress for himself. Several monitors discarded around the stage light up and make it possible to follow the male dancer's trajectory. At the same time, the woman is responding to music that has just been introduced with tiny twitches in her upper body. Her movements slowly grow, expanding in space, as her fingers imitate the act of typing on a keyboard. Her fingertips seem to gain a life of their own as they lead her in various directions initiating her next movement. Her actions become increasingly more erratic, while a series of images from social media and other internet sites is projected on the back wall. In the meantime, the man has finished piling up the equipment surrounding him and engages in a demanding multitasking sequence—talking on the phone, tangling some cables, and manipulating a computer mouse with his foot. He struggles to balance all the actions until the lights fade, swallowing him in darkness.

As the lights brighten again, the performers take off one layer of clothing. The man tucks a shirt into the back of his pants so it hangs off like a tail. The woman takes off her blue woolen sweater and turns it inside out to reveal a red fabric. She ties it around her head in an imitation of the fairy tale character Red Riding Hood, thus metaphorically rendering the man into the Big Bad Wolf. The Wolf slowly creates a path for Red Riding Hood by lining up pieces of equipment in front of her. He supports her every step as she carefully moves over old printers, PC towers, keyboards, and other devices, all forming a path toward the Wolf's den, constructed earlier. A hard disk with dangling cables becomes a purse for Red Riding Hood, which she carries as she continues along her path and uses it to store pieces of computer hardware that she collects along the route. Once she reaches the den, she feeds RAM sticks to the Wolf, who seems to get an energy jolt every time he bites one, roaring with pleasure and opening his mouth wider to accommodate more sticks.

The final RAM sends him off to a gathering frenzy. He collects the pieces that formed the trail to his den as though trying to erase any traces of it. He uses the cables he gathered to tie Red Riding Hood's limbs, making it harder for her to move on her own; she now requires his assistance and support. The red-hooded dancer is so tangled with the wires that she can barely balance herself while the Wolf runs to the den and brings out a wired plank, which he positions on top of some other hardware in the middle of the stage. The hardware supports the middle part of the plank, forming a makeshift seesaw. Simultaneously with the feeding scene, a series of images is projected on the background, which, like puzzle pieces, slowly compose a picture of a Wolf and Red Riding Hood. The video concludes when the characters are replaced by an image of a ballot box, thus alluding to the subjectivity of the represented.

The beastly nature of the Wolf is revisited later in the performance. This time, it is a cyborgian rendition of the creature, who loads the seesaw with equipment on one end and then climbs on the other, reveling in his ability to weigh it down. Red Riding Hood assumes an animal role as well, clucking like a chicken and bending her elbows into wings as she admires his strength. Monitors in the background project unrecognizable fragmented images, and in one corner of the stage, a monitor lights up, projecting a continuously rising twelve-digit number corresponding to the growing debt of Greece. All these visual stimulants render clearly, beyond doubt, the subjectivity of the indebted and, more specifically, the indebted Greek.

Another scene fuses the subjectivity of the indebted with that of the mediatized. The two dancers remove pieces of clothing and replace them with pieces of equipment that they strap on their bodies, parading around in them for the audience. The stage momentarily becomes a fashion runway as the performers proudly strut in their newly acquired pieces. At first, their walking is reminiscent of fashion models on a catwalk, but as they take off more clothes and add more equipment, their movements gradually become less human and more robotic. Wires and cables divide the stage into segments and are used as a clothesline for each item the dancers take off in exchange for a piece of hardware. The clothes hanging on the wire become the canvas for the projection of the constantly increasing number that represents the hundreds of billions of euros of Greek debt (Figure 9).

In the concluding scene, Strimbakou and Apostolatos start taking off all the pieces of hardware. Once freed, they clear the seesaw of any remaining debris and step on it, gazing straight at the audience. Strimbakou weighs

Figure 9. Performer Sania Strimbakou in *On the Seesaw (2014)*. The rising debt of Greece is projected on the hanging clothes. © Angela Svoronou.

down the board while Apostolatos soars slightly above her, singing the German national anthem "*Deutschland, Deutschland über alles, über alles in der . . .*" (Germany, Germany, above all, above all else in the . . .). Shortly before finishing the verse, he weighs down the seesaw. Now it is Strimbakou's turn. She loudly sings the melody of the first bars of the French national anthem, "La Marseillaise," *la-la-la-la-la-taa-ra-da*, only to be overpowered by yet another rise of Apostolatos on the seesaw to "*Deutschland, Deutschland über alles*." When it is her turn to rise again, she responds with the melody of the Greek national anthem. At that, the seesaw starts to tremble, which throws off her tonality, producing a cacophony that sounds like a slowed-down cassette tape. Eventually, the trembling ceases, and the seesaw finds balance, leveling the dancers, who now sing the EU anthem (Beethoven's "Ode to Joy") in unison. The lights dim and take on an orange shade, reminiscent of a sunset, and the performers join hands as the seesaw finds a moment of stillness. The serenity is disrupted when a sudden drop of the seesaw brings one performer above the other, restarting their previous competition over who gets to "rule" by being higher. Each time one of them "rises in power," they return to yelling and swearing until the lights fade at last.

On the Seesaw explores the crisis through an analogy to human relationships. The dancers embody the characteristics of the four subjectivities as they navigate their existence within the precariat. Their indignation, expressed verbally and gesturally, is a recurring motif. Its repetitive nature becomes a commentary on the futility of any type of reaction. In our interview, Gorgia remarked how this motif of overreaction and overexpression is a critique of contemporary Greekness or the stereotype of the "Mediterranean temperament." No matter how strongly the performers react, nothing seems to change. Individual well-being is no longer a priority; the success of private corporations is. Privatization and the transition to neoliberal frameworks are highlighted in the piece's opening. According to Gorgia, the first scene of the fight references the tension between the public and private sector: "It is the moment when anything public is being dissolved here [in Greece], and privatization becomes more prominent" (Maria Gorgia, interview, May 2, 2014). The opening scene directly criticizes the recently implemented austerity measures of the second memorandum of 2012, which included the PSI debt restructurings.

Power and hierarchical structures are latent in how the crisis is explored throughout the performance. The segment in which Red Riding Hood feeds RAM sticks (representing "votes") to the Wolf is a critique of the subjectivity of the represented and the ways that power is used and abused by politicians or figures of authority. As such, it is a direct reference to voters participating in the electoral process yet mistrusting the people in power. Another powerful example of how the piece engages with power structures and approaches center/periphery hierarchical imbalances is the final scene in which the performers balance on the seesaw and sing various national anthems. Recalling the performance's closing, Gorgia noted:

> Right before the lights turn off, they [the performers] return to the initial fighting. Whoever is at the high point of the seesaw starts swearing, which of course, is not leading anywhere and emphasizes the power structure. Additionally, the part with the nations and their anthems is not just a reference to power but also to markets and how globalization has seemingly rendered nation-states' borders meaningless. Borders no longer have the significance they used to because now markets matter; they are the dominant element, not the national borders. . . . For me, the concept of the nation-state implies a sense of sovereignty. . . . So, high up on the seesaw clearly signifies power. Whoever is higher is exercising their power on the others, and then the EU comes to balance it out. That's why I included the colors of a sunset.

It implies that it is a romantic idea, and simultaneously, the romantic idea is that the EU sets. What's going to happen after? (Maria Gorgia, interview, May 2, 2014)

While an answer to this closing question can be given only in time, all the symbols that Gorgia is constructing capture the layered tensions that synthesize Greekness during the crisis. The battle of the national anthems summarizes the struggle of transitioning from a national to a supranational identity, as the seesaw finds balance only once the EU anthem is sung. However, even within the context of the EU, power hierarchies are still prevalent as captured in center/periphery discourses, which, during the crisis decade, manifested as political tension between Germany and Greece. The trembling of the seesaw that occurs when the performers sing the Greek and German anthems points to a critique of the utopian nature of transnational solidarity and the process of European integration. The performance thus does not simply engage with the landscape of the moment by relating existing theories (such as Standing 2011; Hardt and Negri 2012) to represent the Greek crisis experience, but through the choreographic embodied research process, the performers also *produce* discourse.

• • •

Fragile Nothing and *On the Seesaw* suggest frameworks for theorizing the crisis by identifying isolation, indignation, anger, and fear as the primary traits defining human relationships in the early years of the Greek crisis. Both pieces engaged with disoriented subjects who were in flux. The choreographic and dramaturgical strategies employed, such as participant observation, or the embodied application of political theory, ground dance as a site of embodied agency and challenge its concurrent disavowal in the hierarchy of Greek education.

Reviewing the choreographic strategies encountered in these pieces in light of the overall state of dance in Greece, I find that these works challenge dance's devaluation by laying bare the effects that the crisis has had, not just on the emotional aspects of human relations but also the corporeal dimensions of those relations. By highlighting isolation, alienation, the potential of a cyborgian transformation of the mediatized, and what happens behind closed doors (such as the violence and self-harm suggested in *Fragile Nothing*), these works capture a sense of urgency to (re)act.

Contemporary concert dance produced in the first few years following the budget cuts for the performing arts often provided frameworks for theorizing and navigating the precarious landscape of the crisis and the ways that subjects may have felt isolated in their experience. Some other works engaging similar themes are listed below. Athanasia Kanellopoulou's *In lo(e)over-land* (2013) explored female subjectivity and loneliness. Hermes Malkotsis and Yannis Karounis's *Unburied Dead* (Atafoi Nekroi; Άταφοι Νεκροί, 2010 and 2015) engaged with metaphorical cannibalism in human relations. Other pieces focused on the permeating sense of shock and disorientation caused by the crisis, such as Artemis Lampiri's *META* (After, 2014) or Elpida Orfanidou's *One Is Almost Never* (various iterations of the project were presented between 2013 and 2015). In the latter, a solo performer (Orfanidou) responds to a series of obstacles and apparent mishaps. For instance, at the start of the performance, the music is not working, and Orfanidou calls tech staff onstage to adjust the speakers. Then, the speakers are too loud, and the performer yells to the audience but gets no response as they are all uncomfortably and confoundedly staring back at her in silence, waiting for the performance to start. The piece is defined by an overwhelming sense of chaos and disorder. When I witnessed an excerpt of this work at the Society of Dance History Scholars/Congress of Research in Dance (SDHS/CORD)[2] 2015 conference in Athens, I fully believed for a moment that things were not working. Of course, as Orfanidou explained in the subsequent talk-back, this was part of what she was questioning: is there an actual start, or are audiences just thrown into a situation and need to start making sense of it? The purpose of the piece was to capture aspects of the chaotic reality that subjects had to navigate in Greece during the crisis.

Emerging Methodologies

The narrative framework of performances presented in the first half of the 2010s was no longer structured around an abstract, fictional, or mythological premise but around the actual lived experiences of the artists and their collaborators: choreographers, performers, technicians, and audiences. The materializing of personal perspectives and the act of narrating or staging them indicate how Greek artists engaged precarity as a methodological device.[3] Drawing on their personal experiences and observation of other subjects, choreographers and performers abstracted their findings and rendered them into movement. While this is a typical process in creating performance work, what set these works apart was the shared affect and the sense of a shared experience that united performers with audiences and rendered their artworks relatable.

The rise of this highly subjective experiential approach is a common means of engaging precarity, as performance studies scholar Katharina Pewny has observed in discussing the concept of "the self as a role" (2011, 78). The self as a role is a narrative device that structures performances around the lived experiences of people (actors, dancers) rather than a fictional linear narrative with a clear beginning and end. The performativity of narrating one's personal experience allows the narrator to come to terms with their precarious position. Recounting an experience can encourage the narrator to take responsibility for their actions and produce therapeutic effects for performers and audiences. As experiences and memories are often shared in a somewhat fragmented manner (for instance, in the context of a casual conversation), performances employing the "self as a role" framework tend to lack a linear progression and cohesiveness. In many contemporary dance performances in Greece, the oration of personal narratives is complemented by an embodied rendering of personal experience via performative pedestrian acts. The struggle and tension in *Fragile Nothing* and the indignation in *On the Seesaw* evidence such approaches. Practices and images of resistance or criticism of hierarchical power structures, such as the questions raised about the EU in *Memorandum—A Mechanism of Reminder* and *On the Seesaw*, are also indicative of such approaches.

Personal narratives may also be incorporated into performance through audience participation, which has become increasingly common since the crisis decade. Involving audiences and having performers interact with them was often a creative solution to bringing more bodies onstage, thus countering the aesthetic of "precarity solos" and small ensemble work. Van Assche describes this tendency for solo work in her research in Germany and Belgium, "Meager budgets and high competition for subsidies more often than not lead to an abundance of solos created and presented" (2020, 109), which she refers to as "precarity solos." In Van Assche's research, the solos are most often performed by the choreographers themselves. While I observed some instances of precarity solos during my fieldwork in Greece, precarity duets and small casts averaging three to four people were much more common, suggesting the prevalence of the barter economy system amid small groups. Despite the alienation that has been identified as an aftermath of the crisis, choreographic creation still was a collective and collaborative effort.

In instances where solos *did* occur, a choreographer set work on a dancer instead of performing it themselves. For example, in a different production by Amalgama Dance Company choreographed by Maria Gorgia titled *At the Edge of the Springboard* (Stin Akri tou Vatira; Στην Άκρη του Βατήρα,

2015), a woman (Sania Strimbakou) takes on multiple personas through which she interacts with the audience. The work is primarily a solo, with a second performer (Timos Zechas) pretending to be an audience member and reluctantly joining her for a brief duet. In the performance, one persona Strimbakou takes on is that of a therapist who invites an audience member to answer personal questions, then offers a diagnosis. In another instance, she asks audience members to help her read a passage from a book using their cell phone screens as a flashlight. The interactions between the audience and the performer—through brief dialogue or specific tasks that audience members are asked to perform to assist with the development of the piece—add a new dimension to "self as a role." It is no longer only the performer who shares their personal experiences but the audience members join in as well.

Audience participation in dance performances became increasingly common during the crisis, especially as site-specific performances became more prominent in response to budget cuts. One example includes the work *Obey, Deceive, Devour* (2015) by the international CACTUS performance. art. collective, founded by three collaborators: Dafne Louzioti from Greece, Thais Mennsitieri from Brazil, and Noora Baker from Palestine. *Obey, Deceive, Devour* (Louzioti, Mennsitieri, and Baker 2015) was a peripatetic performance in the National Garden in Athens, with intermittent interactive games of embodied call-and-response with the audience. For instance, performers gave prompts, such as "If you feel Greek, line up behind me," "If you are Greek, line up behind her," and "If you have had sex with 0–5 people, stand over there, 6–10 over at the other side"; the audience members responded by positioning themselves accordingly. These games playfully provoked the audience to question their positionality, literally and metaphorically, within a social setting while simultaneously calling for an unconventional engagement with public space and a revisioning of performance space. Similar call-and-response games were often incorporated in live performances, such as the audience poll in *Memorandum—A Mechanism of Reminder*. In many instances, the questions directed at audiences related to the construction of Greek subjectivity during the crisis. This trend attests to artists' permeating sense of urgency to engage with the sociopolitical landscape of the crisis.

While such approaches to audience involvement may constitute long-established practices for European and American audiences, in Greece, they are relatively recent phenomena. Even though improvisational games inviting audience involvement had been incorporated in past productions, the popularity of such approaches among different choreographers with varying training backgrounds in the first half of the 2010s was striking. It is possible that the use of unconventional spaces contributed to the increase of such interactive exchanges between performers and audiences. Such direct encounters are also indicative of the heightened sense of community fostered by the pressures of the Greek crisis. The austerity measures and the financial constraints that were imposed on the population created a new sphere of relationality, a sense of "we are all in this together."

Concluding Thoughts

All performances discussed in this chapter were created following the pause of subsidiary support by the Ministry of Culture. These works capture early responses to the Greek crisis and exemplify creativity under severe financial restrictions. The three works analyzed more extensively, *Memorandum—A Mechanism of Reminder*, *Fragile Nothing*, and *On the Seesaw*, propose distinct frameworks for comprehending, contextualizing, and navigating the crisis landscape. Bridging the specific vision of the choreographers and the performers with broader social concerns, all works effectively propose ways of reclaiming what it means to be Greek or live in Greece in a moment of crisis.

At the onset of the crisis, there was not a lot of scholarship or literature available to assist people with comprehending the forces at play. The main text that circulated in Greece at the time was Naomi Klein's *The Shock Doctrine* (2007). Its Greek translation was published in 2010 and remained on the bestseller list for months. At the core of Klein's argument lies the belief that after a significant rupture (in this case, the Greek crisis), when people are "psychologically unmoored and physically uprooted" (21), people in power find opportunities to remake the world. Her work inundated the media in the early years of the crisis as it provided an anchor for people to understand their experience and an impetus for them to start processing.

The feeling of being unmoored or uprooted was something that many artists identified with, as exemplified by their creative projects, which were attempts to reconceptualize what it meant to live and work in Greece at the height of austerity. The artists emphasized a revisionist approach to history to understand the fraught hierarchies between Greece and Europe; they furthermore pursued introspective exploration of the significance of individual agency in collective action. As the bartering system for artistic collaboration suggests, at the height of the budgetary cuts, what prevailed was a sense of togetherness that fueled artistic creation. The frugality of stage props and scenery made more room for centering the dancing bodies and highlighting personal or collective embodied narratives. Thus the focus fell on movement and corporeality, meaning that the often raw and vulnerable dancing bodies rose in importance and became the epicenter for sociopolitical advocacy.

While the impetus behind this reevaluation of people's bodies and interest in physical activity varies and is subjective, the "return" to bodies and the power of bodily presence is another indicator of the introspection brought about by the crisis. Perhaps paradoxically, this sense of turning inward and focusing on oneself to be able to cope with a chaotic reality deepens one's understanding of sociopolitical agency and makes one aware of one's impact and position within a broader social collective.

Notes

1. The range of shifting subjectivities theorized by Michael Hardt and Antonio Negri in *Declaration* is introduced in the following quote from the work:

> The triumph of neoliberalism and its crisis have shifted the terms of economic and political life, but they have also operated a social anthropological transformation fabricating new figures of subjectivity. The hegemony of finance and the banks has produced the *indebted*. Control over information and communication has created the *mediatized*. The security regime and the generalized state of exception have constructed a figure prey to fear and yearning for protection—the *securitized*. And the corruption of democracy has forged a strange depoliticized figure, the *represented*. These subjective figures constitute the social terrain on which—and against which—movements of resistance and rebellion must act (2012, 9).

2. The Society of Dance History Scholars (founded in 1978) and the Congress of Research in Dance (founded in 1969) were the two prominent organizations in the field of dance studies. In 2017, they merged into one entity known as the Dance Studies Association (DSA).

3. A more extensive discussion of creative methodologies that emerged during the crisis can be found in Zervou (2017b).

Three

Choreographing the Periphery

Displacement and the "Weird"

————

The ways that austerity conditions shaped the Athenian contemporary concert dance scene internally have been integral for formulating a first understanding of the dance landscape during the Greek crisis. However, focusing merely on the internal forces (within Greece) that shaped the scene would do nothing more than provide a siloed, incomplete picture. Therefore, in this chapter, I approach the Athenian contemporary dance scene from the outside looking in, where *outside* denotes the external forces that shaped the scene. These include urban development and gentrification, international imaginings of the Greek crisis, and the so-called brain drain. The conceptualization of the brain drain with respect to the Greek crisis has focused chiefly on the emigration of academics, scientists, and information technology workers, thus largely overlooking the artistic drain set in motion by the crisis and its potential impact on the embodied cultural capital[1] of Athens and Greece broadly.

The surge of creativity that characterized the early years of the crisis did not go unnoticed internationally. In fact, it became a branding point for the Athenian scene, which—in international media primarily—was often labeled as "the new Berlin." Internationally, the notion of Athens as Europe's new arts capital gained quite some traction, while locally, most artists and curators were very critical of the concept because they were aware of its rather superficial character and saw no real changes in the infrastructure supporting artistic creation or artists. The motto "Athens is the new Berlin" was a facade that romanticized the Athenian art scene and exploited the precarious position that Greek artists found themselves in. Such a symbolic decentering of Europe's artistic capital from Berlin to Athens challenges previously established center/periphery hierarchies and attempts to reposition Greece in a culturally superior position to Germany, thus flipping the crisis-established paradigm that places Greece in the EU periphery. Beyond the media fanfare branding Athens as the new artistic hotspot of Europe, however, lies a complex web of displacement within the city limits of Athens (through gentrification practices) and internationally (through waves of emigration during the crisis).

Comprehending the forces of gentrification, which were noted in Athens for the first time in the early years of the crisis, is essential for tracing the subsequent shifts in the Athenian art scene, especially since gentrification in the city was tied to the performing arts. As the opening section discusses, gentrification practices became the primary point of attraction for international artists who gave up their lives in European hubs such as Berlin and London and moved their studios to Athens. The same forces that attracted international artists to Greece drove artists residing in Greece out of their vibrant neighborhoods and, in some instances, out of the country. Thus, the seemingly innocuous discursive comparison of Athens to Berlin became a pitfall for some artists who got caught up in trying to adapt to international expectations about what art coming out of Athens should be and look like.

The tension between imposed external expectations and the lived reality exposed the inherent inadequacies and shortcomings of the local performing arts scene even further. First-person accounts by performers and choreographers who chose to emigrate for various reasons during the crisis decade form the core of this chapter. By sampling productions of emigrant Greek performance artists abroad, I question how they engage with the aesthetics and narratives of the crisis and contextualize their works amid another influential artistic movement that emerged in the 2010s known as the Greek Weird Wave, documented mainly in reference to cinematic productions. Aesthetics akin to the Weird Wave were also prevalent in performance works during the crisis decade. These new approaches to performance creation and cinematic production suggest a potential exoticization of the crisis label. Considering these approaches and the narratives that Greek artists circulated internationally enriches discussion of the commodification and branding of the Greek crisis. The clash observed between, on one hand, local conditions in art production and, on the other hand, romanticized perceptions of the Athenian art scene's vibrancy that circulated internationally further complicate center/periphery hierarchies. In the context of contemporary concert dance specifically, the dichotomy between center/periphery is analogous to a dichotomy between creative approaches and choreographic methods that are trending in European hubs. An example is the so-called *conceptual dance* that is very popular in central European contemporary dance centers (such as Berlin and Brussels) but is still not well established in Greece. The lack of access to such conceptual approaches was named as a primary creative need by many interviewees who had chosen to leave Greece and pursue careers abroad.

The emigration of Greek dancers is also related to an increased interest in the theoretical study of dance. For many, their first encounter with dance studies, performance studies, or dramaturgy takes place while traveling abroad for work or attending institutions of higher learning to acquire master's or doctoral degrees overseas. Having obtained this knowledge, many of them return to Greece or reside abroad and intermittently collaborate with choreographers based in Greece. The latter half of the crisis decade evidenced a gradual shift toward a substantial engagement with the theoretical study of dance through workshops, curated initiatives, and the popularization of dramaturgy. This increased interest in theoretical approaches to dance would not have been possible without the exposure of Greek artists and Greek dance scholars to the methodologies available mainly in international institutions. The popularization of performance theory discourses is hypothesized as an early effect of the international dialogue facilitated through the emigration of Greek artists to European art centers.

Rebranding the City in Crisis: Is Athens the New Berlin?

In the decade of the 2010s, there was an observed surge of artistic activity in the Athenian neighborhoods of Gazi, Kerameikos, and Metaxourgeio (hereafter GKM). Several modern Greek studies scholars and urban studies scholars (Alexandri 2015; Avdikos 2015; Gourzis and Gialis 2017) have noted a flourishing of the artistic scene in these neighborhoods. They have created a framework that focuses on gentrification to theorize the sudden rise in creativity that these neighborhoods underwent and to trace the reasons behind their sudden branding as artistic hot spots in Athens. The GKM neighborhoods lie at the core of exoticizing conceptions that frame Athens as "the new Berlin." Most articles referring to this conception address initiatives in one of these neighborhoods' studios or other spaces.

It is necessary to step back in time to contextualize the conditions that initiated processes akin to gentrification in these areas. Sociospatial and class segregation have been a characteristic of Athenian urban structures since the Second World War when it was common for lower-class households to occupy the lower floors of apartment complexes while the most affluent lived on higher levels with better views. Such spatial class divisions were preserved in the decades leading into the 2000s, yet following the Eastern European migration flows, the nature of segregation shifted from being focused on class to being focused on ethnicity.

The areas of Kerameikos and Metaxourgeio, in particular, experienced two distinct flows of people from the 1980s into the 2000s (Avdikos 2015): a large number of immigrants and a flow of people interested in the red-light district and prostitution houses[2] that popped up in the area's abandoned buildings. According to social and political scientist Vasilis Avdikos, as soon as these population shifts occurred, many of the former Greek residents of the GKM area left seeking a "better quality of life in the Athenian suburbs, while immigrants and prostitutes enter[ed] KM [Kerameikos and Metaxourgeio] and create[d] their own 'heterotopias'" (2015, 119). This move caused property values to drop significantly, especially between 1980 and 1990. Gradually, the lower occupancy rates and the diversity of GKM became a point of attraction for residents in low-paying occupations, such as manual laborers and artists. According to the 2001 census, there was a sharp increase in people holding higher education degrees moving to these neighborhoods. Thus, the early 2000s signaled a rise of a new "creative class" (a term coined by Richard Florida [2002] 2012) in GKM. Further attesting to this point is that between 1994 and 1999, six theater companies settled in these neighborhoods, which provided a strong pull factor for performance artists to move to the area. Beyond actors, who created artistic clusters in GKM, dancers, musicians, visual artists, and other creative professionals similarly moved to the area. They established their studios in some of the large spaces available in the area, whose factory buildings were now empty and abandoned. Notably, the studio of SineQuaNon, which was very active in the 1990s, was in one such space in Metaxourgeio, where they conducted their rehearsals and offered classes to the public.

Creativity and talent were the driving factors of gentrification in GKM. The spontaneous and collective nature of artistic endeavors in these three Athenian neighborhoods increased during the crisis decade when the gentrification efforts intensified. The shifting conditions of the crisis decade presented a branding opportunity that attributed authenticity to the embodied cultural capital coming out of GKM. In urban studies scholarship, gentrification in Western metropolises (such as London, San Francisco, and New York, which form the core of many studies on gentrification) is often tied to race (Stein 2019; Florida 2017). Following geographer Samuel Stein's definition:

> [Gentrification is] the process by which capital is reinvested in urban neighborhoods, and poorer residents and their cultural products are displaced and replaced by richer people and their preferred aesthetics and amenities. . . . The people of color and immigrants who built up neglected neighborhoods are recast as outsiders in their own homes and expelled in favor of White newcomers. Neighborhoods, and eventually, cities become places only the rich can afford, with environments designed according to their desires. (Stein 2019, 41–42)

Even though racial segregation was historically not as pronounced in the Athenian urban landscape as it may have been in American urban metropolises, the diversity of GKM neighborhoods was one of the factors that made them attractive, along with the drop in rent prices. Whereas artists moved to these neighborhoods because of the affordable rent and studio space, scientists, researchers, and business professionals did not choose the city as their base because of the limited opportunities within those fields. The exception to this rule is professionals from Greece working in business or technology companies abroad, who had the flexibility to work remotely. In the 2010s, some opted to reside in Greece and enjoy the quality of life afforded to them with the higher salaries of their international employment.

The focus on creativity as a driving economic force is a neoliberal ideal that captures the new direction of the status quo while simultaneously exposing the inherent contradictions of neoliberalism. Creativity is often tied to ideas of progress and prosperity. Yet, in the Athenian context of the ongoing crisis, such aphorisms became part of the branding narratives of the Greek crisis. During the second half of the crisis (from 2015), when artistic activity had started picking up, there was a surge of festivals being organized all around Greece, which attracted artists from Northern and Western European art hubs such as London, Paris, and Berlin; they in turn moved to Athens and made it the center of their creative production. In mainstream media, this international artistic influx fueled perceptions of Athens as "the new Berlin" because the city attracted young artists from various disciplines, such as visual arts, fashion, textile design, and photography.

International newspapers and media, such as the *New York Times* (Khemsurov 2010;) and *Die Welt* (Krauel 2012) first introduced the idea of Athens as a new cultural center for Europe in the early 2010s. After 2015, the idea of Athens being the new Berlin resurfaced in international media (Dudziak and Wellnitz 2015; Sooke 2017; Wilder 2018). Publications branded Athens as brimming with artistic opportunities, which was an oxymoron since in that period many Greek artists chose to emigrate to pursue careers abroad. Emphasizing the abundant cultural events also became a systematic marketing strategy for tourist sites, promising a romanticized cultural experience in Athens.

The discursive trends observed in such articles were fascinating to follow as they often sensationalized the contradictions inherent in Athenian life as a point of attraction and uniqueness. Examples of such contradictions include the housing of galleries or performance studios in abandoned buildings that look nearly derelict (at least as far as their facade is concerned), which has given rise to a distinctly barren aesthetic in works produced in Athens. Another example is the hosting of performances in alternative sites or unconventional spaces. The urban landscape aesthetics in Athens encompass a different set of contradictions. Take, for instance, the neighborhood of Kerameikos, which is located northwest of the Parthenon and is home to a part of the ancient city walls that constitute an enclosed archaeological space. In the surrounding streets, the sides of what used to be factory storage spaces (which are common in GKM) are adorned with large murals; these images are nowadays overwritten by graffiti. The contemporary urban landscape in GKM encompasses ancient ruins, derelict, graffiti-tagged apartment buildings, and colorful murals, and all can be seen in a single glance. The unrefined beauty captured in these contradictions between pristinely restored ruins, decrepit buildings, and urban anarchy promotes a distinctly Athenian aesthetic that was, in turn, sensationalized.

International media often highlighted the creative surge observed in the neighborhoods of GKM but rarely addressed the contradictions that gentrification laid bare. Authors took a sensationalizing approach that further fetishized these tensions and rebranded them as points of attraction. For instance, in one of the first articles discussing the notion of Athens as the new Berlin the reporter from the *New York Times* notes: "Athens's Kerameikos/Metaxourgeio neighborhood—which still has its share of drug dealers and prostitutes, *like any good arty neighborhood should*—along with the rundown Kypseli district have become the new home for influential galleries" (Khemsurov 2010; emphasis added). *Travel and Leisure* magazine published an article in May 2017 titled "Athens, an Unexpected Renaissance" (Heyman 2017), which similarly celebrated the contradictions in the Athenian landscape. It made a note of the graffitied walls, juxtaposing them to the "mythical ruins" of the ancient city. A block quote highlighted in the middle of the article posits: "You can get so lost in Athens's anarchic beauty that you forget, if only for one evening, that this is a city living through a depression" (Heyman 2017). This language indicates a romanticizing of the rundown aesthetic, which was born out of the necessity to find alternative spaces during the crisis.

Returning to the characterization of Athens as "the new Berlin," one can only wonder what makes such an analogy possible, especially considering the irony that many artists opted to leave Athens *for* Berlin or other European cities. A look at the German newspaper *Die Welt* suggests a comparison on the grounds of the financial impact either city had on the broader economy and how they serve as symbols of unity in their respective contexts given that Berlin became a symbol for the unification of Germany, and Athens, a symbol for the unity of the EU. Published early in the crisis, in 2012, the article claims that Athens *is* the new Berlin because of the impact that it has on the German economy: "As used to be the case with West Berlin, Greece costs us a lot of money" (Krauel 2012; my translation). An alternative approach (Dudziak and Wellnitz 2015) focuses on similarities in the use of open spaces in Berlin—following the fall of the wall—which is paralleled to the repurposing of large, abandoned factory spaces in Athens.

What this comparison between Athens and Berlin achieves is a further romanticization of the Greek crisis as an opportunity to restructure life and the urban landscape; and in doing so, it overlooks the fact that the empty spaces are a direct result of austerity. Thus, the prospect of an "artistic renaissance" or the promise of "creativity equals prosperity" that was popularized in mainstream publications debating the new Berlin idea comes at a much darker cost for locals than travel blogs and newspaper articles openly acknowledge. Furthermore, emphasis on *renewal*—captured under terms such as "modernization," "renaissance" (Heyman 2017), or "emerging from the wreckage" (Wilder 2018)—commonly cited in articles promoting "new Berlin" comparisons assume an implicit backwardness. Such narratives of backwardness reevoke the historically latent Orientalist anxieties about Greece's positionality in the EU periphery and present the arts as Greece's opportunity to reclaim its position as central to Europe's cultural capital.

The rebranding of the crisis as opportunity and the emphasis on renewal appears to be a millennial revisiting of Greece's long struggle to balance between Oriental fantasies and Western ideals. History seems to be relentlessly repeating itself as there is, once again, pressure to conform to European expectations. This time, expectations prescribe what recovery from the crisis should look like in terms of aesthetics—borrowing from the comparison with Berlin's gentrified and reclaimed artistic neighborhoods—and a national narrative of resilience. Ultimately, such narratives have done more harm than good. They gained traction internationally and made space for exploiting the affordable life offered in Athenian art hubs. These same "opportunities," however, are born out of the locals' loss.

Compared with the cost of living in European artistic hubs, such as Berlin, Paris, and London, Athens is a much cheaper city to live and create in. In a short documentary produced by VICE questioning whether Athens is the new Berlin, a group of artists from the aforementioned European capitals reflect on their choice to move to the Greek capital in the midst of the crisis. One of them notes: "Nobody that I know from here, in Athens, is benefitting from making money in Athens" (Laughlin 2017; 5:48–5:52.). This implies that they were still making money internationally but chose Athens as their base because of its affordable rents and a significantly less hectic life, compared with big European metropoles. As another interviewee points out, even though the pay was considerably higher in London, they did not feel like they had time to enjoy life, which they had the opportunity to do in Athens.

So, while at first glance, it may seem like the artistic scene was flourishing and offering many opportunities, the truth is that these opportunities were limited to people whose income and well-being were not dependent on the Greek market. Further attesting to this is the testimony of a Greek realtor who, in the same VICE documentary, admits having repeatedly provided space in building blocks that he owned to artists for free, particularly in the Metaxourgeio neighborhood (Laughlin 2017, 15:30.). Thus, the perception that the arts in Athens were genuinely flourishing and growing is troubled when these transactions are revealed as one-sided affairs: there were limited (if any) benefits for the locals. Additionally, the testimonies captured in the VICE documentary about life in Athens being more relaxed than in international art hubs further supports the romanticizing of Greece during the crisis. Enjoyable conditions of life and a relaxed pace cannot be afforded by everyone, especially not by local artists struggling to make ends meet and having very hectic schedules, frequently working multiple jobs. Questions about potentially capitalizing on the conditions of the crisis therefore cannot be ignored. The crypto-colonial narrative of assumed backwardness (in terms of a struggling Greek economy that needs to rely on EU saviors to survive) becomes a marketing point for the Athenian art scene and is turned into an aesthetic preference that glorifies Athens as "alternative" and vibrant. The subsequent sections further expose the contradictions inherent in this branding of creativity as a step toward prosperity by conducting a brief historical overview of the waves of emigration of Greek artists and by mapping how emigration motives shifted in the decade of the crisis.

Training and Draining the Creative Class: A Brief History

The phenomenon of Greek dancers and choreographers going abroad for career opportunities or further education has been common since the beginning of modern dance in Greece in the early 1900s. Throughout Greece's tumultuous history, emigration in search of better opportunities has been a constant, peaking periodically and targeting specific countries based on the political climate and economic needs of any given era.

Since the mid-twentieth century, the most common reason for artistic emigration has been to acquire terminal degrees (mostly MFAs) or to attend workshops and intensives to cultivate and improve technical prowess. Migration patterns and destinations fluctuate every decade. For instance, dance artists during the 1980s received training mainly in the US and primarily in New York (see Figure 10). Following Greece's entry into the EU in 1981, the 1990s showed a steady decline in emigration to the US and an increase in artists acquiring degrees from other European countries. The establishment of the euro as the common currency in 2001 made traveling and residing in other EU countries more affordable and accessible. The steady decline of emigration to the US—especially after the the first decade of the twentieth century—is most likely related to the tightening of visa processes and border control after 9/11 and to the limited funds and state support for scholarships, which also waned during the Greek crisis decade.

The shift toward a borderless Europe also coincided with the twilight of the artistic movement of postmodernism in the US, which had been a point of attraction for many artists. Simultaneously, in Europe, contemporary dance approaches in the legacy of *Tanztheater* became increasingly popular and gradually nurtured the aesthetics of what could be broadly classified today as European contemporary dance. Beginning in the mid-1980s, the attention of dancers from Greece seemed to slowly shift away from the US as the center for avant-garde experimentation toward the European scene, which claimed that pivotal position in the Western concert dance world.

Between the 1990s and 2010s, according to available data from two scholarship-granting institutions for studies in dance (the State Scholarship Foundation[3] and the privately run Alexander S. Onassis Public Benefit Foundation), most scholarships for graduate education in dance or for continued technical training were granted for studies in an EU country. UK universities and conservatories, such as The Place and the Trinity Laban Center, were highly desired destinations, as English is one of the first foreign languages taught in Greek schools, making English-language education more

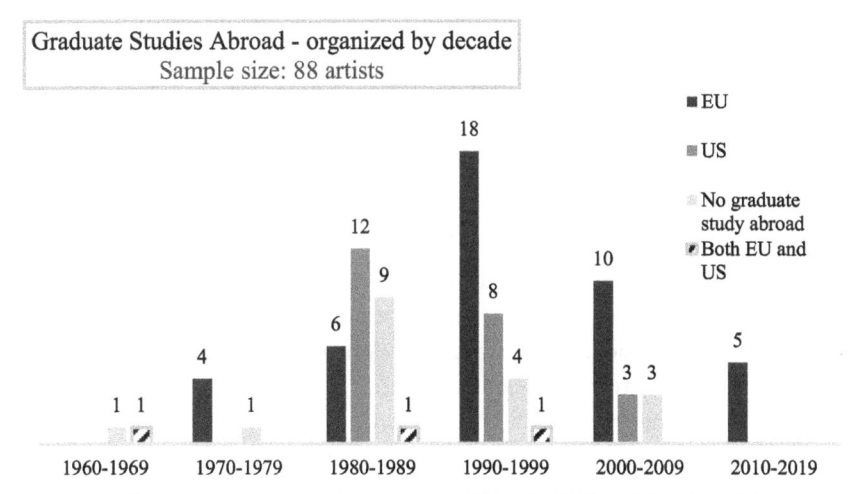

Figure 10. Greek choreographers' graduate study in the EU and the United States, 1960s–2010s. The data was drawn from the artists' biographies found either in anthologies documenting their work (Grigoriou Mirayas 2004; Fessa-Emmanouil 2004) or on their personal websites. The graph encompasses only choreographers who returned to produce works in Greece after studying abroad. Chart created by the author.

approachable for Greek artists. This trend will likely shift in the aftermath of Brexit, so it will be interesting to trace the emigration patterns following the UK's exit from the EU.

During the crisis (specifically between 2010 and 2017), the migration patterns of Greek dancers both intensified and varied. The primary motivation for moving abroad was no longer driven primarily by education, as artists also moved in search of better working conditions or in pursuit of a more secure career in dance. The dance artists who graduated from professional dance schools late in the first decade of the twenty-first century or early in the second decade shape the primary demographics of economic migrants during the years of the Greek crisis. The backgrounds of the emigrant performers and choreographers of the crisis wave vary, as do their destinations and motivations. Some of them studied dance in Greece and left to seek opportunities for more stable employment abroad; others did not have professional dance training but were drawn to dance dramaturgy or dance studies and left Greece to pursue degrees in those fields. Their stories and motivations are captured in the coming section. Tuning in to the recurring themes in my discussions with emigrant dancers, I outline how they are slowly reshaping the field of Greek contemporary dance upon their (intermittent or permanent) returns to the country. Their individual stories create a complex fabric of social and artistic interactions, which I follow thread by thread to describe an exciting shift that seems to be in the works for dance in Greece.

The Motives: Exposing the Limitations of the Local Scene

"What made you decide to leave Greece?" This was one of the few questions[4] I asked all the emigrant artists I interviewed. While responses varied, they usually revolved around a need that each respondent had for "something more" that could not be satisfied in Greece. Many interviewees completed degrees in dance in one of the professional dance schools in Athens, and their graduation coincided with the early years of the crisis. Therefore, the challenges they faced upon joining the workforce were tainted by austerity conditions. For some dancers, the conditions of the crisis were not the deciding factor as they had already made plans to move abroad and their relocation just happened to coincide with the Greek crisis. Even when their emigration was motivated by reasons unrelated to the crisis, their motives still reveal limitations of the Greek dance scene.

The reasons interviewees chose to leave Greece can be grouped into three overarching categories: (1) dissatisfaction with the structure of dance education in Greece—either in terms of the opportunities for artistic research and experimentation or in terms of the infrastructure available to pursue theoretical studies in dance; (2) the working conditions and lack of professional stability, and (3) reasons pertaining to cultural conservatism, such as intolerance toward the LGBTQIA+ community, or political extremism. Familial or personal reasons related to the brain drain (such as finding more professional opportunities abroad) are also encompassed in the abovementioned categories. Interestingly, none of these aspects have been identified as restrictions by the international artists that immigrated to Greece in the context of the "Athens is the new Berlin" trend. The disparity noticed between the motives of the local artists who chose to leave compared to those of international artists who relocated to Athens during the crisis suggests a capitalizing on the precarious conditions that the crisis brought about for the locals. International artists whose well-being was not dependent on the Greek economy were not impacted in the same way.

A Technique-Obsessed Education System

Eleni Mylona left for Zurich, Switzerland, in 2010. She explains:

> The decision was taken with my partner, who wanted to move abroad for professional reasons, but I actually always felt that in Greece, every-

thing was really limiting for me, in the sense that dance in Greece was either expressive or technique. . . . For me, there was always a need to understand [dance] better . . . I wanted to find answers to questions about the body, which never appeared in my dance training in Greece. (Eleni Mylona, Skype interview, October 25, 2018)

Eleni and I were in the same cohort at the professional dance school Morianova–Trasta. In fact, I remember our conversations regarding the limitations of studying dance in Greece when we were in our third (and final) year of studies. I recall her vividly discussing ideas she had come across in André Lepecki's book *Exhausting Dance* (2006), which she found after personal research in performance studies scholarship. We were both very excited about further exploring the intersections between performance and theory. Neither of us had been exposed to performance studies theory before, as dance studies—and really, *any* theoretical framing of dance—were not part of the required curriculum in Greece at the time.

Answering the question of what motivated her to leave Greece, another interviewee Stella Dimitrakopoulou simply responded: "It was the studies that I was interested in pursuing, which I could not find in Greece" (Stella Dimitrakopoulou, Skype interview, December 20, 2018). Dimitrakopoulou graduated from the Grigoriadou Dance School in Athens in 2006 and left to pursue her master's degree at the Trinity Laban Center in London in 2008. In Greece, she had been simultaneously studying metallurgical engineering at the National Technical University of Athens, which allowed her to pursue a study abroad program called Erasmus in 2007 in Vienna, Austria. Erasmus is not an option for professional dance students since dance is not included in university education, so this was an opportunity that Dimitrakopoulou had access to through her enrollment in the engineering program. She took advantage of her time in Vienna and signed up for dance classes at Tanzquartier. This strategy is a common alternative for Greek dance students wishing to broaden their technical training or exposure to dance beyond what the Greek educational system provides. Upon returning to Greece to finish her university studies, Dimitrakopoulou worked as a dancer with some companies in Athens, but her interests concerned practice-based research. She pursued this in her master's degree and later continued her explorations by earning a PhD degree at the Trinity Laban Center.

Martha Pasakopoulou, who graduated from the professional dance school of Niki Kontaxaki in 2006, left to pursue studies abroad at the London Contemporary Dance School (The Place) in 2009. She, too, echoed the sentiment of needing to broaden her horizons following graduation:

> I was looking for a chance to leave [Greece], so it was a good opportunity to further my studies because the truth is that I felt like I was missing a piece. I didn't feel as though my studies in Athens were enough. . . . After I graduated, I stayed in Athens for two and a half to three years to finish my university degree, and I was, of course, still teaching dance on the side and trying to find work. I was working as a dance teacher in dance schools, but—at least at that time—that was not enough. I wanted to do something more, so I looked into going abroad for further studies. (Martha Pasakopoulou, Skype interview, December 10, 2018)

In our interview, Pasakopoulou stated that she considered dance education in Greece relatively narrow in scope, an opinion that she grounded in its intense emphasis on virtuosity and technique with little attention paid to individual choreographic exploration or improvisation practice.

Virtuosity, in this context, is culturally specific and closely tied to how dance education is structured in Greece. It is thus different from understandings of virtuosity established in the field of dance studies and theater studies by scholars such as Ariel Osterweis (2013), Gabrielle Brandstetter (2007), or Susan Bernstein (1998), whose theoretical frameworks imply a sense of excessiveness and infer a level of individualism. On the contrary, the term was used by interviewees to emphasize the focus on technical excellence in performing Western concert dance techniques that shape dance education in Greece. Contrary to the individuality at the core of the abovementioned scholars' theorizations, in the context of the Greek dance education system, virtuosity emphasizes the dancers' uniformity and musicality, as well as the shapes and lines that the dancing bodies are expected to embody and perform.

Ironically, the emphasis on technique and virtuosity that many performers consider limiting *is* their ticket out of Greece. Having partaken in intense technical training, they have developed the skillset required to audition for and secure scholarships[5] to study abroad or to compete with other dancers on the international contemporary dance stage. Evangelos Poulinas, a choreographer working and residing in Germany since 2005, commented on the technical excellence of Greek dancers, whose performances he had observed in auditions or at international festivals:

> The dancers I meet from Greece, who are coming here [in Germany] to audition have an outstanding level of technique, which is great. This should not be taken for granted; it could be very different. (Evangelos Poulinas, Skype interview, May 28, 2019)

While the emphasis on virtuosity can be a celebrated trait and a point of pride, at the same time, it can also be a factor imposing limitations on the way the art form develops locally, as many interviewees noted.

Elpida Orfanidou completed her training in Greece and then moved to Berlin. Her works deliberately push the boundaries of what constitutes dance by adopting an aesthetic that disavows virtuosity. In our interview, she critiqued the emphasis on technical excellence as leading to a creative rut:

> In Greece—at least that is how I see it—there is an intense obsession with technique. There are extraordinary dancers who graduate from some schools, but it is as if you are a victim of that desire to reach a very high level of technical skill and then just communicate that in the performances. I decided I wanted to explore things beyond that, and there are more diverse stimuli abroad. It is not that they don't care about the technique, but they simultaneously present you with a plethora of other layers of thought and experiences. (Elpida Orfanidou, interview, July 10, 2018)

Like the artists introduced above, Orfanidou left Greece to study abroad soon after she graduated from the Grigoriadou professional dance school in Athens in 2005. She began by pursuing a bachelor's degree in choreography at Arnhem School in the Netherlands, continued at the Center for Choreography (Centre Chorégraphique National) in Montpellier, France, and completed a master's degree in performance practice and research in London at the Central School for Speech and Drama. She has been based in Berlin since 2009.

In all the examples discussed thus far, the artists migrated before the crisis or in the first few years after its onset. They were not in the country when the ministerial subsidies for dance ceased, so their emigration was motivated primarily by personal curiosity as well as the lack of infrastructure in the local scene to foster an exploration of their artistic interests. Their dissatisfaction with the state of the dance field in Greece thus exposes the limitations in the local educational system.

Precarious Working Conditions

Some interviewees actively pursued careers in dance in Greece during the early years of the crisis and eventually chose to leave after being disappointed by the working conditions. Ioanna Kerasopoulou left Greece twice. At first, she moved to pursue a professional degree in musical theater in Hamburg, Germany, right after she graduated from high school in Nafplion in southern

Greece. After completing her studies, she returned to Greece to pursue contemporary dance in 2013. Upon her return, she started working at a contemporary dance company while continuously auditioning for other companies and participated in large productions at the Badminton Theater[6] as a performer. She stayed in Greece until 2017, when she decided to leave again. She described those four years in Greece as tainted by financial struggles, such as her pay being frequently delayed or, in some instances, never being disbursed. Echoing the financial shortages in the dance field that have already been addressed, she notes that her salary would often be between 15 and 25 EUR per performance without any compensation for the rehearsal period. Thus she considered the Greek crisis an excuse that people used to ensure cheap labor:

> I think that everyone has surrendered to this situation that Greece is currently in and that many people who are [in positions of] authority are using the excuse of the crisis to put you down, degrade you, and suck you dry, all based on the excuse that there is no money. Especially in dance, where it was always about having favorites, knowing people, and having connections, the situation has gotten out of control. (Ioanna Kerasopoulou, Skype interview, October 14, 2018)

Eventually, Kerasopoulou grew intolerant of these conditions and decided to move back to Germany, this time to Berlin, to seek professional opportunities as a contemporary dancer there. Reflecting on the decision to leave again in 2017, she noted:

> I am very hurt that I had to leave my country because I love something so much. I wish I could combine my passion with [staying in] my country. I did not want to leave, but I had to because there was no other way. I had to choose: either I would have a career or at least more opportunities [in Berlin], or I would remain stagnant. My choice was between these two. And I decided to drop everything: my friends, my house, my life in Athens, my boyfriend, my dog, everything, to come here [to Berlin] and do the thing I loved so much, which is such a pity. (Ioanna Kerasopoulou, Skype interview, October 14, 2018)

Our discussion made it apparent that Kerasopoulou was frustrated by what she experienced in Greece. She acknowledged that she was lucky to have a choice to return to Germany, a point of access afforded to her by her family, as her mother was from Germany. Seeing things unfold in Greece as an outside observer, she also expressed frustration with the "waste of talent," which she identified as due to the lack of infrastructure in Greece to support and absorb dance graduates. She recalled visiting the 2018 KDF after having settled back in Berlin and emphasized her surprise at the intense competition among dancers (who primarily resided in Greece) in the festival workshops. While healthy competition is to be expected in dance classes, she noted how the high rates of unemployment and the lack of contracts for Greek dancers made for an aggressively competitive atmosphere. Reminiscing on the workshop, she commented:

> It is scary to have such rich talent be wasted because they don't dare to leave their country. But good for them! I don't know how easy it would have been for me to leave Greece if it wasn't for my mother. (Ioanna Kerasopoulou, Skype interview, October 14, 2018)

Technical excellence and virtuosity are once more presented as desired traits, yet in Kerasopoulou's observation, the issue of access is brought to the forefront. Emigration requires monetary and linguistic access, which not everyone can afford or is willing to pay. A vicious cycle is revealed: there are a lot of talented dancers, which fosters some healthy competition at auditions and summer festivals, yet there are so few opportunities for dancers, which makes said competition aggressive and creates a negative atmosphere among them.

Kerasopoulou was not the only one to leave after finding the working conditions in Greece unbearable. Yannis Mitsos, a dancer and Butoh instructor who worked on several dance productions in Greece in the period between 2014 and 2017, disclosed that for him, the reasons were both financial and sociocultural:

> [The reasons why I left Greece] varied. I was starting to get tired of what was happening with dance in Greece, not just on a financial level, although that was one of the reasons too. I wanted to work and be able to be compensated better, to work, and to be able to have insurance. . . . To work and be safe. This means having others [choreographers/directors] consider my safety during rehearsals. (Yannis Mitsos, Skype interview, October 20, 2018)

In asking follow-up questions, Mitsos clarified that safety meant a sense of security and welfare, as not all employers covered insurance benefits. He also discussed safety in terms of practicing and rehearsing in spaces designated for dance. An example he brought up was rehearsing in a room with a cement floor, which raised the risk of knee injuries for the entire ensemble.

The financial precarity of the profession (short-term contracts, limited opportunities, the need to work multiple jobs to sustain oneself), along with the physical precarity and risk of injury noted by Mitsos, evoke Anusha Kedhar's (2014, 2020) argument on the hyperflexibility often required by dancers and the risks involved in reaching one's bodily limits when striving to satisfy the diverse demands imposed on them. In Kedhar's argument, *hyperflexibility* is defined by conditions such as short-term contracts that do not secure financial stability for performers yet require them to be on standby and readily available whenever the need arises. Kedhar also references immigration laws and the visas required to work in some countries for a limited time. Immigration laws and visas are not an issue for artists holding Greek citizenship (or citizenship in any other EU member state) who seek work within the EU. Yet the term *hyperflexibility* can be stretched to include other financial obligations that dancers are expected to afford out of pocket to remain competitive. Such expenses may include transportation to rehearsals, festival tickets, or workshop fees to train in multiple styles and remain versatile. In the small, highly competitive, and—as some interviewees hinted—clientelist scene of Greek contemporary concert dance, such hyperflexibility and versatility become a necessity and an agreed-upon requirement.

In this instance, the notion of "flexibility" takes on an additional connotation if one considers the international artists choosing to live in Greece and the emigrant Greek artists returning intermittently. It is not by chance that most international artists who relocated to Greece are in the visual arts or other fields where remote work is possible, rather than in dance. In both instances, the subjects have accumulated experience abroad and have been exposed to various techniques and approaches that perhaps are not as accessible (if at all) in Greece. In auditions or workshops they attend in significant international festivals, such as the festival workshop that Kerasopoulou mentioned, performers with more diverse training are much more "flexible." Concerning the ways that this impacts the climate of competition, it raises the stakes higher for local artists who are entering these spaces (festivals and workshops) from an already precarious position and makes them compete with international artists, or emigrants, who are comparatively much more mobile in the scene with the wages from contracted jobs abroad. This serves only to intensify the competitive structure already in place.

Juxtaposing the experience that many emigrant interviewees had in Greece with the experience they had working for or auditioning for ensembles abroad, most of them spoke fondly of the respect they were getting from international institutions. They appreciated signing contracts at the beginning of employment with clear expectations, being paid for rehearsals, and—more importantly—being paid on time. They also valued the relationships they formed with the choreographers and expressed a feeling of being treated as equals, in terms of their work being recognized as part of the creative process and not performing strictly choreographed routines with little room for improvisation. The so-called expanded approaches to choreography that the interviewees were seeking and finding abroad negate the top-down hierarchy between choreographer and dancers and allow for individual agency.

Of course, what interviewees described as an ideal professional experience did not come without sacrifices. Out of respect for the subjects' privacy, the names of the interviewees who addressed this aspect are not revealed because most were reluctant to discuss this. Several of them, especially those who migrated to pursue careers abroad and therefore did not have the support of an academic scholarship, have repeatedly struggled to make ends meet and have had to take on additional jobs to support themselves. One of them noted: "My main income is from working at the bar, and like everyone else, I also clean the houses of rich folks." Thus the precarity of the profession and the "flexibility" or "hyperflexibility" it requires is not limited to dancers living in Greece under austerity conditions, but it is a reality even for performers pursuing careers in other European countries (see also Van Assche 2020). Based on the accounts of emigrant dancers, they are much more willing to make such sacrifices while pursuing careers abroad because they view the working conditions in the host country as nurturing their creativity and valuing their efforts compared with the conditions they faced in Greece.

Cultural Conservatism

Beyond the working conditions, another limitation that several subjects identified is cultural conservatism. During the crisis decade, homophobia, sexism, and gender inequality were still prevalent, and the overarching structure of society was founded on patriarchal values. While popular discourse on these topics has significantly advanced since the beginning of the millennium, the ethnocentric political turn during the crisis stalled these developments.

To paint a picture of the impact that the crisis has had on social values and the resurgence of cultural conservatism, I briefly delve into a short history of queer and feminist activism in Greece and look at some of the milestones in the developments of these movements. Homosexuality in Greece was decriminalized by penal law in 1950 (Zestanakis 2017), yet even so, it remained a cultural taboo in the following decades. In Greece, queer activism has its roots in the years following the fall of the junta in 1974.[7] The type of activism that occurred relied on grassroots organizations[8] that were not part of larger institutions and thus had limited political influence. During the 1980s and 1990s, there were not many significant advancements in the visibility of LGBTQIA+ identities and rights, and for the most part, they remained marginal, which is indicative of the arrangements around gender and sexuality in the country. Culturally, gender identity and sexual orientation tend to be considered "private" rather than "public" issues. Such systematic invisibilization and silencing of queer identities, in turn, presents a challenge for historicizing queer expression and for grounding contemporary debates on gender equality, sexuality, and nonbinary identities.

Since the early 2000s, queer activism has become more visible, with Pride parades becoming annual in Athens (starting in 2005) and gradually being established in other cities and communities, such as Thessaloniki in 2012 and Crete in 2015 (Giannou 2017). Following their election in 2015, the leftist government (SYRIZA) passed several laws supporting the LGBTQIA+ community. In December 2015, Law 4356/2015 introduced same-sex partnership, and in October 2017, Law 4491/2017 was voted into effect by Parliament, which streamlined the procedures for declaring one's gender in official identity papers. In May 2018, another law was passed, allowing same-sex couples to foster and adopt children. While these significant and long-awaited advancements took place in the latter half of the crisis decade, they were offset by the simultaneous rise of homophobia, as ethnonationalism regained traction and regurgitated the junta-era obsession with the survival of the Greek family. In this conservative rhetoric, the family is very narrowly defined as a heteronormative nuclear social unit.[9]

Beyond such cultural shifts, the austerity measures imposed have negatively impacted the field of human rights and the universal health care system in Greece, deriving from the extensive budget cuts and directly impacting the health of LGBTQIA+ populations.[10] While the crisis did not cause the rise in such instances of cultural conservatism and of limited understandings of intersectional identities, it certainly fostered their resurfacing, as well as heightened aspects of patriarchal and macho Greek culture. Even though dance in Greece has always been a space for challenging conservative ideas and experimenting with queer performativity and expression, there are still many limitations in the ways that queerness is explored and (re)presented, which are not present in other European art centers. A quote by Yannis Mitsos captures this sentiment:

> I would like to work in dance in a way that engages with the hardships of the era. What I am trying to say is that Greece is undergoing a crisis, and this has brought to the surface a lot of issues of Greek culture. However, I haven't seen many [artists] engage these [issues]. Really, I think they either suppress them or don't want to show them. They don't want to show that Greek society has issues; we are artists and should be showing these things. . . . So I thought that because I personally would like to live in a society that is more "open," more liberated, coming here [to Berlin], I would be able to experience something like that. And I have. (Yannis Mitsos, Skype interview, October 10, 2018)

What Mitsos identifies as an openness characteristic of international art centers is something that translates into a distinctly different aesthetic and methodological approach in the works of many Greek emigrant performance artists presenting work in Greece. This distinction may be rooted in the varying stimuli the artists are exposed to and the openness to experimentation beyond the emphasis on virtuosity and technique that dominates the Greek scene.

Before delving into these emergent frameworks for creation characteristic of Greek artists residing abroad, I briefly turn to another trend that directly relates to the waves of emigration: the surge of theoretical exploration of dance in Greece. There is an evident shift in the level of experimentation and the mode of engagement with social issues as an increasing number of dance scholars and dancers pursue academic studies abroad in dramaturgy, dance studies, or other related fields. They then return to Greece to collaborate with choreographers and take up the role of dramaturgs and choreographers' assistants, gradually influencing local aesthetics and approaches.

Emergent Approaches to Bridging Theory and Practice

Beyond dance practitioners pursuing careers abroad during the crisis decade, dance theorists and arts administrators also turned to international institutions to pursue theoretical studies in dance. In this demographic, a significant number of individuals demonstrate a growing interest in theory and dramaturgy and pursue graduate degrees abroad to later work as dance historians, arts administrators, or dramaturgs. Leaving Greece to pursue theoretical studies in dance and then returning to enrich the field is one of the most apparent ways that emigration impacts the local scene.

There seems to be a wave of Greek scholars and practitioners who enroll in part-time dramaturgy courses abroad and either relocate to participate in the program full-time or are based in Greece and travel back and forth to complete their studies if the program allows a residency-type format. Rodia Vomvolou, a researcher pursuing graduate studies in dramaturgy at the time of the interview, left Greece in 2017 after completing her bachelor's degree at the School of Drama in the Faculty of Fine Arts at the Aristotle University of Thessaloniki. She was based in the Netherlands when we spoke and remarked about a two-year master of theater practices program in Arnhem (ArtEZ University of the Arts). According to the program description, the mission is to create "diverse thinking artists that promote performance making as a strategy for equitable societies and resilience" (ArtEZ 2019). In 2018, the first-year cohort of the program included three students from Greece (out of eight students in total) and five students from Greece (out of twelve students in total) in the second-year cohort (Rodia Vomvolou, Skype interview, November 13, 2018). While the demographic of one single program is certainly not enough to prove a shift in interest toward dramaturgy and the theoretical study of performance practices, it is nevertheless indicative of a new direction. Some of the students enrolled in such programs aspired to return to Greece immediately and either choreograph their own works or collaborate with choreographers as dramaturgs upon their return. Another observation attesting to the rise of dramaturgy in Greece is the increased number of choreographers crediting dramaturgs in performance programs.

Vomvolou, who had started exploring dramaturgy as part of her bachelor's degree, considers the surge of interest toward a theoretical contextualization of dance as directly related to the crisis landscape:

> The crisis, and the notion that we must find alternative ways to do things, has given rise to a new discourse around dance. . . . Dramaturgy has started gaining visibility in various ways, even if we don't always name it or recognize it as dramaturgy. Various modes of collaboration and methodological approaches have solid dramaturgical components, which have come out of alternative ways of approaching the creation of works, such as forming a community to counter the crisis. (Rodia Vomvolou, Skype interview, November 13, 2018)

Comparing this claim to some of the shortcomings of the dance field in Greece, such as the many artists not adequately engaging with aspects of the crisis, which Mitsos remarked on, the gradual establishment of dramaturgy as a practice in Greece can be understood as an attempt to create frameworks to engage with the conditions of the crisis in ways that are meaningful for choreographers and audiences.

Vomvolou's point was elaborated by another dance researcher, Elena Novakovits, who has collaborated with Greek choreographers as a dramaturg after completing graduate studies abroad in the UK and the Netherlands. She highlighted the rise of institutional programming for the support of artistic research residencies in Greece. For example, Novakovits (Skype interview, November 22, 2018) named a research residency program for artists and creators run by the Onassis Stegi in Athens, which invites international artists for two to six months and organizes workshops on artistic research.

Another research initiative is directed by Giorgos Sioras Deligiannis, who graduated from the National School of Dance in 2014. He regularly organizes meetups with performers and choreographers, curating dialogues around predetermined topics of interest. For instance, the 2019 series called *Regulatory Bodies | Research Lab Vol. 2* spanned four weekends (from February to March), with each meeting lasting about three to four hours on Saturdays and Sundays. According to the social media page for the event, the workshop was concerned primarily with notions of reconfiguring the framing of performance and choreographic structures and invited participants to explore these concepts in meetings that took place in public, highly trafficked areas. Sioras Deligiannis regularly organizes forums for discussion between choreographers and highlights his interest in the process of choreographic practice and performance as research. The series *Regulatory Bodies* received state sponsorship in 2018.

Both examples, one promoted by an established private institution and the other driven by an artist's vision, demonstrate the rise of interest in the theoretical study of performance and perhaps even an alternative conceptualization of performance practice and dance, which had not previously been made available through the dance education system in Greece. Many interviewees captured this turn with the terms *conceptual choreography* or *expanded choreography*. Such new choreographic direction has been their primary motivator to leave the country to explore the possibilities beyond what they identify as the limitations in their virtuosic technical training.

The gradual "expansion" of choreographic approaches and the exploration of new modes of collaboration and creation, which can partially be achieved by incorporating research and theoretical frameworks to guide and ground the performers' movements, make space for reconsidering the creative process altogether. As Novakovits observes:

> In the Greek scene, other than the lack of a theoretical foundation, there is also a lack of creators/choreographers going to each other's performances. . . . In Greece, we are most [concerned] with the end result and less with the process. And I do miss the [aspect of] artistic research in Greece. It's like boom . . . performance.[11] (Elena Novakovits, Skype interview, November 22, 2018)

The quick turnaround and creation timeline that Novakovits notes were also identified by choreographers and festival curators Christina Mertzani and Evangelos Poulinas, who, at the time of our interview, resided in Germany. They consider this an issue inextricably linked to the funding structures in Greece:

> POULINAS: I think there is a difference [between the Greek scene and international scenes] in terms of time, funding, and infrastructure, which impacts the quality of the work, and the end result.
>
> MERTZANI: The main difference in the works presented abroad . . . is repetition. . . . I remember, for example, working as a dancer [in Greece] in some productions for three to four months [of rehearsals] and doing only two or four performances, and that was all. The instances when there were more performances than that were very few. . . . Another difference that I discern, which is not exactly related to the [dance] scene, but is undoubtedly influenced by it, is something that Evangelos [Poulinas] has already noted: in other countries, there is an infrastructure for dance; a dancer can work for a company year-round. They may make a living out of it and have a steady income for one or two consecutive years through one production. In Greece, this is something that no company can offer. . . . Some projects run for three to four months, and then [the dancers] are paid per performance. Dancers cannot make a living this way. (Christina Mertzani and Evangelos Poulinas, Skype interview, May 28, 2019)

Beyond the nature of the subsidies that push performers to focus on producing only one work per season, another limitation is the audience. There is a limited audience for contemporary dance productions in Greece, which further justifies a low number of performances.

Naturally, the time crunch and the limited resources that choreographers in Greece have for creating their works justify the limited overlaps between theory and practice that some interviewees identified. The research and residency initiatives mentioned here can thus be viewed as efforts to respond to these shortcomings and create the space for artists to come together and engage in dialogue with one another.

Embracing the "Weird"

PIIGS (2015)[12] in Berlin

PIIGS—A European Cheerleading Team, curated by Daniel Kok, was presented in Maxim Gorki Theater in Berlin in 2015. It was a collaboration between Kok and five choreographers and performers, one from each country represented by the "PIIGS" acronym. Jorge Conçalves represented Portugal; Sheena McGrandles, Ireland; Luigi Coppola, Italy; Elpida Orfanidou, Greece; and Diego Agulló, Spain. Kok invited each artist to create a work drawing on their identity as coming from the countries most impacted by the crisis. Then, they wove all pieces into an evening-length production as a group. In the piece, each performer embodies the cheerleader of their country, as the work presents a humorous and absurd critique of the Eurozone crisis by toying with exaggerated cultural stereotypes. The performance opens with Ireland, who hypes up the audience in typical cheerleader fashion and introduces the rest of the PIIGS through a call-and-response game. McGrandles shouts, "Can I get a *P*, can I get an *I*, can I get a *G*, can I get an *S*." As the audience responds with shouts, the other four performers enter wearing jumper jackets with the letter of the country they are representing printed on the back. The music for this segment is the famous song "Eye of the Tiger," which was popularized by the *Rocky* film franchise. It provides an energetic background for a group cheerleading sequence of the five performers waving their blue-and-yellow pom-poms (corresponding to the EU's official colors) while chanting "P-I-I-G-S" over and over (Figure 11).

The solos continue in the order the countries appear in the acronym. Portugal (Jorge Conçalves) is followed by Italy (Luigi Coppola), and each solo performance is interspersed with group work and the official "profile" of every country. During each profile, the back wall lights up, and each performer is framed in a manila-folder-shaped frame whose colors match those of their

Figure 11. The introduction of the PIIGS cheerleaders in *PIIGS—A European Cheerleading Team* (2015), curated by Daniel Kok. Video screenshot from Kok (2015, 13:32).

country's flag. The profile offers information about the country's debt and other facts relating to the Eurozone crisis, all projected on the wall (Figure 12) and narrated by a male voice over the loudspeakers. The staging of each profile is reminiscent of the setup phase of a video game avatar as an electronic *bling bling bling* sound signals each profile's beginning and completion. The performers pose under a stripe of white light and remain frozen until their profile is completed. The projection extends beyond the wall to the floor, where the twelve yellow stars of the EU flag rotate. When each profile concludes, the stars rise from the floor and spin on the back wall, moving faster and growing smaller with each spin until they eventually disappear.

Most performers stand still during their profiles, posing awkwardly, either glued to the back wall (Ireland), in a wide-legged superhero pose (Portugal), with a wide grin bordering the grotesque (Italy), or a simple sideways stance, which becomes a reference to bull fighting, as the performer puts on a matador hat and is given the EU flag to use in place of a red cloth (Spain). Only Greece is unruly during the profile and during many other moments in the performance. Drawing on the stereotype of Greeks as lazy or difficult because of their reluctance to accept austerity measures, the cheerleader for Greece (Elpida Orfanidou) is often off-beat or a few steps behind the others in group sequences.

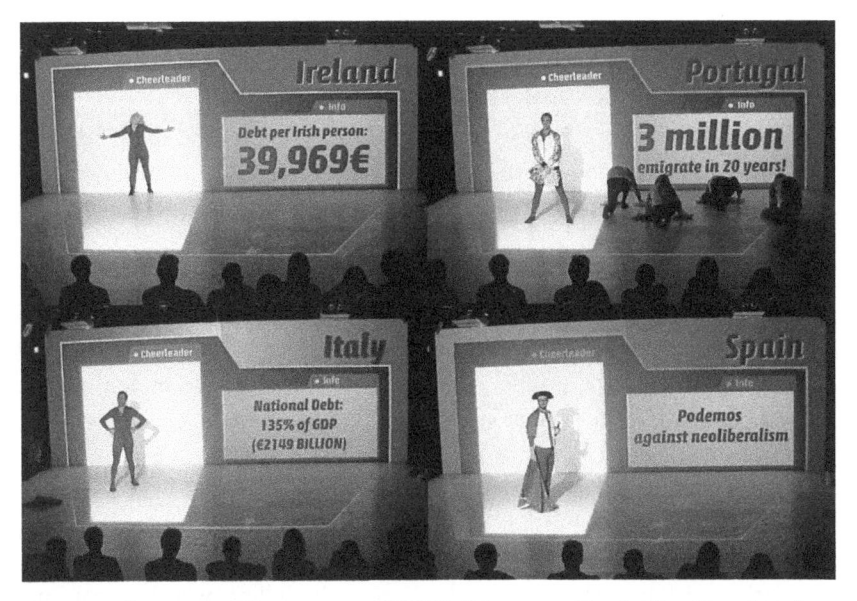

Figure 12. Country profile sections in *PIIGS A European Cheerleading Team* (2015), curated by Daniel Kok. From top left clockwise: Ireland, Sheena McGrandles; Portugal, Jorge Conçalves; Spain, Diego Agulló; Italy, Luigi Coppola. Sreenshots from a YouTube video of the performance (Kok 2015 3:40; 14:23; 54:20; 23:59).

Greek Section of *PIIGS* (2015)

"Hello, I am the ehm . . . Greek," Orfanidou walks in from stage right for her solo and introduces herself to the audience. "I come from Greece . . . there is some ehm . . . a part . . . not a part in the map, but a part of Greeks that they are called complex? . . . Pontiacs, we belong to this group, and we talk a dialect, and we have some traditional elements, and I started to connect more directly to this tradition."

The sound of static interrupts her.

"What's this?"

During this deliberately fragmented monologue, Orfanidou repeatedly pauses, and her body posture communicates confusion through gestures that fill in the blanks in the spoken word conveying a sense of convolutedness. She moves to the side of the stage, grabs her phone, and at the press of a button, the room fills with traditional Pontian music. Orfanidou stops the music and pulls a Pontian lyra from its instrument case. She holds it up so the audience can see and declares: "So this is called lyra! Some people of you may think that it's the ancient instrument."

(Tries to play a note evidently out of tune)

Waving the bow for the lyra in the air, she asks an audience member: "You know how to play the violin?"

She asks audience members to move so she can enter the space between them and seeks someone with "delicate hands" to hold it and tune it. She seems to find a person, yet as soon as they touch the instrument, she changes her mind and asks for it back.

"No, no, we are going to lose valuable time. Now play!"

The sound of a lyra playing fills the space over the loudspeakers, only to be shortly interrupted. The masculine voice coming over the speakers hesitantly asks, "Maybe we do the profile?" The lights turn off, and Orfanidou grabs a striped blue-and-white jumper jacket from the side of the stage, representing the Greek flag.

She puts on the jacket while the voice announces a set of words in English, providing their definition and etymological roots in (ancient) Greek, such as *politics, economy*, and *austerity*. Sometimes the voice-over makes pronunciation mistakes, which Orfanidou corrects by yelling over the recording. Gradually, the corrections turn into a conversation between her and the voice. The last word projected in the background is "Grexit" (Figure 13). Orfanidou is the only one of the five performers who interacts with the voice, thus further supporting the stereotype of the unruly Greek.

Upon the conclusion of the profile, Orfanidou positions herself at the center of the stage and settles into an extraordinarily deep stretch, reminiscent of a warrior yoga pose, yet one so deep that both of her thighs almost touch the ground. Traditional Greek music becomes audible through the loudspeakers. The singer laments: "Δική μου είναι η Ελλάς, και στη κατάντια της γελάς" (Hellas is mine, and yet you laugh at its abjection). Balancing in the deep stretch, she turns to the audience and asks: "Anyone Greek here understand what the song says?" The audience initially responds with laughter, yet when she repeats the question, a few yell "Yes!" in response. After calling over Spain (Agulló) to assist her in getting out of the stretch, Orfanidou leaves the stage and reenters, holding a plate with *mezedes* (μεζέδες, or *mezes*), which she offers to the audience. This concludes Greece's solo, which gives way to Spain.

Political humor, satire, and a taste of the absurd are at the core of all five solos in *PIIGS*, as each performer pokes fun at the common (and often ridiculous) stereotypes circulating about people from the countries represented. Orfanidou, in her insistence on correcting the voice-over, is simultaneously toying with the stereotype of the unruly and "know it all" Greek while also commenting on the trope of Greek as the root of many English-language terms.

Figure 13. Elpida Orfanidou in the profile section for Greece in *PIIGS—A European Cheerleading Team* (2015). Screenshot taken from a video of the Greek section (Orfanidou 2015a; 6:15).

Upon the conclusion of Spain's performance, "Eye of the Tiger" fills the room again, and all performers reenter, each wearing a jumper jacket with their country's flag. They complete a cheerleading drill to the music and then attempt to balance in a deliberately awkward acrobatic shape as they chant loudly, "¡El pueblo unido jamás será vencido! / The people united will never be defeated!" The rhythm of the chant corresponds to the homonymous song by Sergio Ortega, a Chilean composer, which became the anthem for the Chilean resistance against the Pinochet dictatorship. The PIIGS chant this as they try to maintain their balance but fail to do so, which is a telling metaphor for the sovereign imbalances between the EU and its marginalized peripheries.

In my interview with Orfanidou, she disclosed that her involvement in this project came through an invitation to represent Greece. She approached her solo as a continuation of her ongoing choreographic investigation, which experimented with creating a chaotic atmosphere. As she notes, what particularly piqued her interest, was how this crisis created onstage ultimately resulted in a sense of liveliness, turning the experience into something positive and fun for the audience (Elpida Orfanidou, interview, July 10, 2018).

The highly fragmented nature of the narration, the sense of confusion embodied by the performer and experienced by the audience, and the choice to withhold context from the audience and instead keep them guessing are the main traits of the piece. This approach manages to engage audiences through humor, which Orfanidou frequently incorporates into her work, yet, at the same time, this approach may also alienate them. As soon as audiences think they grasp the piece, the environment shifts again, and they are invited to construct a new framework to understand the direction that the performance has taken, an effect that accurately evokes the experience of navigating the landscape of the Greek crisis.

The "Greek Weird Wave"

The fragmentary, nonlinear approach to storytelling seen in the solo for Greece in *PIIGS* is also found in many other performance works produced during the crisis years—such as those discussed in chapter 2. Orfanidou's intentionally chaotic framework and the deliberately elusive environments she created are also observed in what has come to be known as the Weird Wave in Greek cinematic productions that emerged during the crisis. *Weird Wave* is a term popularized by journalists and later widely adopted by film theorists. It describes a group of critically acclaimed movies created by Greek directors in the early years of the Greek crisis. Some highlights include Yorgos Lanthimos's Oscar-nominated *Dogtooth* (2009) and his following film *Alps* (2011), Athina Rachel Tsangaris's *Attenberg* (2010), and Panos Koutras's *Strella: A Woman's Way* (2009). All these films were produced by Greek filmmakers whose works premiered at prestigious international festivals awarding them critical recognition and acclaim. According to film scholar and filmmaker Marios Psaras (2016), one of the central characteristics of this cinematic wave is the thematic motif of alienation. Most films classified as "weird" present a distanced, dedramatized, and anti-naturalistic abstract space, which borders on surrealism. Other defining elements are the stylistic and narrative choices made by the directors. As Psaras observes, "there is a long genealogy of local production that has insistently and self-consciously pitted its oppositional aesthetics against the nation's official historicity and self-representation" (2016, 5). The emergence of the Weird Wave as a movement temporally situated in the crisis years, and actively challenging national narratives through cinematic production is understood by some modern Greek studies scholars as an occurrence intricately tied to the experience of the crisis. For instance, Dimitris Papanikolaou (2021) regards the Weird Wave as a cinema of biopolitics, a window into exploring how social and political practices govern and discipline living beings. The absurdity and surrealism in the environments created in these films is thus understood as paralleling crisis responses.

Returning to the approaches characteristic of the cinematic Greek Weird Wave, Psaras (2016) draws attention to the fragmentary and open-ended narrative structure of most of the examples he identifies as belonging to the movement. Beyond these two evident analogies between the cinematic trend popularized during the crisis and the approach in Orfanidou's *PIIGS* solo, there is an added resonance, which holds true for many productions debating the crisis: facial expression, or more accurately, a lack thereof. With respect to expressivity, the protagonists of the "weird" movies are often deadpan, regardless of the absurdity of the situations that are taking place around them. This is especially relevant to Orfanidou's work, who maintains her composure despite the humor and confusion she creates for audiences. Her face expresses consistent indifference to anything happening in that moment.

Media and communications scholar Afroditi Nikolaidou (2014) highlights that many of the films belonging to the Weird Wave are "bodily centered," which she defines both in reference to the deadpan expression of the protagonists, as well as in regard to the narrative tactics used, which often rely on repetition and highlight the actors' physicality through close attention to gestures. Performative rituals encompassing games, reenactments, and public ceremonies are also commonly included. All these tactics are described as relating to a specific type of acting grounded in post-dramatic theater tradition. This approach often results in acting that highlights the performers' vulnerability and may give the impression of (or may, in fact, be) improvisation. This is another resonance with Orfanidou's work, which at moments appears as a series of unrehearsed and spontaneous actions, performed in a stream of consciousness model rather than following a linear progression.

According to Nikolaidou, the performative aesthetics of "weird" films ultimately "bear the mark of the shock, of destabilization, of discomfort of/ for the present" (2014, 40). The correlation between the country's severe financial crisis and a particular corpus of its cinematic production emerges as an intriguing hypothesis generating many epistemological and ethical questions about the meaning and interpretations of the crisis, but most significantly concerning its social, cultural, and affective manifestations.

At the same time, causal assumptions that the crisis inspired this new wave of artistic exploration should be avoided since the emancipation of Greek cinema is a convergence of multiple factors. Especially since the Weird Wave came from a generation of filmmakers that had primarily studied and worked abroad, it is in direct conversation with international cinematic trends. The Weird Wave coincides with the Greek crisis, Papanikolaou (2021) points out, but it is a byproduct of the discourse that critics, analysts, and journalists (who helped solidify the "weird" label) circulated. Critics and journalists were eager to read allegories of the Greek contemporary nation and crisis in the films produced in that period. At the same time, "the very word 'weird' smacks of somewhat patronizing, even Orientalist, framing" (Papanikolaou 2021, 5). Consequently, the Weird Wave can be viewed as a means for the peripheral (Greek) subject to reclaim their (crisis) narrative and identity during a highly tumultuous time. In the context of the already fetishized Greek crisis, it helps peripheral subjects recenter themselves by exploiting that label and entering dominant and internationally relevant art discourses.

There is an evident analogy between the trend situated at the core of the "weird" cinematic experimentations, which is challenging established aesthetics, and a similar trend that emerged in the works of contemporary choreographers in Greece. Beyond Orfanidou, whose work is one of the most striking examples of this trend, the work of other contemporary dance choreographers from Greece is driven by similar experimentations and approaches, as the next section discusses.

Is "Weird" the New "Conceptual"?

META (translating as After 2014), by Artemis Lampiri (MAN dance company), is a piece for two to four female dancers. In the rendition I witnessed at the Arc for Dance 6 // 'NETWORKing, Festival (May 2014), there were two performers (Candy Karra and Artemis Lampiri) dressed in identical plain black dresses cut above the knee. As the lights came up on an otherwise empty stage, one of them was lying on her side with her knees bent to her chest, feet flexed. Her hands were clenched into tight fists, her knuckles facing the audience, and her arms bent ninety degrees at the elbow. She appeared frozen in a horizontally oriented seated position, ready to fight or defend herself from an attack. The other dancer stood beside her, one leg slightly forward (see Figure 14). The dancer lying on her side slowly straightened one leg and directed her elbow to the floor to support her head. The motion seemed mechanical and purposely devoid of any recognizable human emotion. In response to this slow shift, her partner took a slow step. Gradually responding to one another's minuscule gestures and position shifts, they eventually came together, sharing weight in multiple ways yet never genuinely engaging with one another. Their interactions grew increasingly more complex, involving demanding balancing sequences. The stiffness in the dancers' body postures traversed the borders of the stage as I felt my body clench upon witnessing one dancer place her fists on the other's spine to climb on her back. I winced

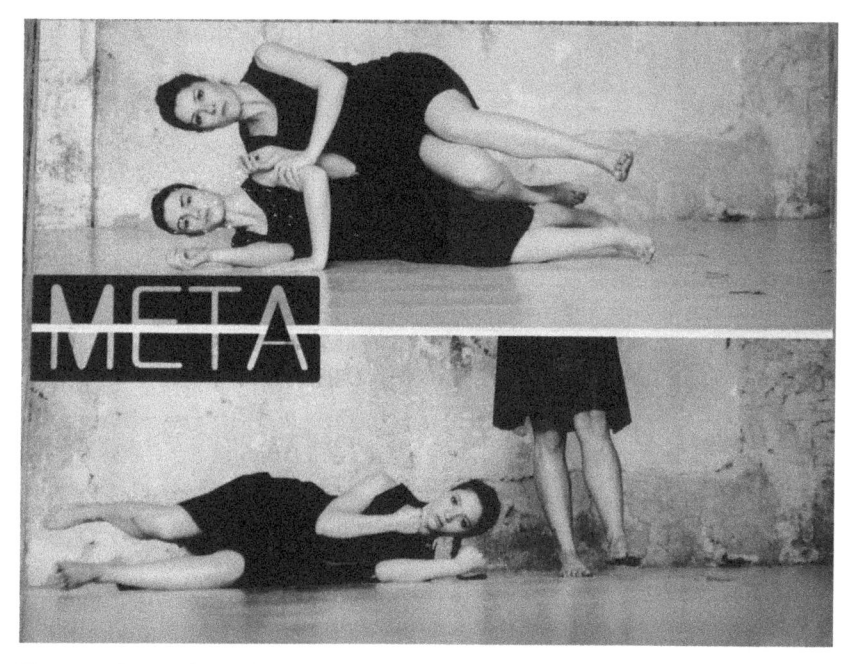

Figure 14. Promotional flier for *META (2014)*. Author's personal archive.

momentarily at the sight, yet the performers showed no signs of discomfort and continued expanding their repertory of seemingly robotic gestures.

The choreographed dissociation between the dancers and the stiffness of their bodies successfully communicated an overarching sense of numbness and shock. The note in the program describes the work:

> META is a dance piece that deals with the state of being, straight after a shocking experience, a big fight, when we realize that life goes on without us and redefine ourselves. META is a moving picture of two women of two of the survivors, with the tension of no intention of moving forward. (Lampiri 2014; original in English)

While there is no direct connection to the crisis in this description, the condition of shock and attempted recovery is a very familiar crisis scenario. The dancers' deadpan facial expressions convey an intense dissociation from their environment and perhaps even a dissociation from reality, which aligns with the familiar crisis aesthetic popularized by the Weird Wave.

Further examples connected to the structure and devices of the cinematic

Weird Wave were the performances presented in the 1st Festival for Emerging/Young Choreographers, held at the Onassis Stegi in 2014. The festival hosted an eclectic selection of four works on two weekends. One of them was *Contreplongeés* (2014) by Panagiota Kallimani. At the time, Kallimani was residing in Paris, and this was her first choreography. *Contreplongeés* is a French term signifying worm's eye perspective in filmmaking and photography. In the program notes, the piece was framed as having been inspired by the crisis and focusing on the experience of people experiencing homelessness. The viewpoint indicated by the title—from the bottom looking up—is a reference to the perspective of the aforementioned group of people. Kallimani had provided several people currently experiencing homelessness with a single-use camera and asked them to take pictures of their everyday lives, and their takes were presented in a photography installation in the theater foyer.

The dance piece bore many references to "weird" narrative structures. One such reference was fragmentation, which was explored by the lighting and costume choices that presented audiences with isolated body parts, such as an elbow or a knee being the only visible limbs of a performer peeking through dark fabric. As a collaboration between three dancers (Laurie Young, Emilio Urbina, and Panagiota Kallimani) and an actor (Alexandros Siatras), the piece used a movement vocabulary that was deliberately not virtuosic but rather pedestrian and abstract. The most notable performer was the male actor. Tied to a piece of wood resembling a tree trunk, he slowly made his way to the front of the stage, dragging the trunk behind him. His movements were so minuscule and slow that he seemed to be still throughout the performance, yet he gradually traversed to the front of the stage. The fragmented nature of the narration and the effect of alienation evoked through the display of fragmented limbs align with the aesthetics of the Weird Wave. In addition, *Contreplongeés* falls under the umbrella of "conceptual" dance rather than a performance emphasizing virtuosity and technical prowess.

Another example is Katerina Andreou's work: *A Kind of Fierce* (2016/2017). The Greek premiere of Andreou's piece was at the Athens and Epidaurus Festival in 2016, which is where I witnessed it; it has also been performed on many European stages (e.g., Berlin, Vienna, Paris, and Nantes). Based on the talk-back that followed the performance in Athens, the central premise of the work was a set of rules that Andreou constructed so she could break them and explore a sense of free will and freedom in her dancing. Similar to Orfanidou's piece, there seemed to be a deliberate resistance to technical virtuosity. Even though Andreou is evidently a trained professional dancer (she graduated from the National School of Dance in Greece before relocating to France to pursue a master's in research and choreography), her movement quality in this piece evoked the careless prancing of a child, dancing with reckless abandon and without a care about fitting into any movement vocabulary molds. Throughout the piece, Andreou's facial expression was consistently deadpan, in contrast to the stark shifts in intensity suggested by the accompanying music choices. The mismatch between the sound score and the movement qualities evoked a sense of alienation that aligns *A Kind of Fierce* with the surrealist, off-beat environments seen in Weird Wave filmography. The playful and exploratory approach taken in the choreography similarly situates this performance in the conceptual dance realm.

The parallels between the emergence of conceptual dance experimentations in the Greek dance scene and the Greek Weird Wave are indisputable. Creators employ nonconventional approaches that resist established narrative structures and dominant narratives. Revisiting Psaras's terminology of "weird" cinema as engaging with "oppositional aesthetics" (2016, 15), it could be argued that a lot of contemporary dance produced during the Greek crisis similarly opposed the prevalent aesthetic of virtuosity. Both the generation of "weird" filmmakers and the emerging generation of contemporary dance makers are pushing their respective genre's boundaries and thus slowly introducing audiences to new modes of thinking about these practices. Of course, it should be acknowledged (albeit with a sense of bitter irony) that most of the performances in question, like the films, were vetted by international audiences prior to being presented at prestigious Greek festivals; or they were developed according to high-brow standards of cultural capital to make the process of presenting these works on Greek stages easier. The artists' and works' international background and exposure are highlighted and often admired as points of superiority, playing into the xenomania and sense of national pride commonly observed among Greeks.

Many interviewees, when asked whether people's perception of them changed after they had moved abroad and whether they were suddenly afforded more opportunities in Greece, confirmed that they became much more sought after for workshops and classes. This is not a coincidence. They also mentioned that disclosing their international experience made it easier to find venues to present their work or to showcase their work at prestigious Greek venues. It is understandable that venues and dance studios would want to invite artists with international exposure to share their knowledge. At the same time, it evokes the question of why, if there is indeed strong interest in fresh perspectives and approaches, the Greek education system is still experiencing a degree of stagnation that causes young artists to emigrate.

If we relate the abovementioned oppositional aesthetics, which were introduced to the Greek scene by practitioners working abroad, to the aesthetics of the crisis evidenced in the performances discussed in chapter 2, it becomes clear how both approaches highlight a heightened sense of alienation. In the works produced by artists from the local scene, alienation is found in how choreographers construct the relationships between their performers. Yet in the works produced abroad, alienation is introduced primarily to challenge the relationship with audiences and to create a sense of confusion. In local productions, the crisis was the overarching framework: the works portrayed a crisis that the performers experienced, which offered a model for audiences to navigate. By contrast, in international productions, the crisis was explored as a concept that structured an environment for the audience to actively experience and become immersed in.

Concluding Thoughts

During the Greek crisis decade, the dance community was at the confluence of a spatial reconfiguration incited by gentrification and a reevaluation of aesthetics and approaches brought about by local artists' displacement and migration. Considering the impact of gentrification and the international migration of skilled populations known as the brain drain is essential in mapping the shifts in the Greek dance landscape during the crisis years. International dialogue and exchange intensified as the crisis became an opportunity to rebrand and reevaluate artistic production from Greece, as exemplified by the trope of "Athens is the new Berlin" and the popularity of the Greek Weird Wave.

The international implications of the Greek crisis expose the complexity of how crisis narratives circulate. Narratives of Greek resilience became a point of attraction internationally. Locally, however, resilience manifested as indignation about the limitations of the art scene and pushed artists to migrate in search for better opportunities abroad. The waves of artists migrating in response to the crisis, in turn, created new hierarchies. One such dichotomy is between, on one hand, artists from Greece who were able to relocate to other European dance hubs, who could afford to live and study abroad, or were in a position to make sacrifices to achieve their professional goals and, on the other, those artists who could not. Thus access to international experience and exposure became a new currency legitimizing and adding value to one's artistic capital upon their return to Greece.

The comparison between the local and other established international scenes inevitably begs for an uncovering of the multiple layers of politics embedded in these tensions. The neoliberal policies of austerity reignited underlying anxieties regarding Greece's marginalization and set in motion attempts to prove Greece and Greeks as European and to establish the Greek dance scene as equally important as its central European counterparts. The direct comparison between Athens and Berlin further unearths another layer of tension between Greece and Germany, as one of the dominant European economies, which assumed a significant financial burden to support the recovery of the Greek economy.

The Greek performance and arts scene, thus, did experience a renewal, yet it was one centered on creative approaches rather than one bearing financial benefits for the locals. Locally, the popularization of the Weird Wave and the ways that "weird" aesthetics translated into conceptual approaches pushed the limits of what was accepted as contemporary dance and expanded the art form in new directions. While there has not been enough temporal distance at the moment of writing to theorize the true impact of these international dialogues on the local scene, a shift toward conceptual approaches is already evident.

Notes

1. The term *cultural capital* is borrowed from Bourdieu (1973) to denote the accumulation of cultural knowledge that confers power and status. It refers to knowledge of artistic trends, which are determined by dominant trends (such as what is valued as high art, which is of course determined in line with the priorities of the dominant culture). I use the term broadly to capture the impact of artists' migration on the cultural output/productions. I also draw on the work of Sarah Thornton (1995), who tied the notion of cultural capital to dance cultures and especially hip-hop. Following Thornton, I specifically employ the concept of *embodied cultural capital*, which refers to consciously acquired and passively inherited (through socialization and tradition) embodied traits that are impressed on a person's habitus (Bourdieu 1984). In the context of contemporary concert dance in Greece, embodied cultural capital encompasses all elements associated with being a contemporary dancer, ranging from the predominant techniques of training to trending dancewear and the overall aesthetics of performance, such as those described in chapter 2.

2. Sex work is legal and regulated in Greece.

3. The State Scholarship Foundation stopped granting scholarships for dance around 2009, so during the decade of the crisis dancers wishing to study abroad had to choose between the Alexander S. Onassis Public Benefit Foundation and Fulbright scholarships. The latter was only available for study in the US.

4. Most of the interviews conducted for this chapter were structured around a core set of questions. All emigrant artists interviewees were questioned about their motivations, the limitations they identify in the Greek scene, their aspirations to return to Greece, as well as the timeline of their migratory journey.

5. The State Scholarship Foundation used to offer scholarships in dance based on an audition process. Students auditioned in ballet, modern/contemporary dance techniques, and improvisation. Applicants had to participate in the audition process even if they aspired to pursue theoretical studies in dance. On the contrary, the Onassis Public Benefit Foundation held an audition process for students interested in furthering or pursuing their technical studies in dance, and an interview process for students interested in pursuing theoretical degrees.

6. The Badminton Theater is one of the largest indoor theaters in Greece with 2,500 seats. It is a repurposing of the Badminton Stadium that was built for the 2004 Olympic Games. It regularly brings musicals and large productions requiring elaborate sets that are hard to stage in smaller-capacity theaters.

7. Regarding the sharing of information during the military junta, social scientist Dimitra Giannou remarks how "even within a context of absolute censorship imposed by the junta, Greek gay students studying abroad and political dissidents living in self-exile provided information to gay people in Greece about the growing level of homosexual activism around the globe and the international discourse on issues of gender, sexuality and kinship" (Giannou 2017, 20). For more on the LGBTQIA+ movement in Greece, see also Dendrinos (2008) and Kantsa (2014).

8. Some of the most notable forums for queer activism included a magazine called *Amfi* (Αμφι, meaning "Bi"), which had the reputation of being among the most informed on topics regarding fluid identities across Europe. The magazine was popularized since 1978. Another organization that was at the forefront was AKOE, acronym for Απελευθερωτικό Κίνημα Ομοφυλόφιλων Ελλάδος (Apeleftherotiko Kinima Omofylofilon Ellados; Greek Homosexual Liberation Front), which convened in 1976. AKOE took important steps in the 1980s to open bars and queer spaces (Papanikolaou 2018a). A few gay bars existed during the junta as well, located in the central neighborhood of Plaka, as the regime thought that this would present a favorable image of Greece internationally, yet AKOE attempted to popularize them and open even more after the fall of the regime.

9. For more on the intersection of LGBTQIA+ activist agendas and the cultural prevalence of the family as an institution in Greece see Papanikolaou (2018a, 2018b) and Papanikolaou and Kolokotroni (2018).

10. As a study published by the American Psychological Association attests: "Because of diminishing services and medical treatment for the general population, health professionals may perpetuate stigma and discrimination against LGBTQ+ population to ration who is considered worthy to receive medical treatment and health care services" (Halkitis, Valera, and Kantzanou 2018, 505). Instances of discrimination were particularly present during the period of 2011–2013, when there was an HIV outbreak among intravenous drug users in Greece (Halkitis, Valera, and Kantzanou 2018) and HIV testing for drug users, sex workers and immigrants

was enforced under police supervision (under the 31A Public Health Act). In a heinous example of profiling, related to this case, in the summer of 2013, the Greek Transgender Support Association reported purges and arrests of transgender citizens under the pretext that the police needed to establish whether that particular person was a sex worker. As Dimitra Giannou, who has written extensively on the health inequalities that the LGBTQIA+ community faces in Greece notes: "Trans women who were presumed as being sex workers by appearance were arrested, left to wait in police departments for more than 3–4 hours to be identified while they were humiliated, threatened and offended by police officers" (Giannou 2017, 19).

11. When giving consent in 2023 for her interview excerpt to be used, Novakovits noted that her views as well as the ways the field operates had changed. Novakovits shared the following statement: "Since the interview took place in 2018, I can notice from my point of view a shift in my views on institutional functioning, the systemic faults and the relevant urgent critique that can be raised from the position in which I operate" (email correspondence, March 27, 2023).

12. The description of the performance is based on two videos: one found on Orfanidou's Vimeo account (Orfanidou 2015), which captures her solo, and the other is documentation of the entire performance available on Daniel Kok's website (Kok 2015). Since many aspects of the performance are improvisational, the description meshes elements from both iterations, as the overall structure of the piece remained the same, yet elements of the solos were diversified.

Four

The Rise of Regional Festivals

———

The sun has set, and the dusk slowly swallows the surroundings of the outdoor Eastern Moat Theater (Theatro Anatolikis Tafrou; Θέατρο Ανατολικής Τάφρου) in the Cretan city of Chania. The audience is slowly gathering for a performance called *tempus fugit* (2016) by cie toula limnaios, a company led by a Greek choreographer based in Berlin, presented under the auspices of the 8ᵗʰ Dance Days Chania (DDC) Festival in July 2018. The work is prefaced by a welcome speech by DDC artistic director Sofia Falierou and a representative from the German embassy in Greece—one of the sponsors of the festival and this work. Honoring the sponsors and openly involving funding agency representatives in the festival events is a rare model that provides visibility to the multiple agents involved in the festival organization. It also speaks to DDC's unique organizational structure grounded on community building and human connections.

The audience comprises an amalgamation of locals interested in dance and festival participants, who attended after a full day of dance workshops and seminars. The festival participants were young dance students (enrolled at professional dance schools, who were broadening their technical skillset by participating in this summer festival) and professional dancers. There seemed to be an even mix of Greek and international audience members, apparent through the diverse languages that could be heard.

The night set and the lights surrounding the theater turned off, indicating the performance would commence. The lively chatting among audience members subsided, and the dancers dressed in beige- and earth-colored raincoats and leather ankle boots came to the stage one by one. Brown leaves lay scattered on the stage, audibly rustling as each dancer rolled through them. The calming music of a violin accompanied their entry. It was a hot summer evening in late July, and even though the performance evoked the fall season, it seemed to naturally blend into the surroundings. The theater was in a trench, and the back of the stage consisted of a brick wall supporting the soil. At the top, the trench's steep face was adorned with wild bushes. The relative quietude of the opening scene was interrupted by the sound of cicadas buzzing, cars honking, and occasionally people yelling on the street. As the performance progressed, there were moments when I found myself fully immersed in the action, assisted by the loud music that covered any potential distractions. Other times, the pulse of the city of Chania won over.

Halfway through the performance, a couple on a motorcycle rode onto the hill at the back of the theater, turned off the engine, and paused to watch a snippet of the performance. Upon witnessing this, I could not resist a look around. I noticed the balconies of a nearby high-rise hotel building occupied by guests getting a glimpse of the dancing from the comfort of their rooms. Even though the performance took place on a relatively conventional proscenium stage, the location of the outdoor theater made it accessible to passersby and tourists. Chance encounters between the unsuspecting public and contemporary dancers materialized and offered a unique setting for theorizing how dance becomes enmeshed in the local community, not just in Chania but more broadly in the various regional festivals that emerged during the crisis decade. The role that contemporary concert dance performance plays in regional communities is ripe for questioning, as is its potential to transcend the traditional stage and veer into the realm of sited work,[1] even though this may go against the performance's initial format.

Instances of dance being performed in outdoor theaters or other public settings, such as in a central square—sometimes in a guerrilla manner—have become a trend that is especially popular in the summer dance festivals in Greece's tourist areas. Such events became particularly prominent during the decade of the financial crisis. This trend further reflects the fluctuating relationship to space introduced in previous chapters, as well as a newly identified need to broaden artistic dialogue beyond the confines of Athens as the capital and the center for artistic expression and to engage audiences from regional communities. Audience engagement is often driven by staging strategies, such as hosting performances in public settings, to foster what I term "forced encounters" between the performers and the unsuspecting public. The choice to engage audiences through the genre of Western contemporary concert dance—a decidedly abstract form adhering to Eurocentric aesthetics and practices— poses a wide array of critical questions about the timeliness of this endeavor (why during the crisis and not in years prior) and the politics of choosing a genre that is still somewhat "foreign" for local audiences in peripheral areas.

Unpacking these questions and initiating a discussion around the increased visibility of contemporary dance as a practice and its festivalization,[2] this chapter maps out the institutional shifts that led to the rise of regional festivals and explores the aforementioned questions by homing in on three regional festivals. First, I provide a brief history of the most influential festivals in Greece, which include dance, and then I open the discussion with a study of the numerous festivals that emerged during the crisis decade.

Institutional History and the Festival Canon

Athens and Epidaurus Festival

One of the most prestigious and long-established festivals in Greece is the Athens and Epidaurus Festival, often also referred to as Greek Festival (Elliniko Festival; Ελληνικό Φεστιβάλ), a name that attests to the importance it holds in the Greek performing arts scene. It is a festival centered on theater, dance, and music performances by local and internationally acclaimed artists and ensembles. Hailed as a "celebration for the high arts" (Athens and Epidaurus Festival 2018; my translation), the festival has its roots in Cold War Greece in 1955. Initially, the space used for the festival was the restored Herodes Atticus Odeon, an outdoor theater. In the years that followed, more sites were added, such as the restored ancient theater of Epidaurus and, since 2006, the repurposed spaces of the old Tsaousoglou furniture factory on Peiraios Street (known as Peiraios 260) in the neighborhood of Gazi.

The early focus of the festival was to invite prestigious international orchestral ensembles and to revive theater repertory from classical antiquity.[3] The orchestral performances were hosted at the Herodes Atticus Odeon, while theatrical performances were presented in Epidaurus. Dance was added to the program in 1956 (the second year of the festival). The works presented were part of a tourist outreach effort and aimed to foster cultural tourism and establish Greece as a country that not only offered beautiful landscapes and archaeological sites but could also become the center of intellectual activities and entertainment. The agenda of the festival was in close alignment with the priorities of the Greek National Tourism Organization (Ellinikos Organismos Tourismou; Ελληνικός Οργανισμός Τουρισμού); it also delicately maintained the balance of the Cold War political climate by ensuring ensembles from both the Soviet Bloc and the US were represented. As the extensive archival research of Tsintziloni (2022) attests, this task was achieved primarily through the invitation of ballet ensembles.

In the first few decades after its inception, the festival invited performances that, in some way, extended notions of classical lineage and fostered connections with much-acclaimed Greek antiquity. This direction has dominated the festival's agenda, which has consistently played an important role in shaping and reaffirming the Greek national narrative.[4] Curation of the performances often revolved around the criterion of historical or thematic relevance to Greek antiquity. Works that possessed such relevance were deemed worthy of being presented in one of the two ancient theaters that constituted the main sites of the festival up until 2006.

Theater and performance studies scholars Eleftheria Ioannidou and Natascha Siouzouli remark:

> Although the so-called "Loukos' era"[5] arguably brought about a crucial shift in long-established practices in the history of Epidaurus, the discussion about the sacredness of the space, the authority of the ancient text, and the Greek ownership of antiquity never ceased to abound in the discourses surrounding the Festival. (2014, 112)

As a national institution, the Athens and Epidaurus Festival was a site for cultural diplomacy, especially in its first decade, during the ongoing Cold War. Greece's geopolitical significance during the Cold War was pivotal for the primarily communist Balkan Peninsula as it was under US economic and political surveillance.[6] The dance productions hosted by the festival during those early years reflect the contested position of Greece within that political climate. In 1956, Harald Kreutzberg presented a work with Koula Pratsika and Dore Hoyer called *The Fate of Mycenae*. In the following years, the festival repertory comprised works by international artists and ballet companies such as the Belgrade State Opera (1957), Jerome Robbins (1959), American Ballet Theatre (1960), Royal Opera Covent Garden (1961), Margot Fonteyn and Rudolf Nureyev (1963), Béjart Ballet (1963 and 1964), and the New York City Ballet (1965), to name a few.[7] The works presented included excerpts from romantic and classical ballets such as *Swan Lake*, *Le Sylphides*, *The Nutcracker*, *Romeo and Juliet*, and *Giselle*, as well as works that related to Greek mythology, such as *Orpheus and Euridice* and *Prometheus*, and more modern—yet still monumental—pieces such as *The Rite of Spring* and *Afternoon of a Faun*.

At the time, the Athens and Epidaurus Festival was the biggest of its kind in the country—and also rose to be among the most significant festivals in Europe. Given this, it clearly set a precedent for what constituted high art, which was confined to Western concert dance practices and primarily ballet (with some instances of incorporating modern dance). This curatorial choice presents a critical dichotomy because, for Greek audiences, Western concert dance practices were an "imported" genre. As Tsintziloni (2022, 41) remarks, the festival was an attempt to cultivate a more "extroverted" and cosmopolitan identity for Greece. Consequently, the festival agenda was driven by and aligned with the agenda for cultural tourism to "elevate" Greece's cultural capital to be on par with what was valued in the rest of the West at the time.

Fast-forwarding to the first two decades of the 2000s, the direction of the festival took a turn toward embracing the contemporary moment by engaging with pertinent topics of the time. Yet one thing that has not changed is that it is still considered one of the leading institutions in Greece; and as such, it sets the bar for dominant art trends and delineates what constitutes "high art." The festival's character and aesthetics have shifted through the diversification of its venues and the move to reclaim more industrial spaces (such as the Tsaousoglou furniture factory on Peiraios Street mentioned earlier). This change was further intensified during the crisis decade.

Ioannidou and Siouzouli, who have studied the festival during the financial crisis, note that in the years after 2010, the festival turned into a "*topos* of transformation and fluidity which seems to elude certain conditions of production and reception pertaining to its past history" (2014, 109). The reason behind some of the main changes in the festival's agenda was the budget cuts. In particular, in 2013, following two years of the festival's operation under austerity conditions, Giorgos Loukos—the festival director at the time—noted in an interview for the free newspaper *LiFO* that the curatorial criterion for the year was "not to spend money" (Dioskouridis, 2012). The budget shortage led to a significant turn toward supporting young artists, which destabilized preexisting institutional and cultural practices. Furthermore, it led to an increase in the work of Greek choreographers represented at the festival. This trend started in 2011 and intensified under the artistic direction of Evangelos Theodoropoulos between 2016 and 2019. The chart below (Figure 15) traces this surge by mapping out the dance performances presented each year between 2007 and 2019.

The increasing representation of local dance artists is in line with the hype around Greek arts production during the crisis. It also indicates a new direction for how the national narrative was negotiated and conceived through influential institutions. Echoing the observations made in chapter 2 about the "inward turn" in the consumer market, the programmatic shifts in favor of an increased number of Greek choreographers exemplify a similar direction in curatorial practices. In the trajectory of the Greek Festival, the national

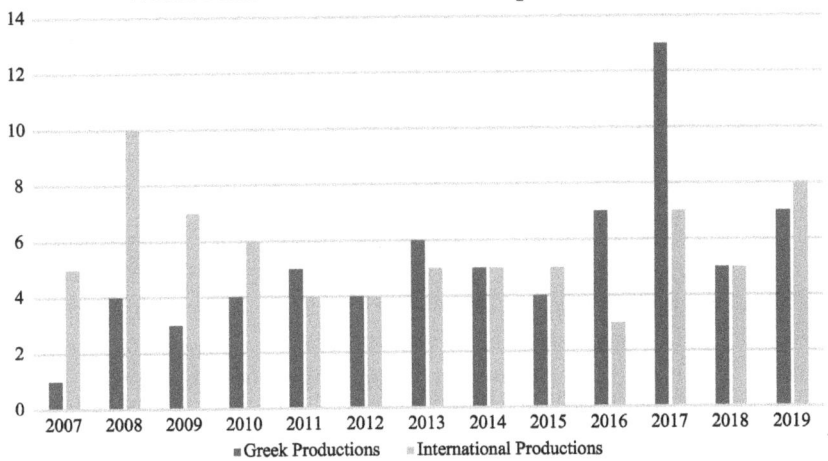

Figure 15. Greek and international dance productions presented at the Athens and Epidaurus Festival, 2007–2019. Chart created by the author.

narrative in the latter half of the crisis decade seems to have shifted out of necessity, gradually moving away from the historical honoring of classical and ancient Greek references toward a curatorial focus more closely related to the present. Beyond this narrative reorientation, the new focus was likewise reflected in the genres and choreographic approaches showcased in the 2010s. The list of performances increasingly included newly founded contemporary ensembles and more experimental choreographic methods, akin to those aligned with the cinematic Weird Wave. This shift in focus further attests to the increasing number of Greek choreographers who pursued degrees abroad and then either returned to Greece permanently or intermittently presented work in Greek festivals.

In the crisis decade, the Greek Festival also expanded to include youth education programs[8] and activities to directly involve audiences, such as talkbacks or seminars. This further mirrors the turn toward building collectives and enhancing the sense of community, one of the primary shifts noted to counter the austerity measures. Notably, since 2017, the festival has included a site-specific component presenting performances in various neighborhoods such as Gazi and Kerameikos, in public spaces, and archaeological sites. The site-specific turn of the Athens and Epidaurus Festival justifies the surge of local choreographers represented in the above chart. Six out of the thirteen Greek productions presented in 2017 were part of an initiative called Anoigma sti Poli (Άνοιγμα στη Πόλη; or Opening to the City), which, according to the official festival website, aimed to "broaden its audience base, and its range, and to encourage more active participation of spectators" (Athens and Epidaurus Festival 2018). This initiative further attests to the rising trend of community engagement and audience involvement in the latter half of the crisis decade.

Kalamata Dance Festival

While dance is only one of the arts represented in the Athens and Epidaurus Festival, it holds a much more prominent role at the Kalamata Dance Festival (KDF), which has been running since 1995 and is arguably the most long-standing and influential dance festival in Greece. KDF focuses on contemporary concert dance and organizes performances, workshops, and discussion forums with local and international artists. According to the festival's mission statement, "from the very start, the Festival was programmed with two considerations in mind: the wide range of trends in contemporary dance and the ever-larger audiences this art form attracts" (Kalamata Dance Festival 2019a). Spanning two weeks in July every year, the festival invites prestigious international companies (primarily from Europe) and Greek ensembles who have usually presented work during the regular season in Athens, as well as a few newly established ensembles embarking on experimental explorations. The schedule for a participant at KDF is filled with classes in the morning and performances in the evening. The concerts take place either in outdoor public spaces in Kalamata or in theaters. When I attended the festival for the first time in 2007 as a recent dance graduate, the performances were hosted in an indoor theater space downtown and the outdoor castle amphitheater.[9] Yet since 2013, most indoor theater performances have been held at the Megaro Chorou (Μέγαρο Χορού) (Figure 16), a structure built with the intent of housing the Demotic School of Dance (Dimotiki Scholi Chorou; Δημοτική Σχολή Χορού) and a theater specifically for dance performances. It is important to note that at the time of the Megaro Chorou's establishment, Athens did not have any spaces dedicated explicitly to dance, which attests to the position of Kalamata and KDF as a central forum for contemporary dance creation. It was not until 2016, when the Stavros Niarchos Foundation Cultural Center was established, that Athens gained a dedicated dance space; the center now houses the Greek National Opera Ballet.

Kalamata is the second most populous city on the Peloponnese peninsula, with an average population of about 54,000. Given the city's large size, the

Figure 16. The Megaro Chorou in Kalamata. Photograph taken by the author in 2018.

festival's scope varies significantly from the Athens and Epidaurus Festival, especially regarding the benefits for the local community. Since Kalamata is an established tourist destination, the festival has not translated into much higher tourism revenue or infrastructural improvements but has significantly enhanced the city's image and elevated it to a high-profile visitor attraction.[10] KDF has become a branding tool enriching the city's cultural capital. The fact that the festival usually takes place in mid- to late July enhances its international appeal as it is at the peak of the tourist season.

In its nearly three decades running, KDF has become one of the most influential festivals of the Mediterranean South and has built bridges between Greece and the international dance community. As one of the attendees (Ioanna Kerasopoulou, Skype interview October 10, 2018) noted in the previous chapter, KDF is often a forum for young Greek dancers to form connections with international artists, which may blossom into future collaborations or employment opportunities. While the agenda of the Athens and Epidaurus Festival has evidently been aligned with national values and historical narratives of national identity, KDF is very clearly focused on the current moment and the ways that the movement practices of the present will evolve into potentially new approaches in the future. It is also a hub for Greek audiences to attend the performances of prestigious international dance ensembles that are not hosted in other venues in the country.

A look at the history of KDF's workshop component reflects a shift in interest toward dance research approaches. All workshops held since 1996—no data was available for any workshop in 1995—focused almost exclusively on contemporary dance approaches and improvisation (Kalamata Dance Festival 2019b). They were hosted primarily by international artists specializing in techniques that were either not widely accessible in Greece (such as Frey Faust, who taught aspects of Alexander technique in 2007) or coming from renowned companies (such as Jeremy Nelson in 1999, 2001, and 2005; David Zambrano in 2006; and Laida Aldaz Arrieta in 2015 from P.A.R.T.S.[11] to name a few). Notably, until 2008, there was only one workshop for the festival's duration, except for 1998, when a classical ballet workshop was held in parallel to a contemporary dance workshop. Since 2008, the scope of the workshops has broadened, and there has consistently been a contemporary dance workshop and one or more workshops with different foci.[12] These included choreography workshops for the teaching of repertory or choreographic composition, dance research workshops, and a dramaturgy workshop with Hildegard de Vuyst in 2014; and in 2018, for the first time, a dance workshop for children was introduced along with one for people with physical disabilities. Despite the financial hardships during the crisis decade, there was increased activity in the realm of theoretical inquiry at the time, reflected in the broadening of the activities of KDF. At the same time, the crisis severely impacted the resources available for the festival and, in effect, shortened it: in the early years of the millennium, the festival had lasted ten to eleven days, but it was only eight days between 2010–2015.

A review of the companies hosted at KDF since its inception evidences a definite shift in orientation in the festival's second decade. In the first few years, the festival comprised modern dance, folk dance, and ballet ensembles, while in the last decade, there has been a clear prioritization of contemporary concert dance. A look at the festival archives (Kalamata Dance Festival 2022) and the performances hosted over the years helps map the prominent artistic influences on the Greek dance scene. In the early years of the festival, the international companies invited comprised various dancers and ensembles from the US, including proponents of the postmodern movement like David Dorfman (1996), Trisha Brown Dance Company (1997, 2000, 2004), Twyla Tharp (1998), and Merce Cunningham Dance Company (2002) as well as others such as Stephen Petronio Company (2002). In the festival's second decade, however, there was a gradual phasing out of American companies in

Figure 17. Public performance in a central square of Kalamata during the 24th Kalamata Dance Festival in 2018. The work is *99 corners of a possible self* by Athanasia Kanellopoulou. Photograph taken by the author.

favor of European ensembles and choreographers or proponents of the Israeli contemporary dance legacy, such as Batsheva Dance Company (2001, 2007) and Hofesh Shechter Company (2008). Some of the high-brow European artists that were invited included Akram Khan Company (2001), Xavier Le Roy (2003, 2009), Jérôme Bel (2001, 2004), Wim Vandekeybus/Ultima Vez (2001, 2007, 2013), and Les ballets C de la B (2005, 2007, 2010, 2014).

A look at the comprehensive listing of the performances and workshops hosted in KDF's second decade shows an increased interest in site-specific and sited work as well as performances held in public spaces, such as the central square, as depicted in Figure 17. These site performances "interrupt" people's daily routines and are accessible to broad audiences as they can be viewed from the comfort of one's home balcony or a coffee shop, or as a break from shopping.

Returning thus to the notion of utilizing a festival as a way to contribute to the construction of a national narrative, evidences that, while the Athens and Epidaurus Festival historically worked to incorporate and strengthen the construction of Greek national identity, KDF focused primarily on cultivating a sense of artistic identity that was in dialogue with international trends. It also assisted in making the Greek contemporary dance scene visible internationally. Both festivals continue to educate audiences and cultivate an understanding of international "high art" trends, delineating what constitutes valued cultural capital. Even though KDF is a regional festival, its history and scope of influence distinguish it from the festivals that form the core of this chapter.

As most artistic activity and dance creation is concentrated in Athens, the breadth and success of KDF inevitably raises the question of whether the festival has decentered artistic activity away from the capital. This question permeates my exploration of the dance festivals included in this chapter. In terms of making Kalamata the locus for the Greek premiere of many international performances, KDF does achieve a certain level of decentering. Audiences from around Greece travel to Kalamata annually to view the productions from trend-setting ensembles and renowned international performances. Since the establishment of the Megaro Chorou, dance has held a more prominent role in Kalamata throughout the year, even though it still reaches its peak during the summer. Most of the Greek performances presented at KDF are restagings of works that premiered in Athens during the regular season (September to May). KDF thus makes performances available to audiences not based in Athens, but the creative process remains centralized in the capital of Greece. Nevertheless, one of the festival's main contributions to the Greek dance scene has been the fact that it takes place in a regional community, thus offering participants the opportunity for more direct contact with the invited artists. This is true for many of the festivals that developed during the crisis decade, which revolved around building a sense of community for participants and performers.

One last aspect to explore before delving into the rest of the case studies for this chapter is the funding for these two established festivals. The Ministry of Culture is the primary sponsor for both the Athens and Epidaurus Festival and KDF. Secondary sponsors vary from private institutions (only for KDF), banks, airlines, and various other organizations, such as hotels (which sponsor accommodation needs), public and private TV channels that assist with communication, dance blogs and culture blogs, and websites.

Although there is no definitive evidence to prove a direct correlation, the

Table 1. Select Dance Festivals Active During the Crisis Decade

Name of festival	Place	Year est.	Time of year	Status (as of 2023)
Akropoditi DanceFest	Syros	2013	Summer	ongoing
Arc for Dance Festival	Athens (Gazi)	2008	Spring or fall	ongoing
Athens Video Dance Project[1]	Athens (Gazi)	2010	Winter	ongoing
Dance Days Chania	Crete	2011	Summer	ongoing
Dance Laboratory Rhodes	Rhodes	2015	Summer	ongoing
Dancing Days	Naxos	2010	Summer	last occurred in 2012
one small step	Corfu	2010	Summer	last occurred in 2018
R.I.C.E.[2]	Hydra	2013	Summer	last occurred in 2017
Zante Dance Festival	Zante	2016	Summer	ongoing

1. Athens Video Dance Project (AVDP) was first organized in 2010. It focuses on showcasing video dance productions, dance documentaries, as well as hybrid, interactive technological projects, or installations. It comprises two programs: AVDP.edu, which centers on "educational workshops and lectures organized for students and professional artists in Greece and abroad" (AVDP 2019), and *AVDP on TouR*, which tours special editions of video dance works in local and international festivals. Since AVDP is organized in Athens, it is excluded from the analytical scope of this chapter.

2. R.I.C.E. is an acronym that captures a multiplicity of potential meanings. According to the website (Rice on Hydra: The Choreography of Humans 2013), the definition is as follows:

    1. (abbr.) an acronym of endless meanings
        Raw, Relevant, Real, Radical
        Instinct, Institute, Inquiry
        Choreography, Civic, Commonwealth, Cybernetic
        Engagement, Enquiry, Epistemology, Elbow
    2. (n.) the most common nourishment on earth

funding structures supporting the festivals during the crisis may have contributed to the emergence of multiple smaller festivals in several regional areas, such as on islands. As noted in chapter 2, various choreographers turned to European Strategic Investment Funds to fund their productions in the intermittent period (starting with the 2010–2011 season until the 2015–2016 season) when ministerial subsidies ceased. These grants were also utilized to support the funding of smaller festivals, most of which emerged within the same time frame.

Some of the festivals founded in the early 2010s continue to occur annually, while others have ceased. Table 1 and Figure 18 provide a selective overview of the initiatives active or established during the crisis decade. The following sections are a selective examination of three of these festivals. I trace their modes of curation, the ways they were embedded in cultural tourism initiatives, and, last, the ways they framed contemporary concert dance in regional Greece during the crisis decade.

Figure 18. Map of regional dance festivals in Greece. *Country boundaries shapefile data is from Natural Earth Dataset. Projection is a Miller Cylindrical World Projection.* Map designed by Lauren Gerlowski.

Dance Days Chania

What has come to be known as the Dance Days Chania (DDC) international festival did not start as a festival but as a necessary response to the crisis, according to the artistic director Sofia Falierou:

> [DDC] did not start as a festival. The idea and the necessity came about in 2011 when the crisis broke out in Greece, which had been brewing for a while. A sense of panic overcame the country on multiple levels. You are aware of the repercussions [the crisis had] on a social, cultural, political, and financial level. A breadth of obstacles was presented in front of us and mangled us. Fear comes and locks our senses. . . . On the one hand, this surprised us, but on the other, we had to come up with something to do about this situation. So in this framework of looking for alternatives and in one of the many discussions we had with the Union of Greek Choreographers during that period—since we[13] had been working on figuring out what kind of prospects there might be in a time when there didn't seem to be any

hope, *we started thinking how each of us would be able to make small interventions in our local communities through our art.* Theaters were closing, the subsidies [from the Ministry of Culture] had already stopped, spaces for rehearsals were very hard to rent. It was a crucial moment on multiple levels. *I think that because of fear, we forgot that art finds its role, especially in times of crisis.* I believe that big social and political changes set off the most meaningful modes of research and creativity in art. Such fermentations brought about the need for decentralization, for new cores that would operate throughout the country. (Sofia Falierou, Skype interview, October 3, 2018; emphasis added)

In this quote, Falierou identifies multiple factors that contributed to the rise of DDC. The primary ones were, first, the use of art as a site for intervention and activation of the local community and, second, the need to decenter artistic production to make it accessible to people in Chania, without requiring travel to Athens.

DDC was more of a gathering than a festival in its first iteration. There was a group of choreographers that had agreed to travel to Chania to present seminars at the Association for Expressive Dance SYN-KINISI (Syllogos Ekfrastikou Chorou SYN-KINISI; Σύλλογος Εκφραστικού Χορού ΣΥΝ-ΚΙΝΗΣΗ), the company founded by Falierou in 2002. Falierou got in touch with the Cabinet of Culture of the Chania Municipality and asked for the artists' transportation to be subsidized. The vice mayor approved a budget of 700 EUR and offered them an indoor theater space. They were thus able to host an event called Four Days of Contemporary Dance in 2011 at the Venizelos Odeon in Chania. Falierou notes that, at that point, she had not even considered the prospect of curating a larger festival. The first gathering consisted of performances from the four ensembles invited and the workshops at SYN-KINISI.

The following year, in 2012, they had fifteen participating choreographers. The event lasted eight days and was renamed Days of Contemporary Dance. In the third year (2013), the event grew further through word of mouth and attracted international artists who had heard about the gatherings through their peers. Since interest was spreading and there were not enough financial means to support the initiative, starting in 2013, the people involved with SYN-KINISI and others interested in supporting the gathering's growth, opened their homes to international artists to defray accommodation costs and make the event possible. In this third iteration, the gathering was first framed as a festival and became Dance Days Chania.

The growth of DDC has since been exponential. As Falierou noted, in 2018, they received 510 applications from around the world, and the festival was extended to two whole weeks. Out of these hundreds of applications,[14] the selection committee, comprising the festival organizers, invites only around twenty artists to present work. The committee also extends invitations for approximately twenty slots for workshops (sometimes artists offer both a workshop and a performance, although the two do not always line up) or other activities (such as a photography exhibition on the body, for instance). The workshops usually take place in the morning, and the performances are presented in the evening. Each workshop lasts three to four days, and workshops take place at various times throughout the day so that participants can stagger them and attend multiple ones. The workshops' shorter duration allows participants to create their own schedule and to choose a limited time frame for participation (such as a few days rather than being there for the entire two weeks).

The volunteer model that is the principal means for providing festival accommodation to artists extends to multiple other activities. Most of the labor associated with running the festival is based on volunteerism. The city of Chania is also involved: shops, hotels, restaurants, and entrepreneurs offer their services to the festival in the form of free breakfasts, discount coupons for food, or lodging discounts. Since the festival takes place during the peak tourist season in mid- to late July, these offers are particularly valuable because it can be difficult to secure accommodation. In reference to the culture of volunteerism surrounding the festival's organization and administration, Falierou remarked:

> We are gradually learning to fend for ourselves through this festival. It is a precious lesson. What I mean by this is our need, our desire, our philosophy to work so hard and with such consistency. We are all volunteers, and that is a very clear condition. I do not consider it heroic, nor do I believe in volunteering without limits. For me, volunteerism should not be the state's crutch as far as its responsibility and obligation toward art, culture, education, and artists is concerned. However, for the time when the festival started, if it were not [for volunteerism], the festival would not have been possible. (Sofia Falierou, Skype interview, October 3, 2018)

The base of volunteers for DDC grew along with the festival, and the services they offered varied. For instance, artists and scholars residing abroad assist with translations of festival materials. Since 2018, when DDC added a conference to the festival, the base of volunteers expanded to include academics who were consulted on the creation of the call for papers and formed a selection committee to evaluate the submitted proposals. Even though I could not attend the festival in 2019, I was invited to the growing base of volunteers and offered assistance in drafting the call for conference papers.

After speaking to some other volunteers who worked on different aspects of the festival organization, I came to understand that each individual is personally invested in the festival's vision and the value it holds for the local community. They view their involvement with the festival as a reciprocal relationship, and their reward is the satisfaction and fulfillment they get from supporting this initiative. Many of the volunteers have roots in the local community and are either from Chania or have come to love Chania as a repeated vacation destination. They are frequently migrants themselves and thus engage in volunteerism for DDC to give back to their country and community. Freda Antypa, who studied dance in New York and returned to Greece in 2008, has been a volunteer at DDC since 2014. Reflecting on her experience, she observed:

> The experience is excellent, with a positive impact on many levels. Every year the mode of work and my participation become even more substantial . . . , and this offers satisfaction to everyone involved. On a human level, the teamwork, the strong friendships, and the collaborations foster powerful feelings. . . . Looking at the effort, the drive, the diversity, the positivity, and the constant willingness to communicate through dance in Dance Days 3, I immediately wanted to join and offer [my service] to this endeavor. (Freda Antypa, email interview, October 5, 2018)

This quote suggests that volunteers build a sense of solidarity and community between them, which fuels the festival. It also hints at the formation of a liminal commons, a community built across physical space, which manifests for a short period each year, then dissolves.

The volunteer aspect of the festival extends beyond the organizational components into the overall culture surrounding the endeavor. Many international artists view DDC as an activist project, and even though it has grown significantly (compared with the tight-knit community it was in its first few years), some artists *still* approach it as a grassroots activist initiative. Falierou reflected on this tendency:

In the past few years, most artists were hosted at our [the volunteers' and organizers'] houses. Now that the number of participants has increased to over a hundred, this is no longer feasible. A significant number of participants still wish to be hosted. They treat DDC as an activist project. They choose to send proposals for productions presented at some of the most prestigious venues in the world. By respecting our conditions, which have only slightly changed throughout the years, they create work and perform at the stages of the rural theaters without compromising the quality of their works. Despite [being well-established in the field], they travel under these circumstances [offered by the limited resources of the festival], reside in these spaces, and are paid by the ticket sales. . . . Artistic directors of other festivals and choreographers visit [DDC], even when their works have not been chosen, thus supporting the organization. This is significant. Year by year, the community of DDC becomes broader. (Sofia Falierou, Skype interview, October 3, 2018)

The conditions of austerity during the Greek crisis fueled an aspiration for decentralizing the artistic community, which was then perforce structured on a culture of volunteerism, as that seemed to be the only viable option to navigate the stark landscape and the budget cuts. Whether this was deliberately an activist endeavor or one born out of necessity is difficult to determine. Nevertheless, it is worth noticing the ways that DDC's volunteering structure was perceived internationally and how it was romanticized in line with branding narratives of the Greek crisis and a fetishizing of artistic struggle and resilience.

For DDC, a festival in a popular tourist location, the politics surrounding its branding amid the crisis are very complex. It is worth mentioning that Crete is home to some of the most beautiful beaches in Greece, an attraction that the DDC organizers are aware of and utilize in promotional materials and flyers when advertising the festival. It is not an accident that the thumbnails chosen for the promotional videos feature images of waves crashing at a beach or an aerial view of people and beach paraphernalia forming the festival logo, as seen in Figure 19.

The festival thus does not only promise professional development and networking through its rigorous workshops and performances; it also weaves a narrative of festival participants becoming part of a community of artists while enjoying aspects of the local culture in an idyllic location. In the video, the location is emphasized with a plethora of outdoor shots of dance activi-

Figure 19. Promotional videos for the 2019 Dance Days Chania festival. Screenshots from separate videos on the festival's Vimeo page: Image on the left is from (Dance Days Chania 2019b, 0:10) and image on the right is from (Dance Days Chania 2019a, 0:48).

ties taking place throughout the old city amid stone-walled buildings, or on the beach. Thus it offers the promise of cultural tourism.

DDC's impact on the community of Chania is not only experienced by the participants, but it extends to the unsuspecting public. There is an important distinction to be made here: audiences who attend DDC performances, even when they have never encountered contemporary dance before, are willing participants; they have made the conscious choice to attend the event and are open to the encounter. The broader community, on the other hand, which I previously referred to as the "unsuspecting public," comprises people who are forced into unexpected encounters with contemporary dance and dancers.

Both types of encounters are part of the vision of DDC. Beyond the decentralization of contemporary dance to foster dialogue with new audiences, DDC takes a bold step to bring dance to the people. As Falierou explains:

> For a large percentage of people, the theater is a "forbidden" space. Because of this, we make it a point to go to their neighborhoods. [To go] where grandmothers are sitting and knitting, where the children are playing in the open fields, where art would not reach under other circumstances. . . . Initially, there were significant difficulties in this approach both for the performers and for the community. It looked like an alien spaceship had landed in their neighborhood. [Performers were met with] suspicion and reservation; [these are] elements that make up all small communities." (Sofia Falierou, Skype interview, October 3, 2018)

Calling the theater a "forbidden" space is a strong word choice that reiterates the unspoken hierarchy that classifies concert dance as "imported" and thus "foreign" or illegible. What Falierou infers is that often in regional communities, such as Crete, where the traditional culture (including both music and dance) holds a prominent role in social occasions, attending a dance performance in a theater space, where there is a clear separation between audience and performers, can have an alienating effect on locals. Especially on the island of Crete, where there is a strong sense of local pride and tradition permeating everyday life through folk songs and dance, the openness to a "foreign" genre becomes an even bigger challenge.

Falierou provided anecdotal examples of how DDC countered this challenge and made concert dance approachable and legible for local audiences. Performers went to remote villages around Chania to perform amid the locals, who were going about their day unaware. There, performers were met with skepticism, and locals threatened to call the police on them. Yet, gradually, the locals grew accustomed to the artists and even invited them to their homes for a warm meal. Falierou asserts that this is the type of art and intervention she and her team are interested in making through DDC and that such encounters create the most fruitful dialogues. Indeed, receiving feedback from audiences with no prior exposure to the genre is undoubtedly valuable as it informs the creative process in different ways. The fostering of such encounters is achieved not only in the few days when DDC takes place, but it also extends to the rest of the year through other initiatives such as dance workshops for children of refugees or dance programs for the elderly. While encounters between lay audiences and esteemed artists are definitely creating opportunities for contemplating the value of contemporary dance, there is an underlying colonizing dynamic in the urgency to acquaint untrained audiences with the concert dance genre. It prompts the question "Why is it so significant to expose regional audiences to contemporary concert dance and to have them engage with it?"

The emphasis on contemporary concert dance, which is indisputably classified as a subgenre of Western high art, assists in overturning negative narratives surrounding Greece during the crisis and forming more positive associations tied to artistic resilience in the crisis narratives that circulate internationally. The focus on cultural tourism is also highlighted in the following case study, where it is more overtly tied to the overarching agenda of the festival.

one small step

Ena Mikro Vima (Ένα Μικρό Βήμα; one small step; abbreviated as OSS) was a regional festival on the Ionian island of Corfu, founded in 2010. It occurred last in 2018. It was co-organized by artistic directors Christina Mertzani and

Evangelos Poulinas, both graduates of the National School of Dance in the first decade of the 2000s who have since traveled extensively to further their art and their studies. When I interviewed them in 2019, they were both based in different towns in Germany. Having had extensive exposure to international festivals and performances, they were incentivized to offer something similar to Greek audiences. They decided to base the festival in Corfu because Mertzani had grown up there, and it was a place that Poulinas had visited and grown fond of.

The mission statement for OSS declares: "Dance should be accessible to all. This is why [the festival] organizes free of charge performances that everyone is welcome to attend and workshops for professional dancers as well as for non-professionals" (one small step 2018). Marketed as an "international urban dance festival," OSS uniquely held all performances at public sites. Here, *urban* does not refer to vernacular dance styles as it often does in dance studies. Instead, it is used to convey the sited character of the contemporary dance works presented at OSS. The term refers to performances held outdoors in the capital of Corfu, so that dance is woven into the regional cityscape. The works performed were finished productions that had been presented on international stages and not works created to be performed at those sites.

Beyond performances, the festival also included workshops, photography exhibits, video dance screenings (in collaboration with Athens Video Dance Project), tours of local landmarks, and excursions in nature or by the sea that were organized for all participants and workshop facilitators. One of the stated goals of OSS was cultural tourism. The relevant blurb on the website states:

> *one small step* is proud to be able to attract to Corfu dancers and audiences from all over the world. By offering contemporary art (performances and workshops) of high quality, the festival enhances the cultural production of the island, making it an attraction for [an] international audience. (one small step 2018)

The communal activities offered to the participants provide a glimpse into how the cultural tourism agenda was approached. Even in promotional materials for the festival, such as Vimeo videos presenting excerpts of the performances and workshops, there is often a section dedicated to the social aspect of the festival. Participants are captured strolling at a beach, jumping off a cliff into the sea, or enjoying traditional Greek dishes at a tavern, scenes that are depicted in screenshots from the 2017 promotional video (Figure 20).

Many pieces hosted at OSS had already been performed internationally

Figure 20. Promotional video for the 2017 one small step festival. Community-building and recreational activities are emphasized. Video screenshots from one small step (2017, 01:14; 01:13; 01:11; 01:16).

before they were presented in Corfu. Each year, one piece was explicitly created for OSS. In our interview, Poulinas described the process:

> We would bring over a choreographer, and every year, a different number of dancers worked on a piece of fifteen to twenty minutes that would premiere in Corfu. This way, the locals had a chance to watch something new that was presented in their town for the first time, created by esteemed artists. (Christina Mertzani and Evangelos Poulinas, Skype interview, May 28, 2019)

The dancers participating in the repertory work produced on site were international and were selected through a remote audition process. Interested performers submitted a CV and an audition video. This ensured that the quality of the work would remain high and offered a chance for professional dancers to collaborate with internationally renowned choreographers.

The repertory aspect of the festival had very little involvement with the local community (not just of Corfu, but of Greece more broadly). Mertzani estimated that out of the average sixteen participants in the repertory piece, only two or three were from Greece each year. This indicates that professional development opportunities for locals attending the festival were limited. Other festival activities, such as the seminars and workshops, were more open to the local community. Some seminars targeted professional dancers and were attended by many dancers from mainland Greece. The high level of skill required at those workshops made them inaccessible to the people of Corfu since the island does not have any vocational dance schools. OSS also offered seminars for amateur performers or beginners, which extended the festival's reach to the local community members. All workshops at OSS revolved around aspects of contemporary dance techniques and approaches. On this point, Mertzani and Poulinas remarked:

> MERTZANI: There was this need for the people of Corfu and the [local] schools. They were attending classes and seminars, but not the performance projects. Attendance at the [seminars] that culminated in a performance was limited. There were [workshops] for intermediate level, and we held some for beginners in the last few years. It was a beautiful movement because we would realize that people wanted to dance every time. It is a way to express themselves . . . . It was delightful, and many people of varying ages attended.
>
> POULINAS: The seminars for nonprofessionals were primarily [attended by] people from Corfu. Others, such as Greeks [from other regions], would come to Corfu for a vacation that week and say, "This is great! I can go on vacation and take classes!" There were also some people from abroad that would take the beginners' classes, but for the most part, it was locals. (Christina Mertzani and Evangelos Poulinas, Skype interview, May 28, 2019)

Corfu is relatively developed as far as arts education is concerned for an island of its size (population 102,071, according to the 2011 census).[15] There are multiple philharmonics local to each municipality and more than a dozen dance schools, some of which offer contemporary dance classes. Even under these exceptionally favorable circumstances, local audiences are not versed in contemporary dance; thus, educating them and making contemporary dance broadly accessible was among the festival's primary directives. As Mertzani highlighted in our interview, contemporary dance is often considered limited to the theater space and targets dancers as the primary audience. Even though there have been examples of established international choreographers who have broken this mold, she still believes that contemporary dance is not *as* accessible as theater performances are. This rings particularly true for Greek audiences, given the theater's role in Greece's cultural history.

During our interview, Poulinas expanded on the festival's aim to broaden the audience for contemporary dance and discussed how that factored in their choice to present performances outdoors:

> In conversations we've had with Christina [Mertzani], we were wondering how to present [contemporary dance], what to do, and how to bring contemporary dance closer to the people and to develop its audience. So we decided to have performances outdoors, in the city, on the street, in *plateies* [squares]. We saw the reception it had the first year; people of all ages wanted to watch. Ok, we know that contemporary dance may appear alien for lay audiences, but despite that, they embraced it, and the festival became a favorite throughout the years. Performances would occur in front of the Museum of Asian Art or the pillars of old castles. We were not using the space in a site-specific sense, but we were utilizing the existing architecture as a backdrop. (Christina Mertzani and Evangelos Poulinas, Skype interview, May 28, 2019)

To this, Mertzani added another layer, the fact that presenting performances in outdoor spaces, free of charge, makes them accessible to many more people. Year by year, as the festival grew through word of mouth, the audiences became larger, and frequently, tourists would plan their vacations around the festival so they could attend.

Even though Corfu is a relatively cosmopolitan island with comparatively more exposure to arts than other regional areas, OSS organizers noted the need for audiences and locals to get used to contemporary dance and progressively grow less "scared" of it. This observation, which echoes a similar remark by Falierou, leaves unanswered the question of why contemporary dance was chosen to engage the local public. Mertzani and Poulinas's response to this question draws on notions of an assumed universality of contemporary dance. Poulinas mentioned that, in his personal opinion, "dance is an art that does not have borders like language" (Christina Mertzani and Evangelos Poulinas, Skype interview, May 28, 2019). He suggested that it relies on a sense of immediacy, thus implying that it can be widely understood and is relatable.

Perhaps what Poulinas refers to as "immediacy" is also reflected in the choice to not host any OSS performances in a theater space. An argument could be made that contemporary dance as an art form offers itself more readily to a guerrilla or pop-up presentation. Alternatively, "immediacy" may also relate to ideas of spectacle in terms of what draws the audience's attention. OSS presented dance by companies and choreographers known for highly physical and virtuosic work, such as Rootlessroot,[16] so even though lay audiences may not have been able to discern the conceptual framework of performances they are witnessing, they may be attracted to what the highly trained professional dancers' bodies can achieve.

Organizationally, OSS was similar to DDC in a number of respects, as both relied on the community to a great extent. Contrary to DDC, however, choreographers presenting work at OSS were paid through participants' seminar payments since performances at OSS were free for audiences and there were no ticket sales. At the same time, the performers selected through the video audition process to participate in works created specifically for the festival were not paid. Their participation involved essentially a barter system: they invested their time and effort to gain experience working with acclaimed choreographers and expand their professional opportunities. The pool of applicants in the auditions was international and comprised primarily professional dancers, while a few participants were dance students in their final years of professional training. The conditions of this exchange are questionable as the choreographers were being compensated for creating their works, yet the performers who participated in workshops lasting four hours a day for the duration of the festival were awarded through experience. No matter how one labels this exchange, it remains unpaid labor at its core. While this type of transaction is certainly not novel, its occurrence amid the crisis prompts questions about the exploitation of artistic labor and the perpetuation of artists' self-precarization.[17] This format further provokes questions about how the artists themselves value their creative labor, as well as the motives behind the cycle of production and reproduction of works at one of the numerous festivals established during the crisis.

Akropoditi DanceFest

Akropoditi DanceFest (ADF) on the Cycladic island of Syros was founded in 2013. It is still ongoing at the moment of writing after a brief pause in 2020 due to the COVID-19 pandemic. The organizers are a team of five women, most of whom are based on the island year-round. Angeliki Sigourou, Ariadni Psychogiopoulou, and Ioanna Antonarou are the team of artistic directors, and their collaborators, Maria Mavri and Vivi Sklia, offer financial administration and marketing support, respectively. ADF did not receive any subsidiary financial support in its first year. It was fueled solely by the vision and hard work of the team leading the Center for Dance and Performing Arts Akropoditi. Even though it was founded during the crisis, there was no direct correlation between the two events, as two of the artistic directors (Ariadni Psychogiopoulou and Angeliki Sigourou) admitted during our interview:

> PSYCHOGIOPOULOU: For us, the crisis was never factored into our discussions, meaning that we started something on our own, not knowing whether we would make it or not, not having any support at the beginning. It was an insane risk. We didn't know what our income would be, our expenses, nothing. All of it [was fueled] by our enthusiasm and our need to make it happen.
>
> SIGOUROU: The first year, we didn't have any support whatsoever. (Ariadni Psychogiopoulou and Angeliki Sigourou, Skype interview, January 16, 2020)

In its first year (2013), the festival was run solely with the fees paid by the participants. The organizers and everyone else involved behind the scenes worked as volunteers. As Sigourou mentioned, there was a team of volunteers (beyond the core five organizers) who came together to make the festival possible. Initially, the organizers were responsible for every little detail, as there was no budget to hire anyone. After the festival became more established and began receiving subsidies—either from the municipal government (in the form of, for example, performance space in local museums or financial support) or, much later, from the Ministry of Culture (only after 2017 and, even so, requiring an annual application)—they were able to create some paid positions. As Psychogiopoulou described, the first few years were extremely demanding and exhausting:

> We did everything on our own, from the tech support to the provisions, to the organizing, the cleaning of the space, everything. As the years go by, more and more positions become available, and things have been getting better. [The festival] relied on the human factor when it started. Its budget was tiny. There were no positions for tech staff or lighting designers, which was not right. Of course, you need a lighting designer for a festival! (Ariadni Psychogiopoulou and Angeliki Sigourou, Skype interview, January 16, 2020)

The culture of volunteering was once more the driving force and the main support structure for a nascent artistic initiative. As the previous examples have also demonstrated, support from local and national governance only came after ADF proved its value, and even then, it was limited.

Unlike the other case studies discussed, ADF is not limited to contemporary dance but is open to various genres. The offerings change each year based on the lineup of the teachers and have included, for example, ballet, flamenco, physical theater, hip-hop, Indian dance, whirling dervish workshops, and acrobatics, among others. The festival usually spans two weeks and comprises several practice-based and dance theory workshops, performances, improvisation jams, and other activities held throughout the island. It is international in scope and offers classes for amateurs and professional dancers. Workshops usually take place during the week (lasting five days, Monday–Friday) or over the weekend (lasting two days, Saturday–Sunday). A typical day starts at around 9 a.m. with workshops and ends at night with a performance or other events, such as an open improvisation jam or a documentary screening.

Most workshops occur in the space hosting the Center for Dance and Performing Arts Akropoditi, housed in a reclaimed tannery. There are limited theater spaces available to host the performances, so the organizers either convert their studio spaces into performance spaces or hold concerts in the Cyclades Art Gallery, which is allotted to the festival by the local municipality. There is a ticket fee for performances, which contributes to the festival budget. Site-specific performances are something that the organizers are interested in exploring yet have rarely included because of a financial dilemma. ADF compensates the artists partially through ticket sales and it would be challenging to monitor and charge audiences for site-specific performances. To ensure compensation for the artists, even with a very tight budget, the artistic directors of ADF were, until 2019, very conservatively choosing only one to two performances to be held in a public setting.

In terms of the festival's appeal and target audience, even though it is international in scope, ADF's mission is entangled with the growth of the local community. As the capital of the Cycladic Islands complex, Syros is a cosmopolitan island with a rich theatrical tradition. Even so, the local perception of what constitutes art is rather traditional, as Sigourou observes:

> The truth is that [Syros] has a rather classical perception of what constitutes art, even as far as theater is concerned. Even nowadays, the theater that we have [Apollon Theater] is very reluctant to allocate space for alternative or experimental productions, especially in periods of tourism, such as in the summer. . . . The people of Syros are very attached to theater because of their tradition and are very reluctant to accept anything new or to be educated in something new. There are

many theatrical ensembles comprising professionals and amateurs in Syros, many more than for dance—there is no comparison. Yet there is a sense of hesitation. I think that this has slowly started to change. I can't say to what extent [the change is related] to the festival, but I think it has contributed. Both the festival and the performances of our dance ensemble [have contributed]. (Ariadni Psychogiopoulou and Angeliki Sigourou, Skype interview, January 16, 2020)

To this, Psychogiopoulou added how significant it is that the Center for Dance and Performing Arts Akropoditi is active throughout the entire year: "As the years pass, more and more people trust us with their children, get to know us, or get to know contemporary dance through their child taking classes, and afterward they support the festival too" (Ariadni Psychogiopoulou and Angeliki Sigourou, Skype interview, January 16, 2020).

The above comments capture the inherent reluctance of smaller communities to attend concert dance performances, a point noted also about other festivals in regional communities. The ADF directors' approach methodically has built connections with the local community through a continuous presence to negotiate this reluctance. They view contemporary dance as a broad framework through which to introduce audiences and participants to embodied modes of engagement and do not treat contemporary concert dance as the canon of artistic expression. Through this approach, they have begun to dismantle high art hierarchies that alienate audiences or render contemporary concert dance inaccessible. The prominence of contemporary concert dance in some other festivals during the crisis decade seems to mirror a colonial dynamic (insisting that lay audiences acknowledge the value of contemporary dance as a pinnacle of Western embodied expression). Contrary to these approaches, ADF has been striving to decolonize the hierarchies currently in place for valuing dance. Sigourou and Psychogiopoulou speak to the importance of valuing all types of expression and offering an opportunity to both audiences and participants to choose what appeals to them the most:

> SIGOUROU: Contemporary [dance] is something that evolves. It does not have the rigidity of classical ballet. Even neo-classical dance, which we could argue is more flexible, is still somewhat limited. Contemporary is never contained. It is not targeted at specific people, body types, or ages. It is much more connected to the earth, to personal expression, to each person's uniqueness. It is much more

anthropocentric; it is not a form. It continually evolves into something else. Contemporary nowadays encompasses so many things. It starts from stillness, and even nothingness is part of it. As such, its breadth is vast.

PSYCHOGIOPOULOU: I agree with Angeliki [Sigourou], and one thing I would like to add is that this is why we did not want to limit the festival to contemporary dance. Each person should be able to find their own personal expression, through their own unique means; however, they choose to through their bodies. (Ariadni Psychogiopoulou and Angeliki Sigourou, Skype interview, January 16, 2020)

Contrary to other festival models that share a similar mission of making contemporary dance more accessible, ADF takes a different approach that is focused on the education of audiences year-round and on offering diverse opportunities for nonprofessional dancers to join various dance workshops to explore the mode of embodied expression that suits them the most.

Postscript: A Note on Hierarchical (Im)Balances

All three regional festivals examined in more detail in this chapter started out small. They were all fueled by the vision of a team of artists who wanted to create more opportunities for their peers to showcase work and introduce concert dance approaches to their respective communities. In some instances, the initial lack of financial support pushed the organizers to seek alternative spaces to hold performances, whether outdoors or in reclaimed spaces. What started out of necessity slowly turned into a trend, with performances in nontraditional spaces becoming the norm and something that participants expected. Gradually, outdoor performances became established as a trademark of regional dance festivals across Greece, which have continued to emerge even beyond the crisis decade.

The regional festivals held on the Greek periphery all seem to share a lack of initial support from national or municipal governing bodies until they proved their international appeal and tourist value for the local community. Then, they fostered collaborations with local stakeholders and grew the base of festival participants. Even though most regional festivals work closely with the tourist sector (hotels, restaurants, etc.), they rarely seem to embrace local cultural embodied practices, instead celebrating the "imported" genre of contemporary concert dance. "Imported" here is not only referring to the international artists presenting work at these festivals but is also a commentary on the fact that artistic activity in contemporary is rarely endemic to the sites hosting these festivals, thus further attesting to a center/periphery distinction within the country (since most Greek works presented come from Athens).

The prominence of contemporary dance in regional festivals reveals multiple hierarchical struggles. For Greek choreographers and dancers, these festivals fill a gap in the artistic scenes of regional communities and elevate the value of their cultural capital. It is essential to clarify here, though, that this gap is identified by proponents of the genre residing in these areas and is not necessarily a broadly identified need for local audiences, who most often are not versed in contemporary concert dance. To put this in context, alongside other performance practices such as theater, some of the most influential theater productions presented in Athens go on a summer tour after the season in the city is over, so audiences in other regions have a chance to see the plays. There is not a similar practice for dance, as performances (especially those receiving sponsorship from the Ministry of Culture) are presented only a few times during the season; after this, they may, in some instances, be hosted in festivals either abroad or in regional Greece. Until the early 2010s, when most regional dance festivals came about, choreographers did not have organized opportunities to present their work in other areas of the country. The emergence of the regional summer festivals thus has fulfilled this need; and in instances where the festivals also offer classes for dance enthusiasts, they have made room for a different level of audience engagement with contemporary dance.

Most regional festivals focus on broadening audiences for contemporary concert dance and making the genre more accessible. Especially since audiences are often unaware of the genre, offering performances for free in public spaces increases its accessibility to broader audiences since there is no monetary obstacle. Marketing these festivals as enriching the cultural capital of these areas is a strategic choice to capitalize on existing tourism flows. However, the discourse of audience access and the ways that discourse is entangled with many of the festivals' declared missions to make dance more accessible and to educate unsuspecting audiences about contemporary concert dance may, at times, have colonial undertones. Audiences are perceived as passive entities upon whom artists can have a transformative effect.

In light of the reconfiguration of Greek identity during the crisis, the festivals' agenda to educate audiences could be perceived as an attempt to approximate Europeanization. There is a hierarchical imbalance between the peripheral regions and urban centers in Greece, which closely mirrors the dichotomy between popular art (in the sense of being more accessible and therefore perceived as lacking refinement) and high art. Thus the mission to educate regional audiences on genres that are indisputably categorized as the part of the canon of Western concert dance may be connected with an aspiration to elevate the perceived cultural capital of those areas as equivalent to high art. Outreach to peripheral communities and an extended invitation to them to participate in various formats of dance activity is one of the main trends I observed during the crisis; this is also the focal point of the next chapter. This curatorial shift in the context of austerity is both an act of equity as well as a marketing strategy since this type of outreach makes applications for funding more appealing.

Last, as far as the role of these newly established festivals in supporting the national narrative is concerned, there is undoubtedly a hierarchical shift that negates the previously established connection between high art and urban environments, on one hand, and regional areas and traditional art and folklore, on the other. With these shifts, new connotations emerged, and reframed regional peripheries as sites of cultural capital production, creativity, and contemporary experimentation.

Notes

1. I used the term *sited work* to convey performances created with the intention of being presented on a proscenium stage yet had to adapt their presentation to a different setting when they were invited to one of Greece's regional festivals. I use this term to indicate a conscious distinction from site-specific work, which is created in relation to a specific location, or community and is oftentimes based on extensive on-site research, according to scholarship by Kwon (2004) and Barbour, Hunter, and Kloetzl (2019).

2. *Festivalization* is the English adaptation of the German word *Festivalisierung*, coined in 1993 by German urban scholars Walter Siebel and Hartmut Häusserman. The term captures how festivals impact the area where they take place and how they interact with the political, economic, and social sphere of the place. More often than not, festivals create a subcommunity within the community they are held, and this can manifest at various scales.

3. As noted on the festival's "About" page (Athens and Epidaurus Festival 2018; my translation).

4. See Tsintziloni (2022) for more.

5. Giorgos Loukos was the artistic director of the Athens and Epidaurus Festival from 2005 (curating his first festival in 2006) until 2016.

6. See also Prickett and Tsintziloni (2016) and Tsintziloni (2022).

7. The repertory list from the first decade of the Athens and Epidaurus Festival is based on a conference presentation at DDC 8 (Tsintziloni 2018; 2022).

8. An example of a youth program is the Epidaurus Lyceum, an international

summer school on ancient drama inaugurated in 2017. It operates annually under the auspices of the Athens and Epidaurus Festival and invites the participation of recent graduates (both undergraduate and graduate) from drama, theater, dance, and performance departments in Greece and abroad.

9. The mayor of Kalamata announced that 2017 would be the last year that the Kalamata Castle Theater would be used for performances of any kind. The reasons given were safety concerns, as there was not enough room to accommodate the increased audience interest (MessiniaLive 2017).

10. See also Georgoula and Terkenli (2018).

11. P.A.R.T.S. stands for Performing Arts Research and Training Studios. It is a school for contemporary dance established in 1995 in Brussels by Anne Teresa De Keersmaeker. It offers a three-year Bachelor's in dance training that focuses on technique, and a two-year Master's in dance that focuses on choreography.

12. The exception was in 2009, when there was only a contemporary dance workshop and no additional ones.

13. "We" refers to Falierou's collective, the Association for Expressive Dance SYN-KINISI, which Falierou founded in 2002 in Chania, Crete. The team behind SYN-KINISI has also been organizing DDC since 2011.

14. There are four distinct categories for presenting work at the festival: (1) presenting a performance (either on a stage or as a site-specific work), (2) hosting a workshop, (3) submitting a video dance work, and (4) curating a project as "new creator in the city." Applicants are required to submit a video of the entire performance. If accepted to the festival, they must perform the submitted piece unaltered in its entirety.

15. The population of Corfu (and of Greece more generally) has been steadily declining since 2011. According to the 2021 census, the population of Corfu was 99,847 (Hellenic Statistical Authority 2021).

16. Linda Kapetanea and Jozef Fruček are the founders of Rootlessroot and the creators of the somatic practice Fighting Monkey.

17. Performance theorists Bojana Cvejić and Ana Vujanović have discussed and situated the trend of self-precarization in the context of European performance production as follows:

> Performance workers in Europe have looked at current forms of free-lance work, as well as lifestyles, conditioned by the neoliberal market, and mistaken them for innovative and creative formats: production of artistic research in residencies, laboratories, and other temporary working situations; festivalization and the coproduction of projects that atomize and multiply work without end or limit. . . . This paradoxically leads not only to increased economic self-precaritization . . . but also to political complicity with neoliberal capitalism, for which performance practices today supply a training ground. (Puar 2012, 167)

Five

Choreographies of the European Refugee Crisis

In the old stock market's main room, the phrase "MONEY—MONEY! THAT IS ALWAYS THE DANGER WITH YOU" has been painted for the 2013 Athens Biennale. The digital price boards noting the price ranges in green and red fonts are still hanging on the walls and functioning. A circular wood and metal structure (approximately ten feet in diameter and forty-five inches tall) on wheels occupies the space's center. A masculine voice becomes audible through the loudspeakers. The pronunciation is careful, reminiscent of someone learning Greek, and an accent is detectable. He talks about the extremist right-wing party Golden Dawn, about becoming Greek, and how "we are all immigrants."[1] Toward the end of the audio, the voice proclaims that the word he finds the hardest to spell is ΘΑΛΑΣΣΑ (*thalassa*, meaning "sea"). The diverse performers calmly interact, changing their positions inside and outside a wooden and metal banister structure in the middle of the space. Some of them are balancing on the railings; others hang from them or help each other pass through (Figure 21).

Amid the commotion, a female voice, imitating a news reporter cadence, announces: "The dead have risen to over 300. There are women and children among them." The report is swallowed by what at first sounds like ocean waves, produced by two men shaking a large piece of orange tarp on the other side of the room. The performers gradually increase their movement speed, traversing through space with a sense of urgency that turns into panic. They rush toward the central structure. When the tarp noise ceases, the reporter's voice is audible again: "359 immigrants dead, 143 survivors."

The panic fades, and most performers are either inside the banister or clinging to it from the outside. All but one come to a halt. The only person

Figure 21. Performers balance on the wood and metal structure at the center of the space in *They forced us out of here. Walking the routes of the displaced: Small Seeds*, performed by ELANADISTIKANOUME at the Old Stock Market building, October 13, 2013. © Dimitra Tsiaouskoglou.

moving is a White man carrying the body of a motionless Black performer toward the tarp. As soon as the stiff body touches the tarp, a heartbreaking lamentation ensues. In the meantime, the rest of the group has formed a long human chain, holding on to one another in various ways, frozen momentarily, like sculptures (Figure 22).

One by one, the performers make their way to the tarp and lie next to the motionless body of the Black man, who was placed there first. Some are tenderly positioned there by others, a few lie down gently on their own, and the rest fall on the tarp violently. A gray-haired White man stands in front of them, covering his eyes with both hands, deliberately blocking out the sea of corpses forming beneath him. The singer approaches him, and her lament echoes louder with each step: "The path led me to your love's door, and I found it locked."

This description captures the arc of a performance titled *They forced us out of here. Walking the routes of the displaced: Small Seeds* (Mas Edioxan Apo Do. Perpatontas stis diadromes ton ektopismenon. Mikroi sporoi.; Μας έδιωξαν από δω. Περπατώντας στις διαδρομές των εκτοπισμένων. Μικροί σπόροι.;

Figure 22. The closing scene of *They forced us out of here. Walking the routes of the displaced: Small Seeds*. ELANADISTIKANOUME at the Old Stock Market building, October 13, 2013. © Dimitra Tsiaouskoglou.

hereafter referred to as *Small Seeds*), presented at the 2013 Athens Biennale. It was a collaboration between many interdisciplinary artists including ELA-NADISTIKANOUME[2] (which can be translated as "Come See What We Do"), one of the most diverse dance companies in Greece, made up almost exclusively of immigrants and refugees, and the Nomadic Architecture Network.[3] *Small Seeds* was a memorial tribute to the 2013 Lampedusa tragedy, in which a ship full of immigrants sailing from Libya to Italy sunk near the Italian coast.[4] Of the 500 people on board, more than half drowned. Even though the performance occurred in 2013, it remained relevant in the latter half of the 2010s. Such tragedies in the Mediterranean Sea have persisted, many with even more fatalities.[5]

Performances addressing aspects of the refugee crisis had become increasingly common in the 2010s and reached a peak around 2013–2015, when the European refugee crisis intensified. The topic of immigration became increasingly popular and prevalent in many dance performances in the 2010s since the overlap of the two crises intensified latent social, political, and racial issues. Discourses around citizenship, understood as the legal process of acquiring nationality and as a cultural construct at the core of perceived difference, became mainstream at the time. The late 2000s and early 2010s marked a significant shift in the legal process of citizenship acquisition for immigrants, which, in turn, became a topic that some choreographers engaged with.

In some unfortunate instances, the increased visibility and media hype around the European refugee crisis resulted in a rather superficial treatment of the topic. Similar to the aforementioned critique of the fetishizing of the crisis in contemporary performances, in some cases, engaging with refugee experience became a trend. Not every artist approached it responsibly, thus frequently bringing up questions of possible tokenism or exploitation of refugee narratives. At the same time, many choreographers and artists used their works as forums to initiate a dialogue about human rights and the conditions refugees faced in Greece and to question the racial construction of Greekness. It has only been since the dawn of the twenty-first century that Greekness has progressively become detached from narrow associations with Whiteness and cultural heritage.

Some groups of artists/activists engaged with immigrant and refugee communities and created safe spaces where their narratives and stories could be told to educate audiences about the refugee crisis. The bodily vulnerability of immigrant and refugee populations, along with the challenge of language (many immigrants and refugees did not speak Greek, or if they did, they were still in the process of learning it), rendered dance a potent site for engagement with such communities, as their bodies and bodily archives were the primary tools mined in the creative process.

Yet despite its potency, dance presents an intriguing paradox as a site for engaging with refugee communities. As an art form grounded in movement, dance's ephemeral essence often contrasts with the immobility and abiding state of suspension that many refugees experience. In the performance examples discussed in the following sections, there are multiple levels of potential tension between the participants. Many immigrants and refugee participants who find themselves in Greece as part of their migratory journey experience what legal anthropologist Heath Cabot (2014) has termed "legal limbo."

Having studied asylum and citizenship in Greece, Cabot notes that being recognized as a refugee conveys the right to protection in the host country, yet the category "asylum seeker" is highly transitory. Cabot reports that "asylum seekers . . . occupy a neither fully legal, nor illegal position of non-belonging, suspended in limbo between multiple bureaucratic stages conveying possible acceptance, rejection, or appeal" (2014, 56). Populations in this state of limbo often arrive in Greece, yet they do not hold the required documentation to have their asylum claim processed. As such, they find themselves "stuck" and cannot work while in Greece, nor can they move on in their journey until they acquire the required legal documents. The legal constraints limiting their mobility render them in a particularly vulnerable position.

During the crisis decade, the state of legal limbo experienced by refugees arriving in Greece and seeking to make their way to other EU countries contrasted with the hypermobility that professional dancers holding Greek citizenship may have enjoyed, especially within and across the open borders of the EU. The closing lament of *Small Seeds*, which contains the lyrics "I found the door locked," thus serves as an apt metaphor for the treatment of refugees attempting to enter some EU countries and further complicates center/periphery discourses. For many refugees, Greece served as the main entry point to the EU. Because of the ongoing financial crisis, however, Greece significantly lacked the infrastructure to support such a massive population movement. Support and monetary assistance by the EU were required, thus further marginalizing Greece and complicating the crypto-colonial hierarchies of its past.

In what follows, I highlight the tensions and instances of immobility that migrant subjects encounter; and in doing so, I refrain from celebrating the momentary freedom of movement they enjoy through their participation in dance events. By paying attention to the methodological and choreographic frameworks utilized, I delve into the ethics, aesthetics, and politics of representation of populations in precarious positions and question whether and how dance productions work to dismantle the hierarchical binary between *self* and *Other*, thus showcasing awareness of the stakes that dance holds in both local and global citizenship.

Before Dance: Contextualizing Racial Diversity, Xenophobia, and Citizenship

Performances concerned with racial diversity or questioning the racial construction of Greekness were popularized in the early 2010s. The beginning of that decade also marked a turning point for racial representation in performances (including contemporary dance, theater, and even TV productions).[6] Casts became increasingly more diverse compared with the past, when diversity was present on the level of ethnicity (if at all) and thus still grounded in Whiteness. This shift toward inclusivity indicates a convergence of multiple layers of social change occurring sequentially in the decade leading up to the crisis. One such layer, locally, is the gentrification of the GKM neighborhoods, discussed in chapter 3. Internationally, an example is the accession of new members to the EU in the 2000s, which broadened the borderless access of EU citizens. The European enlargement extended supranational citizenship and, in doing so, heightened national awareness of sovereignty among EU member states. The perceived threat to national sovereignty, in turn, enkindled xenophobia and simultaneously heightened awareness of immigrants' rights. When these dynamics were negotiated within the EU, ongoing civil conflicts in other parts of the world (such as Syria, Kosovo, or Afghanistan) caused people to flee and seek refuge further West.

While the above description is a rather simplistic rendering of the chain of events that occurred in the years leading up to the coalescing financial and refugee crises, it introduces the complexity of the topic. Since it is nearly impossible to fully untangle all the interlaced threads in a few pages, I selectively trace some strands that I consider essential for contextualizing perceptions of race in the landscape of the Greek crisis and propose a framework for theorizing how these tensions manifested in the field of dance.

The rise of nationalism in Europe has been an observed phenomenon since the early years of the twenty-first century (Balibar 2002). The phenomenon is in part attributed to the consecutive enlargements of the EU, which rendered hypervisible the inequalities within Europe. Up until 2004, the EU comprised fifteen members.[7] Since then, thirteen new members have been added,[8] thus exponentially increasing EU citizens' accessibility to a borderless union. The "internal migration" (between EU member states), which presented a new multiethnic reality, challenged the newly founded infrastructure of the borderless EU and exposed its structural inconsistencies, as the popular vote for Brexit in 2016 exemplified. The failure of European integration inevitably led to the surfacing of differences between cultures and their symbolic structures.

During the mid-2010s, the xenophobia associated with extreme nationalist outbursts intensified, along with racist violence and collective manifestations of racism. The targets of this violence have most often been immigrant workers, economic migrants, and refugees. The extremism and violence against immigrants further intensified during the financial crisis because rising unemployment rates[9] provided an occasion for populist forces (of both right and left political orientation) to become aggressive and gain votes in the elections.

Even though the European refugee crisis is documented as occurring in 2015, Greece has been dealing with a "crisis of asylum" (Cabot 2014) that dates back to 2004. As Cabot (2014) has observed, the wave of migrants coming into Greece steadily increased from 2004 to 2007 since Greece's northern borders (by Evros, which borders Turkey) are among the most trafficked in the EU. There was a minor drop in the population influx between 2008 and 2010. After 2010, the percentage steadily rose again, reaching unprecedented heights in 2015 (BBC 2016). Given the challenges already imposed on Greece because of the financial crisis, the country lacked the infrastructure to deal with these mass population movements and thus became fertile ground for extremist ideologies to surface and populist rhetoric blaming immigrants for Greece's continuing crisis to gain footing.

Economic insecurity undoubtedly contributed to xenophobia and the rise of nationalism, yet in Greece, both phenomena have roots in the early 1990s, when the first massive wave of migration was noted from Eastern Europe, North Africa, and the Middle East. The borders between Greece and Albania opened in 1992, after the fall of Albania's communist regime, which led to the influx of large numbers of immigrants and economic refugees to Greece. As has been the case for other EU states, Greece saw people arriving from many Eastern European countries (such as Bulgaria, the Republic of North Macedonia, Romania, Ukraine, Armenia, and Georgia) at that point as well. Anti-immigrant rhetoric surfaced in the early years following the relocation of the incoming Eastern European population. The signing of the Maastricht Treaty in 1992 (which went into effect in 1993) provided European citizenship as a supplement to the national one and further fueled the rhetoric of discrimination.

Xenophobia became publicly integrated into political rhetoric in September 2000, when a former New Democracy party member, Georgios Karatzaferis, founded the populist right-wing party LAOS. Advocating for national sovereignty and patriotism, the party leader's popular addresses openly blamed immigrants for the rise in delinquency rates and suggested measures to prevent further population influx. LAOS's popularity rose in the coming years. In 2007, the party entered the Parliament with 3.8% of the votes (ten seats out of 300), which rose to 5.6% (corresponding to fifteen seats) in the 2009 elections.

The most significant rise in xenophobic rhetoric, however, was observed in the early years of the crisis, when the extremist right-wing party Golden Dawn entered Parliament with 6.9% of the vote (eighteen seats out of 300) in the 2012 elections. The alarming popularity of Golden Dawn during the crisis decade stemmed partially from party members' use of overtly racist practices masked as good deeds to manipulate voters in their favor. They claimed to be offering protection to vulnerable groups of Greek citizens, such as the elderly or the unemployed living in low-income neighborhoods populated by immigrants. The party's "protection services" included walking civilians to ATMs to ensure their safety from perceived threats, offering food to those most impacted by the financial crisis (yet only to those with government-issued identification as proof of Greek citizenship), and the so-called practice of cleaning out neighborhoods by illegally prosecuting and exercising violence against immigrants and refugees. These acts were strategically orchestrated to groom the population in those neighborhoods to feel indebted to the party and vote for them. The atrocities and the overt use of violence were no secret, and the inaction of law enforcement fueled rumors about possible police cooperation with Golden Dawn members. Most such rumors were put to rest after several Golden Dawn members, including the party leader, were imprisoned and tried for multiple charges ranging from the constitution of a criminal organization to illegal weapon possession and murder. The Golden Dawn trials were a lengthy process that began in 2015. They concluded in October 2020 with a verdict celebrated across Greece with mass gatherings despite the COVID-19 pandemic restrictions. The Guardian hailed the trials as the "biggest trials of fascists since Nuremberg" (Smith 2020), as it concluded with the conviction of the party's founding members, who faced up to fifteen years of imprisonment for directing a criminal organization. Additional crimes (such as murder, violence against immigrants, and targeting minorities) were examined separately by the criminal court and added to the existing sentences.

The introduction and popularization of Golden Dawn rhetoric in the political discourses of race and nationalism has contributed to a transition from a formerly ethnic-centered understanding of racism in Greece to one increasingly focused on skin color as a visible marker of perceived difference. As a result of this transition, incidents of violence on the grounds of someone's skin color have increased. I trace this shift of attention toward visuality at the core of perceptions of national unity. According to the extremists' reasoning, the entry of racial others threatens to "contaminate" the country's racial profile and purity, and difference based on appearance is thus persecuted. The ethnocentric rhetoric of the Golden Dawn emphasized national unity and purity and organized populations against what was perceived as an external threat found in Athens's racially, ethnically, and culturally diverse population.

A possible reason for Golden Dawn's unprecedented popularity in the 2010s lies in a significant change in Greek citizenship laws. In 2010, the ruling socialist government (PASOK) passed a bill facilitating immigrants' naturalization and citizenship. Up to that point, children born in Greece to migrant parents could not apply for citizenship until they turned eighteen. Then they had to demonstrate continuous legal residence in Greece for at least ten of the twelve years preceding their application.[10] The amended bill reduced the required years of residency to seven for children whose parents resided in Greece legally for five or more years prior to the application or who successfully completed at least six years of schooling in Greece. The importance of education in Greek nation-building has historical roots.[11] Without access to education, children of immigrants cannot get Greek citizenship. Yet access to school is often hindered by bureaucratic restrictions, which denies school registration to anyone without a birth certificate. Obtaining a birth certificate is not always viable for refugees who have fled their country and cannot return.

In the tumultuous political climate of the early crisis years, these legal amendments to the citizenship acquisition process became a point of heated disagreement and were eventually deemed unconstitutional, requiring further revisions in 2014 and 2015 (Nikolova 2015). According to Greek Law 4332/2015, requirements for obtaining citizenship for a minor include enrollment in a Greek school for the first grade, the parents' legal residence in Greece for a minimum of five years before the birth of the child, and legal residence status at the time of application. These revisions made it easier for children born in Greece to immigrant parents to become citizens. At the same time, as more people of color identified as Greek and obtained Greek citizenship than ever before, they also gave rise to the discourse of racial construction of contemporary Greekness.

This brief summary of the continuing legislative struggle surrounding Greek citizenship indicates the fluidity and instability of the construct of citizenship. The historically intense policing of citizenship laws and the close ties to education are inextricably linked to national anxieties concerned with cultural and racial "purity" dating back to the early 1830s and the establishment of the independent Greek state. Consistent with European imaginings of reviving Greece as the cradle of Western culture, Greek citizenship was constructed according to Eurocentric ideals of cultural, racial, and religious homogeneity grounded in whiteness and (Orthodox) Christianity (see also Dyer 1997; Leoussi 1998). Any deviation from this paradigm was perceived as a threat that would destabilize not just the pillars of Greek national identity but also of Europe since many Eurocentric values draw on ancient Greek ideals. Giving access to Greek (and thus also European) citizenship to "non-Westerners" was perceived as a challenge to the long-established ties between Greek nationality, Whiteness, and Orthodox Christianity. The new citizens from varying cultural, religious, and racial backgrounds introduced a previously unencountered diversity.

The increased targeting of people of color during the crisis decade fueled preexisting discrimination on the grounds of ethnic background and gave rise to demographic anxiety. According to sociologist and political theorist Athena Athanasiou (2006), discourses of population decline (such as those forwarded by Golden Dawn and previously by the right-wing LAOS party) are organized around fantasies of endangered national sovereignty. They have come to haunt individual and collective imaginaries in the public life of Greece since the 1990s. Such demographic anxiety spans beyond the level of national sovereignty and identity and seeps through to the social sphere as it also impacts gender politics and brings to the surface discourses of heteronormativity. According to Athanasiou, "Demographic anxiety over the imperiled national future works to stabilize discourses of national and (hetero-)sexual normalcy as timeless structures of cultural intelligibility at a variety of levels of self, kinship affiliation, and national belonging" (2006, 231). Heteronormativity has always been at the core of modern Greek identity, as heteronormative familial structures are central to cultural values of kinship. This presents an interesting paradox in dance, an ideal case study for illuminating the latent ties between xenophobia and heteronormativity that Athanasiou points to.

In concert dance, ethnic diversity has historically been a norm in Greece. Many Greek National Opera Ballet members, especially high-ranking male company members and directors, have often been from Eastern Europe or neighboring countries.[12] Yet, consistent with ballet's global history, racial diversity has not been introduced in Greece's ballet casts up to the point of writing. In contemporary dance, ethnic or cultural diversity has been present in company casts since quite a few students from neighboring countries such as Albania completed their studies in Greek professional dance schools; however, racial diversity is an occurrence dating to the 2010s.

Drawing on anecdotal evidence and years of observation in the field, I have noticed a tendency to apply more pressure on men who engage with dance rather than women, as the discipline has stereotypically been considered "effeminate" and thus inconsistent with traditional views of Greek masculinity and masculine gender expression. Such beliefs often determine the level of acceptance or marginalization of dance practitioners. Eastern European men's involvement in Greek dance ensembles has always been accepted and encouraged, compared with the participation of Greek men. This attitude relates to the stereotype that dance (especially ballet) is a practice that Eastern Europeans have a strong tradition in, and they are admired for their discipline in the art and their technique. Second, allowing "foreigners" to hold positions in Greek dance ensembles such as Greek

National Opera Ballet or other contemporary companies is not presumed to pose a threat to Greek masculinity. Xenophobia thus manifests selectively and completely flips to its counterpart, that of xenomania (fascination with and adoration of foreigners), when it serves to "protect" Greekness and its perceived fundamental pillars.

The involvement of ethnic Others in staged dance practices thus has generally been met with indifference or has been welcomed because they filled the gap of male participation in concert dance practices. While ballet and contemporary dance have generally been more inclusive of ethnic Others, most of the time, the inclusion of "Otherness" has nonetheless remained within the confines of Whiteness. Since the 2010s, however, especially as the refugee crisis intensified, the groups presented on Greek stages have been increasingly more diverse, as the examples discussed in the rest of the chapter demonstrate. Of course, fostering this diversity has not come without new challenges, such as incorporating nontrained dancers or ensuring their safety from racist audience attacks. The inclusion of diverse bodies has also given rise to new hierarchical imbalances within Greece (distinguishing between natives and nonnatives) and beyond (in terms of offering new subtext for the center/periphery discussions).

A Quiet Voice (2014)

In the abandoned furniture factories of Peiraios 260, Ermira Goro's *A Quiet Voice* premiered in 2014 under the auspices of the prestigious Athens and Epidaurus Festival.[13] The stage had concrete floors and foggy, old factory windows in the back. A group of children was playfully chasing one another and playing tug-of-war on the concrete stage as audience members made their way to their seats. A deep hum from the loudspeakers scared them off the stage, and the audience's attention shifted to the figure of a Black man standing outside, behind one of the back windows. He was anxiously knocking on the window, trying to be heard, yet in the vast space, the sound was absorbed. Next to him, more silhouettes appeared behind the windows, some knocking soundlessly on the glass and others placing their open palms on the window, trying to push through. Eventually, all the performers behind the windows disappeared and entered the concrete stage in a long line holding hands.

The transitions between the scenes were quick, and the entire piece evoked a hectic sense of constant movement, reminiscent of the migrant journey and the need to always be on the move. Indicative of a sense of necessary mobility, the underlying sense of flux that permeated the piece was at odds with the reality of some asylum seekers and refugees, who are confined to one country and cannot move on because of bureaucratic challenges. Acknowledging the limbo that many refugees experience, Goro choreographed deliberate moments of stillness and immobility. The transitions from one scene to the next and from one group of performers to another often involved taking turns. Some performers, visible to the audience, waited at the margins of the stage for their turn to perform, thus effectively mirroring the limbo intrinsic to Greece's refugee experience.

Toward the piece's conclusion, all performers are being pushed off the stage by a White woman. Only a Black man remains and resists every push. The woman persistently attempts to force him to leave, but she manages only to slightly take him off his track, as he consistently recovers and continues to occupy the stage. He does not appear bothered by her forceful pushes, and in the end, she succumbs to him as she jumps on his shoulders and lets him calmly carry her off the stage. Approaching the edge of the stage, he drops her to the ground. Leaving her behind, he walks to the center, where he finds a spot to lie down gently. Most other performers join and scatter around him, lying on the concrete floor.

Two women enter, playfully running, and jumping over the motionless bodies, chasing each other. They catch up to each other in the middle of the stage. Standing face to face, they touch their lips in what appears to be a kiss. Their proximity is interrupted as one of them takes a deep breath and starts blowing air into a balloon. Its expanding shape pushes the other's face back, but her lips remain attached to the other side of the balloon holding it in place (Figure 23). The balloon continues to expand, its walls thinning, until it eventually pops. The explosion of sound resounds in the theater, and is followed by a sudden blackout, which momentarily engulfs audiences in complete darkness, depriving them of both auditory and visual stimuli.

The darkness is permeated by the flickering light of three candles. A woman walks on to the stage, balancing one candle at the crown of her head and holding the other two in her palms. She carefully makes her way forward. As she walks toward the center, illuminating her surroundings, all performers who were previously on the floor are now seen standing. One by one, they approach her, take out a handkerchief, and hold it up to the candle flames until it catches fire. Their arms are outstretched, holding the burning cloth away from their body. When the flames get too close to their fingers, one by one, they release the ember-colored remnants. Floating like bright fireflies, all handkerchiefs eventually succumb to the pull of gravity and turn to ash

Figure 23. The performers in *A Quiet Voice* (2014) supporting a balloon with their lips. Photograph taken during performance rehearsals. © Anna Psaroudakis.

on the ground. The woman with the candles reaches the front of the stage and exits. Everyone, except for one White man who stays behind, follows her.

The man performs a solo that resembles an abstracted version of a Balkan folk dance. His focus is internal, and he appears withdrawn. Slightly crouching forward, he swings his arms in large circles in a gesture reminiscent of someone trying to create a gust to fuel a fire. Growing progressively bigger, his movements become a call that heralds the others. The movement is contagious as everyone imitates him forming a cluster in the middle of the stage. Popular club music blasts from the speakers and the group turns into a festive party complemented by flashy lights that flicker and make the dancing bodies appear as though they are in slow motion.

The children who opened the performance with their playful demeanor are seen sneaking from the side holding water hoses with gun-shaped regulators. They shoot water at the performers, causing them to freeze on the spot; they quickly run off the stage laughing. Soaking wet, the performers take off their shoes and exit the stage. The shoes remain on the stage as the lights dim to signal the end of the performance, serving as a stark reminder of the absence of the bodies that had earlier filled them.

A Quiet Voice comprised seventy-five performers from various cultural and ethnic backgrounds. Some of them were professional dancers from Greece, while others were refugees and immigrants residing in Greece who had neither received dance training nor performed before. During the performance, the difference in training sometimes became apparent as one could see glimpses of hesitation and trepidation surfacing in their performance as "untrained" bodies, which starkly contrasted the professional dancers' confidence and stage presence.

Here, the term untrained is a deliberate choice to capture the divide between the dancers who have pursued professional dance training and the participants in dance performances without equivalent training. In using this term, I am fully aware of the hierarchies inherent in the word choice, such as the fact that it prioritizes Western concert dance training over other types of dance or embodied practices. In fact, my goal is to render these hierarchies visible by using this term to challenge the prevailing views about concert dance in Greece, historically characterized by an emphasis on virtuosity and technical excellence. The term untrained thus allows me to lay bare hierarchies that may be taking shape between Greek subjects and perceived Others.

In *A Quiet Voice*, to bridge the divide between the various levels of training, the choreography was structured around a series of group pieces involving almost all participants simultaneously. These were often based on pedestrian movements, emphasizing group dynamics instead of individual movement sequences. The group pieces were interspersed with numerous solos, duets, or trios, showcasing each performer's strengths. The solos and the small group pieces that often intercepted the larger group pieces came out of task-based improvisation exercises Goro used to identify the strengths of each untrained participant. She then pieced the elements together to highlight each person's individuality. Each performer was thus empowered to be expressive in a way that felt comfortable to them. This allowed the participants' cultural diversity to become visible through the various dance practices they embodied. Acknowledging each person's skills was a celebration of their culture and history. This in-depth engagement with people's strengths starkly contrasted with commonly observed processes and trends, where refugee identity was reduced to narratives of hardship in the context of the European refugee crisis.

A Quiet Voice achieved a delicate balance between narratives of hardship and celebration of human perseverance. The juxtaposition of solos with group sequences visually rendered the process of Othering and openly acknowledged experiences of discrimination and alienation that are often central to the migrant experience. Moving beyond that, Goro also brought to fore narratives of loss, highlighting the courage, perseverance, and resilience that are required of migrants and questioning the magnitude of who and what are left behind in any process of migration. The handkerchief-burning sequence and the piece's conclusion, where the shoes were the only remnant of the bodily presence of the performers, suggest two ways that loss was engaged. *A Quiet Voice* honored the complexity of the migratory experience by acknowledging the multiple convergent layers that comprise it instead of rendering it a simplistic narrative of hardship or Otherness.

Crisis narratives, such as the idea that an unprecedented event may dramatically change the course of one's life, also permeated the piece. The scene when the balloon explodes, as well as the closing scene in which children use a water hose to shock a group of people enjoying a careless moment of dancing, reminds audiences that nothing should be taken for granted. Even though the magnitude of the refugee crisis and the experience of Othering that a refugee may endure are not easily fathomable, the framing of such events through narratives of loss or as a rupture to the established order highlight the deeply human aspect of the experience. It thus evokes empathy rather than fostering attitudes of further Othering through spectacularizing human hardship for mass consumption.

PASStresPASS (2013)

A similar approach, layering personal and collective narratives and experiences, is central to a series of recurring projects called *PASStresPASS*. This work is a collaboration between Despina Stamos, a New York–based choreographer and cofounder of the Modern Dance Awareness Society, and Panagiotis Andronikidis, a Greek choreographer, contact improvisation teacher, and the founder of ELANADISTIKANOUME dance company in Athens. In early occurrences of the project, the two choreographers collaborated with New York–based filmmaker Jill Woodward, who compiled the performance footage into short films and dance documentaries presented at international festivals. In what follows, I focus on a live performance iteration of this project under the auspices of the 2013 Anti-racist Festival.

Outside the Olympic Stadium in Irene, on the side of the Calatrava arch, a group of performers descend a long flight of stairs, carefully putting one foot in front of the other on a piece of red-and-white tape running down the stairs.[14] Their arms are stretched out to their sides at shoulder height to assist them in balancing on the tape. Once everyone has made it down the stairs, they form a long line that begins to move from one side of the space to the other. During each crossing, a different individual is left behind to perform a short solo sequence, mainly consisting of pedestrian movements reminiscent of daily tasks, such as picking up flowers or looking at oneself in the mirror, until the line sweeps past them again and they rejoin the group, leaving a new person behind. After numerous crossings, the line sweeps past one last time, and each individual stops until they are all spread out over the open space designated for the performance. The boundaries between the performers and audience members become blurred as festival attendees cross through the area, making their way to other events. Amid the commotion, the performers begin to loudly introduce themselves in Greek:

—*Me lene Despina.* (My name is Despina.)
—*Me lene Dudu.* (My name is Dudu.)

Each of them holds a piece of the red-and-white tape they initially balanced on, which flutters in the light breeze. Gradually, the group rejoins to form a cluster in the middle of the open space designated for the performance, and they crumple up the pieces of tape in their hands. They raise their fists as a voice-over narrative starts playing in the background. It is a male voice talking about a migrant's journey in broken English. The voice notes how challenging it is to miss one's family and loved ones; meanwhile, the performers gather into a tight-knit group, leaving out one individual. The group members extend an arm out to invite the individual to join them. He offers a piece of paper to them, and they all raise their index finger and shake it from side to side, signaling rejection. The individual lets the paper fall to the ground. As soon as the paper touches the gravel, the group's demeanor changes and they now signal him to come closer, with their palms facing up, waving their slightly bent fingers. He takes another paper out of his pocket, which is once more met with rejection, and the sequence alternates between a welcoming demeanor and stark rejection until the participants turn to the next improvisatory task.

Some of the tasks that follow include a playful sequence in which some performers pose and others gently lean on them, sharing weight, or moving around them, filling in negative space. Toward the end, they form a circle, holding hands; at times, break the circle by letting go, and a couple of the participants raise their joined hands, forming momentary gates and allowing others to cross under them. The piece culminates with all performers sitting on one side of a long table and the audience joining them on the other side. They are given a chance to introduce themselves, talk with one another, and share their stories. Through this simple tactic, the choreographers facilitate an encounter between people who may have otherwise never connected.

In this performance, the interplay between personal and collective narratives of hardship and stories of migration is created through improvisatory tasks. The performance is structured around a set of actions, broken down into small objectives, that the performers need to complete. For untrained participants, this helps to create a sequence that is easy to remember. The narrative draws on participants' experiences, making it easy to perform and memorize the tasks since the prompts derive from personal stories. This task-based improvisation is easily relatable to daily life and could be perceived by untrained practitioners as a strategy that allows for relative freedom of expression since they are not required to follow strict choreography.[15]

For the choreographers, the biggest challenge was bridging the performance skill levels of the diverse participants. Based on what they told me during interviews, the project directors adopted an approach employing task-based improvisation to allow the participants to move "freely" (i.e., within the confines of the given task) and get a sense of their movement qualities (Panagiotis Andronikidis, interview, April 9, 2014; Despina Stamos and Jill Woodward, Skype interview, July 5, 2014). The prompts that participants were called to embody related to their migrant journey experience; this was true for the various iterations of *PASStresPASS*. The participants were often asked to physicalize emotions or other pivotal themes stereotypically associated with migrant subjectivities. Examples of this are the pedestrian sequences in which participants were singled out from the sweeping lines, and the scene where one person presented the group with a series of papers and repeatedly got rejected. This is a clear allusion to the struggle of asylum seekers and the difficulty of navigating a host country's bureaucratic and legal processes.

A later iteration of the collaboration between ELANADISTI-KANOUME and the Modern Dance Awareness Society was *bodies of resilience* (2015). This short dance documentary created in collaboration with filmmaker Jill Woodward provides yet another example of using improvisation to draw on real-life experiences. The short film opens with two questions: "How do bodies live in the environments and situations they find themselves in? How do they find softness and resiliency when they are surrounded by harshness?" (Woodward 2018, 0:20–0:40). This prompt is explored outdoors. Dancers, primarily refugees and asylum seekers in Greece, are seen improvising and positioning themselves on pebbled paths, rocks, or narrow sidewalks throughout Athens. The physical harshness of the environment becomes a metaphor for the harsh living conditions they have adapted to in coming to

Greece. Rather than mirroring the rigidity of their environment, the dancers embrace the landscape with their bodies. They become one with the rocks and curl into their nooks, finding comfort and softness despite the terrain's roughness. The embodied negotiation of space that this task requires indicates the adaptability that can be cultivated through improvisation, which is then applicable to contexts beyond performance.

Engaging Precarious "Otherness": Improvisation as a Narrative Device

Continuing to examine the central role that personal narratives play in incorporating untrained bodies, I revisit Katharina Pewny's (2011) approach of "self as a role" introduced in chapter 2. Having refugee participants perform as themselves by physicalizing aspects of their experience or narrating their story in an embodied manner can have a therapeutic effect. Participants in *PASStresPASS* initiatives reported gaining a sense of belonging to a community or experiencing euphoria through engaging in an embodied practice. Yet beyond such positives, staging refugees and asylum seekers as precarious subjects in a dance performance setting within the already precarious landscape of the Greek crisis raises ethical questions, as it might trigger past trauma. The self-precaritization of the artist (as discussed by Van Assche 2020) is very different from the staging of an already precarious subject whose involvement in the creative process occurs within a curated framework determined by the choreographers.

The emphasizing of personal narratives, which can be perceived as a practice of relative freedom and a means for subjects to claim agency, can also be criticized as a practice of essentialization. Most performances involving refugees I observed during my fieldwork in Greece confined their narratives to topics related to the European refugee crisis or issues related to belonging and migration. Participants seemingly had the freedom to express themselves in any way they chose through improvisation, yet they were still confined to narratives of hardship, migrant journeys, and insecurity. They were fixed to the subjectivity of a refugee or an immigrant and were not presented as individuals beyond this label that perpetuated their Otherness. I recognize the value of such choreographic endeavors in raising awareness among audiences, yet the limitations that such initiatives create for the participants should not be overlooked.

While pairings between natives and migrants can spark questions about dance as a site for political agency, they simultaneously raise the issue of the hierarchical relation in which trained choreographers are the ones *making space* for and *giving voice* to untrained bodies. Such questions are especially pertinent given how technical excellence and virtuosity are valued more than improvisatory approaches in Greece. The shift toward new modes of embodied organization that extend an invitation to the Other, which coincided with the height of the European refugee crisis, poses questions of exploitation. The divide between professional dancers and untrained bodies is analogous to racial hierarchies. The predominantly White professional dancers are juxtaposed to the Black and Brown participants' untrained bodies. Thus, it is imperative to question the incorporation of vulnerable population groups into contemporary concert dance performances. As avant-garde contemporary performance is central to constructing the genre's European canon, the example of the already marginalized Greek choreographers inviting and curating productions with participants in states of extreme precarity renders migrants and refugees hypervisible and potentially even more peripheral in these hierarchies.

Considering the xenophobic rhetoric circulating in Greece when these performances premiered, the aforementioned pieces could also be described as different approaches to staging encounters with the "Other," who, in this instance, are subjects experiencing a very precarious mode of existence. What choreographic means are employed to achieve such encounters, and what are some potential challenges inherent in the staging processes?

To explore these questions in depth, I turn to the improvisatory practice most often employed in works involving immigrants and refugees: contact improvisation. It is intriguing that this collaborative approach, often credited to Steve Paxton in the US during the early 1970s, gained popularity again in Greece during the crisis, especially among initiatives involving refugees. There are quite a few parallels that can be drawn between the structure of contact improvisation as a practice and the choice to engage refugee populations through it. According to Paxton, one of the core ideas is openness to adaptability and disorientation. In his essay "Drafting Interior Techniques," Paxton observes how "Contact Improvisation constantly challenges one's orientation: visual, directional, balance, and where in the body consciousness is positioned" (2003, 178). This sentiment not only applies to embodied orientation but also considers mental attitude. As dance scholar Danielle Goldman asserts, training in contact improvisation prepares one to respond to "a range of shifting constraints. . . . [O]ne begins to see the power of a bodily training such as contact improvisation that *seeks calm, confident choices even in situations of duress*" (2010, 97; emphasis added). It seems that the structure of contact improvisation recalls aspects of the experience of Greeks trying to navigate the crisis landscape and the imposed austerity measures, as well as skills that migrant participants may have had to employ in their journeys on the way to Greece and Europe.

Another central concept in contact improvisation is the notion of "sharing a dance," discussed by dance scholar Cynthia J. Novack (1990). According to Novack, the body in contact improvisation is not independent because the practice is a constant negotiation between two bodies. Part of the practice's appeal is that the practice was advertised very early on as something that everyone (regardless of their level of training or prior experience) could participate in. Despite contact improvisation's egalitarian values, however, the participants were, for the most part, White middle-class artists. The rhetoric of contact improvisation as a practice "for everyone" still circulates in Greece, and contact jams are advertised as open spaces for dancers and untrained bodies. Given the close ties between contact improvisation and American cultural values of the 1970s and 1980s, which Novack examines in depth, it is remarkable that the practice is at the epicenter of engagements with migrants. Returning to the notion of sharing, it was, according to Goldman (2010), initially considered threatening in the US context of the 1970s as it was tainted by racial, social, and class hierarchies.

Considering the rise of ethnocentrism and xenophobia, the idea of sharing a dance with an "Other" could be similarly fraught in the context of the Greek crisis. Contact improvisation as a practice to mediate that fear has been employed by both Panagiotis Andronikidis (the founder of ELA-NADISTIKANOUME) and Konstantinos Michos (director and choreographer of Lathos Kinisi), whose alternative approach to engaging with the topic of immigration is described in the coming section. Contact improvisation seems to be a way to take a political stance as they facilitate meetings between locals and "newcomers," fostering encounters between individuals that may otherwise not have crossed paths.

The 2013 iteration of *PASStresPASS* described earlier involved weight bearing and sharing akin to early experimentations in contact improvisation. Virtuosic or acrobatic sequences were absent from this piece. More challenging sequences are present in other works by Andronikidis, as some ELANADISTIKANOUME members developed an interest in contact improvisation and continued taking classes to build their skill set further. Since the participants of *PASStresPASS* come together over only a few weeks, however, the level of training they acquire is limited to certain aspects of contact improvisation: weight sharing, points of contact, or initiation through touch. This restricts the performance to a pedestrian aesthetic. Nevertheless, I consider the choice to employ contact improvisation and improvisation, in a broader sense, in such initiatives as an exercise in preparing audiences, performers, refugees, and immigrants alike for the practice of navigating the present moment and the fluctuating political and social landscape of the crisis. It is training for learning to problem-solve in the moment.

One point that should not be overlooked is the fact that the spaces where such performances and contact improvisation jams occur are still relatively marginal compared with the highly advertised dance festivals or private institutions that frequently host internationally renowned companies. Arguably, the choice to foster such encounters at spaces like EMPROS—the abandoned theater reclaimed as a performance space—or under the auspices of the annual Anti-racist Festival—where *PASStresPASS* was presented—are strategic choices to ensure the safety of participants. Incidents of violence (either verbal or physical) against refugees and immigrants in performances have occurred, so facilitators strive to ensure the participants' safety and well-being. Unfortunately, despite the well-intended motives behind the necessity of opting for marginal venues, these choices mean that such valuable initiatives remain in the realm of lesser-known works that become advertised through word of mouth rather than through institutional support. *A Quiet Voice* was an exception to this as it was one of few dance performances engaging with refugees that was presented at the renowned Athens and Epidaurus Festival. Thus, the lack of prestigious institutional support further urges the question of *who* creates space and *for whom*.

Until the 2010s, the Greek dance scene was not characterized by diversity, as most productions involved predominantly White performers. There was ethnic diversity but not racial diversity, which became more common in the 2010s to create works more representative of the country's increasingly diverse demographic composition. At its onset, this trend primarily took place through initiatives involving untrained bodies, thus often perpetuating inequalities and highlighting distinctions between the self (the native Greeks/professionally trained dancers) and the Other (the predominantly Black and Brown bodies of immigrants and refugees, who did not have professional dance training). As the breakdown of this book's chapters also suggests, the presence of diversity in concert dance stages in the mid-2010s was limited mainly to performances involving narratives of migration and engaging the refugee crisis, rather than performances engaging the Greek crisis at large, where the casts were predominantly White professional dancers.

Situating this divide in the context of Greece's history and fear of being "orientalized" or the desire to preserve its glorified position in the West, the crisis reignited anxieties about Greece's marginalization or potential Othering with respect to the EU. The contrast between the highly trained, virtuosic White (mostly also Greek) bodies and their untrained newcomer counterparts could be regarded as an attempt to recenter Greece's position in the Western canonical hierarchy. Based on my fieldwork, I can assert that this was not the choreographers' intention, as most of them were genuinely interested in the well-being of their participants. Choreographers pursuing work with migrants and refugees considered their work a noble effort in educating audiences and providing a forum for the participants to share their experiences. Nevertheless, the act of providing a forum perpetuates hierarchical inequalities of someone (in this case, a primarily White Greek choreographer) needing to create space for the Other to share their experience.

Questioning the means of fostering encounters between spectators and Others by applying Levinas's phenomenological approach to intersubjectivity, Katharina Pewny suggests that "theatrical performances are an encounter with the other if possibilities are opened up to the spectators to respond to the vulnerability of the other. *How* these possibilities take shape are both the ethics and aesthetics of the performance" (2012, 263; emphasis in original). Continuing to explore how such encounters take shape and the resulting aesthetics of these performances, I turn to another example, which suggests a different approach for staging an encounter between the self and an Other in Levinasian terms.

With Them or *For* Them:
Toward a Critique of Performances on the Refugee Crisis

The performances I have discussed thus far were driven by collaborations *with* the refugees. An alternative approach to this paradigm was suggested by Konstantinos Michos, who created a work *for* them titled *Audition Bacchae* (Audition Βάκχες, 2010–2011). In our interview (May 11, 2014), Michos noted that there is a fine line between creating work *with* immigrants as opposed to creating work *for* them. He considered the former rather problematic as it can potentially cross over into exploitation, and in *Audition Bacchae*, he opted for the latter.

Audition Bacchae's premise is that a group of performers repeatedly attempts and fails to choreograph Euripides's ancient tragedy *Bacchae*. The process takes place as a peripatetic tour in the heart of Athens. Audiences met the performers at the dance studio of Michos's homonymous dance company,

Lathos Kinisi, and were taken on a tour down Euripides Street, which, at the time, had the reputation of being a rather dangerous neighborhood where drug transactions frequently took place. During the performance, audience members sometimes witnessed illegal transactions or caused panic among the drug dealers, who hid their stash and ran upon the sight of a large group of audience members wandering the streets. The choice of the site was strategic. According to Michos:

> You cannot talk about immigration *with* immigrants because immigrants are really something Other; if you go about it this way, you make it familiar.[16] The whole experiment was that the audience had to move through this space on their own at night, without protection, and they were thus called to truly experience the Otherness of the immigrant. (Konstantinos Michos, interview, May 11, 2014)

In this alternative approach of creating work *for* the immigrants, the process of othering is still very much present, yet it is flipped, as the audiences momentarily become the Others in the setting they are navigating. Even though the audiences temporarily experience fear and agony, it is an experience they have chosen to subject themselves to, which they have paid for, and which lasts only for the duration of the performance. It is not their daily reality and is thus incomparable to the forced uprooting of the refugee experience.

Through *Audition Bacchae*, Michos evokes momentary empathy on behalf of the audience attendees. Such an affect could be productive in initiating discussions among audience members on issues of precarity and vulnerability after the performance is over, yet the distinction between the self and an Other persists. In this instance, the Other is not only in danger but is also perceived as dangerous and delinquent. Connotations of this type draw a fine line between the empathy that the work seeks to evoke and a further marginalization of the Other.

Another interesting facet to consider is who the untrained bodies are. In *Audition Bacchae*, the untrained bodies are the audience members and the dealers and residents of the neighborhood who, by virtue of being in the street when the performance takes place, involuntarily become part of it. The choreography and the score are also conceptually expanded in this instance. There is a score that the performers follow, and improvisation is required when audiences happen upon the drug dealers, and they both have to decide how to best navigate that encounter.

In those fleeting moments when decision-making is required (the dealers pack up their stash and run, or the audiences perhaps choose to look the other way or change their walking pace), a different sense of precarity manifests. Driven by the awkwardness of the unplanned encounters and the audience members' momentary experience of fear upon witnessing a potentially illegal transaction, the audiences and the dealers become the untrained bodies. This constitutes a remarkable reversal of the previously explored dynamics between lack of training and virtuosity and presents another approach for framing precarity in and through performance.

Nevertheless, with the exception perhaps of *A Quiet Voice*, which successfully shed light on the participants' cultural backgrounds and heightened their individuality, the other works discussed, be it *for* immigrants or *with* them, inadvertently perpetuated neocolonial hierarchies of self as opposed to Other. Creating works *about/with/for* refugees is common in international art discourse. Such works are often classified as humanitarian action or a means to "give voice to the voiceless" and, as such, presuppose inequality. Instead, why not propose an organizing principle for such performances that follows "a fundamental axiom of Equality," as theater studies scholar Maurya Wickstrom (2012, 3) pointedly suggests.

Indeed, in the performances discussed thus far, the hierarchical relationship between choreographers and participants is analogous to the relationship between trained and untrained bodies. Hierarchy is also apparent in the need for someone, whether local or not, with access or institutional power to provide a forum for the displaced voices to be heard. Here, it should be noted that one of the *PASStresPASS* directors, Despina Stamos, is Greek American and migrated to the US at a very young age with her parents, escaping the junta in Greece at the time. *A Quiet Voice* choreographer Ermira Goro was born in Albania and came to Greece as a teenager once the communist regime collapsed. The choreographers' personal migration stories shed light on the potential motives behind their interest in taking on such subjects in their works. The dichotomy between natives and migrants becomes further complicated in these instances and urges an awareness of the creative frameworks used to engage with the refugee performers, which mostly follow Western concert dance etiquette.

This predominantly Western framework challenges the supposed freedom of improvisation and individual expression, as subjects are allowed to express themselves only in confined ways or through narrowly defined frameworks. Thus a pending question revolves around the efficacy of such initiatives for participants and audiences. The answer to this question is not always clear and can be subjective, as some of the participants report that their involvement in art projects had a therapeutic effect on them. In terms of monetary benefits, it often depends on the context. For works presented under the auspices of a festival, there was monetary compensation for the participants. For performances presented independently, however, participants likely entered a barter system and were compensated for their time in alternative ways. For example, they may have been offered support in navigating public services in Greece, or they may have been shown appreciation for their participation through shared food. As for audiences, the answer is still twofold. As demonstrated through the description of the performances and the discourses they engage, these works succeed in raising awareness of immigration and the European refugee crisis. At the same time, the ways that these encounters are staged (regardless of well-meaning intentions) may perpetuate and reinforce long-established colonial hierarchies and practices of discrimination.

In Closing: Beyond Performance

Immigrants' and refugees' involvement in performing arts during the decade of the Greek crisis was commonly observed in dance productions, yet most participants did not have professional dance training. The lack of training prompted choreographers to make room for individual movement skills and styles to surface. In the context of refugee performances, the move away from prioritizing technical virtuosity toward valuing the individual processes of untrained dancers and their diverse cultural practices produced a uniquely hybrid result that was much more representative of the diversity of the contemporary Athenian urban landscape.

While the hybrid movement vocabulary and the new methodological approaches may be evident primarily to spectators who are dancers or dedicated dance enthusiasts, the cultural, racial, and bodily diversity in dance performances during the Greek crisis decade did not go unnoticed. The bodies on and off the stages were increasingly more diverse, positively affecting representation as audiences became increasingly diverse as well. The viewership for contemporary dance expanded as audiences were able to see themselves represented onstage. The variety of movement vocabularies presented in Athenian venues has, in turn, changed how diversity is understood. One notable example was the change in the Athens and Epidaurus Festival's presentations of cultural diversity in dance. In the past, the concept of diversity was sometimes explored by hosting cultural dance ensembles that shared their dance practices. During and beyond the 2010s, diversity has been celebrated through works involving people of many backgrounds and skills, albeit still through a highly curated lens. This enforces an understanding of diversity as grounded in personal narratives, experiences, and individual skill sets. Thus the emphasis shifted from community and unity (as embodied in folk practices) to individual performers and their often-fragmented subjectivity—an embodiment of how neoliberalism affects societies and cultures.

Other than *Small Seeds* and *A Quiet Voice,* both presented at well-advertised festivals, many initiatives involving refugees were relatively marginal and accessible only to audiences that sought them out since they did not enjoy the same level of publicity. While marginal community projects can at first glance seem problematic, ostensibly perpetuating the very cycle of invisibility that such works are trying to dismantle, presenting these works in lesser-known venues was often necessary to ensure the safety of the performers and spectators. With the dangerous rise of ethnocentric rhetoric and the increasing support for the extreme right-wing party Golden Dawn, choreographers worried about violence in the early years of the Greek crisis.

For instance, in an iteration of *passTRESpass* in June 2015, most meetings were held at the House of Immigrants, a voluntary collective that offered language classes, art workshops, and support programs for immigrants. Other examples included presenting immigrant projects at the annual Anti-racist Festival or at EMPROS, both institutions with an openly leftist political agenda. To some extent, these venues allow choreographers to choose their audiences. As noted, this is sometimes necessary to protect participants from racist attacks, especially since, in their private lives, members of the ELANA-DISTIKANOUME collective have been attacked and stabbed by Golden Dawn members (Panagiotis Andronikidis, interview, April 9, 2014). This harsh reality of physical violence and verbal abuse is embodied in their performances, as the descriptions in this chapter have suggested. Violence was a recurring theme found in performances engaging with the refugee experience. Fostering encounters between locals and migrants was thus imperative for countering hate rhetoric, and it illustrated dance's activist and didactic function.

Opening contemporary concert dance to nonprofessionals stretched the boundaries of what constitutes contemporary concert dance performance, allowing new aesthetics to emerge. Emphasizing individuality is a neoliberal trait, yet at the same time, it is also a way to recognize a kind of agency that no longer focuses only on the work of the choreographer or director but instead brings forth a collective communal vision that very evidently presents distinct subjectivities and points of view.

By becoming increasingly participatory, performances actively reshape perceptions of Greek identity and citizenship. As spaces of advocacy, performances are rendering previously marginalized peoples and histories visible. Performances involving untrained and diverse bodies also play a pivotal role in pushing artists in Greece to reconsider what constitutes performance and how the relationship between audience and performers is understood. Most importantly, the performances challenge Otherness discourses by laying bare what it means to be human through the embodied stories the performers choose to share.

Last, the emergent divide between trained and untrained bodies further complicates the hierarchies between center/periphery discourses both locally and internationally. Locally, virtuosic bodies are centered and associated with high art, whereas untrained bodies or embodied practices outside the concert dance cannon are rendered peripheral. It seems, however that this paradigm is being challenged by the participation of untrained bodies in productions and venues deemed avant-garde. Creating an analogy between these hierarchies seen in the dancing bodies and broader hierarchies or discourses of citizenship reveals an inadvertent centering of the Greek body in a way that distinguishes it from its Others. This analogy points to a hierarchical positioning of trained bodies, who can participate in the central European network of avant-garde/high art cultural production, while untrained bodies remain peripheral to these conversations.

Notes

1. This description is based on excerpts from the piece *They forced us out of here. Walking the routes of the displaced: Small Seeds*, made available to me by Panagiotis Andronikidis, the director of ELANADISTIKANOUME. *Small Seeds*, presented in October 2013, was part of a wider artistic initiative dating back to June 2013 under the auspices of the Nomadic Architecture Network (Diktyo Nomadiki Architektoniki; Δίκτυο Νομαδική Αρχιτεκτονική). In an earlier iteration (June 2013), *Small Seeds* was presented as part of the Anti-racist Festival and comprised a peripatetic performance across several Athenian neighborhoods inhabited by newcomers awaiting their legal papers. The project later evolved into the staged performance presented at the 2013 Athens Biennale, which took place at the old stock market, part of the trend of using abandoned buildings as performance sites.

2. Founded in 2009 by Greek choreographer and contact improvisation teacher Panagiotis Andronikidis, ELANADISTIKANOUME visibilizes marginalized political topics and critiques the dysfunctional infrastructure (mis)serving immigrants. Its founding year coincides with the rise in percentage of votes won by LAOS, as Andronikidis felt the need to counter the rise of xenophobic rhetoric through his work. In the past, ELANADISTIKANOUME's works have addressed analogies between Greek emigration and the refugee experience in *Xeni-*

tia (Ξενιτιά; roughly translating as "the experience of living abroad" 2009) (Panagiotis Andronikidis, interview, April 9, 2014); the exploitation of cheap immigrant labor in *The Bridge* (I Gefyra; Η Γέφυρα, 2011) (Panagiotis Andronikidis, interview, April 9, 2014); and the role of traditions in exploring cultural difference in *Roots* (Rizes; Ρίζες 2015), a collaboration between Andronikidis, Teti Nikolopoulou, and Niki Stergiou.

3. The Nomadic Architecture Network is a collective that organizes series of activities, such as common meals, cultivation of urban gardens, and communal walks.

4. According to news coverage of the event, the boat had sailed from Misrata, Libya, and the migrants on board were primarily from Eritrea, Somalia, and Ghana (see, for example, Harding 2013; Yardley and Povoledo 2013).

5. In September 2014, 500 refugees drowned near Malta; in February 2015, 300 people died on a ship sailing from Libya to Europe; on April 12, 2015, 400 drowned on the same route; and on April 19, 2015 another 700 drowned as their boat approached Italy (Tomara 2015; Lustgarten 2015). According to CNN, 2016 was the deadliest year to date: data gathered in October showed a record high of 3,800 people having drowned in their attempt to cross the Mediterranean (Smith 2016).

6. There is scarcely any research focusing on the intersection of race and performance in Greece. Given this, racial representation is theorized here primarily by drawing on personal observations. The appearance of people of color as characters in Greek television series can be traced back to the 1990s. Since then, until the mid-2010s, the characters portrayed by people of color have most often been caricatures. Examples from privately owned broadcasters include a Black woman housekeeper (Niki Sereti) speaking only in broken Greek and often causing misunderstandings between her boss and his dates in the series *Ekeines ki ego* (Εκείνες κι εγώ; They [indicating females in the Greek language] and Me) (Pretenderis 1996–1998); an unintelligent Black man (Michalis Afolayan), who is the sidekick of the main character in the Greek spin-off of the US series *My Name Is Earl: Me Lene Vaggeli* (Με λένε Βαγγέλη; *My Name Is Vangelis*) (Tsaousoglou 2011–2012); and the Asian school-aged daughter (Hin Yu Fong) of a male protagonist who is one of the smartest students at her school in the 2013–2014 series *Me ta pantelonia kato* (Με τα παντελόνια κάτω; Pants Down) (Hasapoglou and Spiliopoulos 2013). An example of a series that moved away from the stereotypical caricaturing of ethnic others was *Ethniki Ellados* (Εθνική Ελλάδος; Greek National Team) (Kapoutzidis 2015). In contrast to other series in which people from different ethnic and cultural backgrounds were caricatured stereotypes, this series attempted to accurately depict contemporary Athens with a diverse cast of complex characters. One of the leading female characters realizes that she is in an abusive relationship as she comes to terms with the fact that her husband and son are followers of the fascist party Golden Dawn and engage in violent acts against immigrants residing in their neighborhood. This character lives in constant fear of her husband and is friends with a group of immigrant women from China, India, and Africa, who own small businesses in her neighborhood. What made

this example stand out to me is that it was one of the first mainstream series to respectfully engage with the issue of racism, discrimination, and racist violence and to avoid an exaggerated and caricatured depiction of Athenian life in the 2010s.

7. The European Economic Union (as it was originally named) was founded in 1958 by Belgium, France, Germany, Italy, Luxemburg, and the Netherlands. Since then, it has undergone four expansions as follows: Denmark, Ireland, and the UK joined in 1973; Greece became a member in 1981; Portugal and Spain were incorporated in 1986; and Austria, Finland, and Sweden became members in 1995. The UK left the EU in 2020 following the 2016 popular vote known as Brexit.

8. Ten members joined in 2004: Cyprus, Czechia, Estonia, Hungary, Latvia, Lithuania, Malta, Poland, Slovakia, and Slovenia. In 2007, Bulgaria and Romania became members, and Croatia joined in 2013.

9. According to Eurostat, in 2009, when the crisis started, the overall unemployment rate was under 10%. It peaked during the summer of 2013, reaching 27.9%. Statistics documenting unemployment rates among youth (ages fifteen to twenty-five) are even more staggering, peaking at 58.8% in the summer of 2013 and remaining in high rates in the latter years of the crisis. Indicatively the percentage of youth unemployment in June of 2017 was still at 43.3% (ELSTAT 2017). As a baseline for comparison, in 2008, the same percentage was around 20% (Eurostat 2014).

10. For a thorough analysis of the legal processes to obtain citizenship in Greece, see Cabot (2014).

11. The importance of education and its connection to cultural purity have roots as far back as classical Greece, when education was perceived as an indication of a "civilized" person and was the major point of distinction between civilized cultures and "barbarians" (non-Greek people were deemed barbarians because of their lack of education). Nowadays, receiving a Greek education ensures that children are taught Greek history, learn Greek customs and traditions, and become fluent in the Greek language.

12. For example, in 1939, Czech dancer and choreographer Saša Machov was appointed as the first ballet director of the Greek National Opera Ballet. For a detailed history of the institution and its directorial legacy, see Savrami (2019).

13. The description is based on documentation of the live performance provided to the author by the choreographer, as well as field notes following the live performance at the festival.

14. The performance description is based on video documentation of the event available on YouTube (Andronikidis 2013).

15. The idea of improvisation as a practice of freedom is introduced in accordance with how it is understood in modern dance theory. I acknowledge that this essentialist concept has been rightfully problematized in dance theory, such as in the work of Danielle Goldman (2010), which I explore later in this chapter.

16. The Greek word used in this instance was οικειοποιείσαι (oikeiopoieisai), which could also be translated as "to appropriate."

Epilogue

Ministerial subsidies for the performing arts were restored in 2017, so there was a semblance of "normalcy" for three years before artists were called to navigate yet another crisis in 2020. The COVID-19 health emergency severely limited artists' ability to occupy shared spaces with their bodies and work. In the last few weeks of 2020, Greece was under a second lockdown that imposed strict measures, including a mandatory curfew and movement restrictions. During the lockdown in Greece, whoever wanted to leave their home was required to send a text to a five-digit number, providing their name, address, and a numbered code that corresponded to the reason they were leaving their residence. Permissible reasons included taking children to school (when schools were back in session), taking a pet for a walk, exercising alone outdoors, driving to work, doing grocery shopping or going to the pharmacy, and visiting people who needed assistance. Individuals would then receive a confirmation code that they could show to authorities if questioned. There were fines for anyone who could not provide a confirmation code upon request or other proof for being outside. These measures are indicative of the intensive policing of everyone and only hint at the severe impact that these measures had on performers whose work *was* the movement of their bodies.

What will the impact of the pandemic be on the Greek dance scene as it transitions from a state of heightened physicality, creative experimentation, and collective collaboration to a state of imposed restrictions on one's movement, ability to share space with others, and intensive isolation? How will the embodied combativeness identified as a characteristic of dancers and choreographers in the Greek scene transcend into this new era of unprecedented challenges? How will this global health crisis reshape the Greek dance community?

While it may be too early to map the impact of the pandemic on the

Greek dance scene, it is far from the first challenge artists have been confronted with in the aftermath of the financial crisis. The delayed start of the 2019–2020 academic school year for students at the Greek National School of Dance is indicative of such a challenge. During my last research trip to Greece in January 2020, before the world went into lockdown, I attempted to visit the archive of the National School of Dance. Not only was I informed that the librarian's contract had expired and that the library was closed, but the student body had also gone on strike and occupied the school to protest curricular deficits. According to the students' list of very reasonable demands, the main reason for the occupation was that the current structure of the curriculum was not on par with academic requirements both in terms of hours of instruction and classes offered. Teacher and musician hires had been pending since the beginning of the academic year (September 2019), which resulted in dance classes being taught without live musical accompaniment. Furthermore, studio facilities were inadequate, as there was insufficient space for classes for all enrolled students, and some of the premises were deemed structurally unsafe. The Ministry of Culture's failure to address these issues in a timely manner resulted in a significant delay in the academic year, which had started on November 19, 2019. As the students' demands indicated, even though the semester had finally begun, the conditions were still not on par with what a professional dance school should offer.

Later in the same year, after the first lockdown in May 2020, the UWFD released a list of demands in response to the cessation of all artistic activity and theater closures due to pandemic-related restrictions. The government issued subsidies for all workers (similar to stimulus checks), yet as the union noted, many dance workers did not qualify to receive them. An added blow to the arts was a law passed in July 2020, which mandated that art classes (in Greek captured by the term kallitechnika; καλλιτεχνικά) would no longer be taught at the high school level. Set to be implemented in the 2020–2021 school year, this decision affected not only students but also art workers across Greece as it rescinded hundreds of positions for artists in secondary education.

These examples illustrate the Sisyphean reality of art workers in Greece. The irony is that amid this outrageous devaluation of artistic labor, a video surfaced on social media created in celebration of the 200th anniversary of the 1821 start of the Greek revolution against the Ottoman Empire. Set to music composer Dionysis Savvopoulos's "As Kratisoun oi Choroi" (Ας κρατήσουν οι χοροί; translating as "May the Dances Never Stop"), the video captured a grandiose production that took place at the restored ancient Kalimarmaro theater and the Olympic Stadium Arch, designed by Santiago

Calatrava for the 2004 Olympics. Eight different participating choirs[1] voiced the song, while choreography by Artemis Ignatiou is the focus of the work. Ignatiou is a member of the Hellenic Olympic Committee and the choreographer of numerous Olympic flame lighting ceremonies. The video was sponsored by the Greece 2021 committee, the official ambassador appointed by the government to plan the festivities for the national celebration of Greek independence. The airing of a video (Greece 2021b 2020) with hundreds of performers in the same space, even as social distancing guidelines were being enforced, and the overall extravagance of the production seemed completely out of touch with both the post-crisis climate and the reality of the pandemic.

The chosen song was initially released in 1983. It is an allegory for the history of the Greek nation through the celebrations and dancing of a *parea* (παρέα; or group of friends). The song's title ("May the Dances Never Stop") captures the perseverance of Greeks despite hardship. There is an evident nationalist and patriotic undertone that celebrates past achievements and uses them to propel a sense of perseverance. For example, the lyrics note: "Be it through ancient [ruins] or through orthodoxy, the Greek communities are building other galaxies," and "But our [love] has a name, it has a body and a religion and a grandfather in sovereign regions within the Turkish occupation."[2]

The video opens with an aerial shot of the ancient theater dressed in blue light. A Greek flag is seen waving in the breeze on a pole at the front of the stadium, as instrumental music introduces the song. The logo of *Greece 2021* appears with the subtitle "200 Years after the Revolution." The opening shot is replaced by dozens of choir members and dancers dressed in black-and-white pedestrian clothing who are carefully spaced in distanced rows walking at the center of the stadium. Reminiscent of the large movement choirs at Olympic opening ceremonies, the performers all sing the lyrics as the camera alternates from shots at the same level as the performers to aerial shots that capture the spatial patterns and formations created by the bodies in space. The choreography follows the lyrics of the song closely. For instance, when the lyrics mention how Elena, the *parea*'s dancer, leans over to Tasos with her eyes closed and they sing together, the camera pans to a woman (portraying Elena) performing a short prancing solo and momentarily leaning off balance toward a man (Tasos), who has just singled himself out from the group. The choreography presents an interesting contrast as it is at once overly stylized—in terms of the performers' bodily comportment and exaggerated performance of simple movements—and at the same time rather simplistic. I hypothesize that the word-for-word interpretation of the lyrics through movement and the lack of abstracted movement, which is otherwise characteristic of contemporary concert dance, are indicative of the wide audience reach intended for this work. The emphasis is on a performance that is easily accessible and relatable while still clearly belonging to the concert dance genre. As such, it can secure associations with high-art and a presumably refined central European aesthetic.

Once more, history seems to be repeating itself as the national narrative is constructed based on an imagined Greek body that never existed to begin with. The *Greece 2021* celebration is supposed to recall the founding of the Greek nation-state after its liberation from the Ottoman Empire. Other than the portraits of some of the historic revolutionaries of 1821 projected on the empty seats of the stadium in the closing of the video, little else in the celebration's staging points to that moment in history. The song is a 7/8 rhythm, which is a *kalamatianos*, one of the first folk dances to be adopted as a panhellenic dance following Greece's independence from the Ottoman Empire. Yet instead of incorporating folk dance references in the choreography, a highly stylized concert dance approach is taken. The dissociation from the embodied practices of folk dance, which would much more accurately capture the era that the production is supposed to recall and celebrate, is striking. This choice is also indicative of the continued anxiety to present Greece through movement language that is perceived as broadly legible, compared with the regional specificity of folk dance.

Throughout this book, I have argued for a rupture from previously established practices of constructing Greece's national narrative with reference to ancient Greek ideals and a move toward an approach that embraces previously marginalized aspects of Greek identity. This example partially negates my thesis as it proves a strong governmental directive to construct national identity in strictly Apollonian terms and as pertaining to the invocation of "refined" aspects of Greek identity. Drawing on the temporality of this occurrence—after the crisis decade and at the dawn of a global health crisis—there is added pressure to avoid associations with Dionysian indulgence, which could paint contemporary Greeks in a negative light internationally and resurface derogatory views, such as those popularized during the crisis (i.e., Greeks as lazy or as one of the PIIGS). As a consequence, even though the music has a recognizable folk rhythm, the choreographic choices abstain from any engagement with folk tradition and favor more abstracted and refined movements more likely to be broadly understood internationally. As the example of *Greece 2021* showcases, while the discourse around national identity shifted during the crisis decade—at least in the field of contemporary concert dance performance—the mainstream governmental directive has continued to promote a mix of antiquated values and aesthetics.

Bookended by the end of the Greek financial crisis and the dawn of the

COVID crisis, this book speaks to the cyclical nature of history and of crises. When a crisis breaks out, there is an initial period of extreme cautiousness and uncertainty as those experiencing it develop the skills essential for navigating it. This stage may also be theorized as intensive introspection, as people withdraw from the public sphere and close in on themselves until they learn how to negotiate the new circumstances. Gradually, the steep learning curve levels out, and people find themselves in a position to move past the initial shock and to approach the situation critically, to theorize it, and to create works about it. Sometimes, as it happened with the Greek crisis, the emergency becomes fetishized and, in effect, exploited as a marketing strategy. Toward the end of the cycle, once individuals and their bodies adjust to the new reality, the focus shifts to regaining a sense of normalcy, which in some instances means reverting to old and comfortable patterns.

In Greece, the state of introspection and the cultivation of new skills to navigate the crisis prevailed during the first half of the crisis decade. What followed was a saturation of works exploring the crisis, and this gave way to a slow reversion to old patterns, as the above example of Greece 2021 choreography shows. This reversal can be perceived as an attempt to reclaim a sense of normalcy and find a home in the new order of things. The same thing seems to have happened with COVID-19 and the way people, especially artists, seem to have responded to this new crisis. In each crisis cycle, our bodies acquire new techniques for coping; they rehearse new ways of being in the world and of navigating the environment and the shifting conditions around them. In each crisis, the conditions we must adapt to differ, yet from a macro perspective, the cycle looks very similar. Perhaps knowing what to expect can, in some ways, prepare us and make it easier to respond when a new cycle is set in motion.

Notes

1. The participating choirs included La Familia, the National Odeon Choir, Children's Choir of Spyros Lambrou, Musica, OTE (Hellenic Telecommunications Organization) Choir, Athens Odeon Choir, Estia Neas Smyrnis, and the Choir of the Ministry of the Interior. As the Greece 2021 website notes, these groups participated without being compensated (Greece 2021a 2020).

2. The quoted lyrics in Greek are as follows: "Κι είτε με τις αρχαιότητες είτε με ορθοδοξία των Ελλήνων οι κοινότητες φτιάχνουν άλλο γαλαξία" and "Μα η δικιά μας έχει όνομα έχει σώμα και θρησκεία και παππού σε μέρη αυτόνομα μέσα στην Τουρκοκρατία."

References

Albright, Ann Cooper. 2013. *Engaging Bodies: The Politics and Poetics of Corporeality.* Middletown, CT: Wesleyan University Press.

Albright, Ann Cooper. 2019. *How to Land: Finding Ground in an Unstable World.* New York: Oxford University Press.

Alexandri, Georgia. 2015. "Reading between the Lines: Gentrification Tendencies and Issues of Urban Fear in the Midst of Athens' Crisis." *Urban Studies* 52 (9): 1631–1646.

Anderson, Benedict. (1983) 2006. *Imagined Communities: Reflections on the Origin and Spread of Nationalism.* London; New York: Verso.

Andronikidis, Panagiotis. 2013. "*PASStresPASS 2013—Performance.*" Filmed June 28, 2013. YouTube video, 27:07. https://www.youtube.com/watch?v=HQ5ErXuYk Ck&t.

Antzaka-Vei, Evangelia (Αντζάκα-Βέη, Ευαγγελία). 2010. "Oi Ellinikoi Choroi sto Lykeio ton Ellinidon. Ta Prota Peninta chronia" Οι Ελληνικοί Χοροί στο Λύκειο των Ελληνίδων. Τα Πρώτα Πενήντα Χρόνια [Greek Dances at the Lyceum of Greek Women. The First Fifty Years]. In *To Lykeio Ellinidon 100 Chronia* Το Λύκειο των Ελληνίδων *100* Χρόνια *[The Lyceum of Greek women 100 years]*, edited by Efi Avdela, Nikos Andriotis, Aspasia Louvi, Eleni Beneki, Eleni Tsaldari, and Teti Chatzinikolaou, 233–267. Athens: Politistiko Idryma Omilou Peiraios.

Argyriou, Tzeni. 2015. "*memorandum.*" *Vimeo* video, 3:41. Uploaded September 8, 2015. Accessed September 10, 2022. https://vimeo.com/138592484.

ArtEZ. 2019 "*Theatre Practices.*" Accessed February 2, 2019. https://www.artez.nl/en /course/theatre-practices.

Athanasiou, Athena. 2006. "Bloodlines: Performing the Body of the 'Demos,' Reckoning the time of the 'Ethnos.'" *Journal of Modern Greek Studies* 24 (2): 229–256. https://doi.org//10.1353/mgs.2006.0015.

Athens and Epidaurus Festival. "History." 2018. Accessed September 2, 2019. http://greekfestival.gr/istoria/.

Avdikos, Vasilis. 2015. "Processes of Creation and Commodification of Local Collective Symbolic Capital: A Tale of Gentrification from Athens." *City, Culture and Society* 6 (4): 117–123. https://doi.org//10.1016/j.ccs.2015.07.003.

AVDP (Athens Video Dance Project). 2019. "About AVDP / Festival." Accessed December 5, 2019. http://www.athensvideodanceproject.gr/.

Balibar, Etienne. 2002. *Politics and the Other Scene*. Translated by Christine Jones, James Swenson, and Chris Turner. New York: Verso.

Barbour, Karen, Victoria Hunter, and Melanie Kloetzel. 2019. *(Re)Positioning Site Dance: Local Arts, Global Perspectives*. Chicago: Intellect Books.

Barboussi, Vasso. 2014. *I Techni tou Chorou stin Ellada tou 20ou Aiona* Η Τέχνη του Χορού στην Ελλάδα του 20ου αιώνα *[The art of dance in Greece during the 20th century]*. Athens: Gutenberg.

BBC. 2016. *"Migrant Crisis: Migration to Europe Explained in Seven Charts."* March 4, 2016. https://www.bbc.com/news/world-europe-34131911.

Bernal, Martin. 1987. *Black Athena: The Afroasiatic Roots of Classical Civilization*. New Brunswick, NJ: Rutland Local History & Record Society.

Bernstein, Susan. 1998. *Virtuosity of the Nineteenth Century: Performing Music and Language in Heine, Liszt, and Baudelaire*. Stanford, CA: Stanford University Press.

Bhabha, Homi. (1994) 2004. *The Location of Culture*. London: Routledge.

Bourdieu, Pierre. 1973. "Cultural Reproduction and Social Reproduction." In *Knowledge, Education, and Cultural Change*, edited by Richard Brown, 71–112. London: Routledge.

Bourdieu, Pierre. 1984. *Distinction: A Social Critique of the Judgement of Taste*. Cambridge, MA: Harvard University Press.

Brandstetter, Gabrielle. 2007. "The Virtuoso's Stage: A Theatrical Topos." *Theatre Research International* 32 (2): 178–195. https://doi.org//10.1017/S03078833070 02829.

Braude, Benjamin, ed. 2014. *Christians and Jews in the Ottoman Empire*. Abridged edition. Boulder, CO: Lynne Rienner Publishers.

Brewer, David. 2010. *Greece, The Hidden Centuries: Turkish Rule from the Fall of Constantinople to Greek Independence*. London: I. B. Tauris.

Butler, Judith. 2004. *Precarious Life: The Powers of Mourning and Violence*. New York: Verso.

Cabot, Heath. 2014. *On the Doorstep of Europe: Asylum and Citizenship in Greece*. Philadelphia: University of Pennsylvania Press.

Carastathis, Anna. 2014. "Is Hellenism an Orientalism? Reflections on the Boundaries of 'Europe' in an Age of Austerity." *Australian Critical Race and Whiteness Studies Journal* 10 (1): 1–17.

Clogg, Richard. 2002. *A Concise History of Greece (Cambridge Concise Histories)*. Cambridge: Cambridge University Press.

The Constitution of Greece. (1975) 1986. Adopted March 14, 1986. Accessed September 15, 2022. http://www.hri.org/MFA/syntagma/artcl25.html#A16.

Cowan, Jane K. 1990. *Dance and the Body Politic in Northern Greece*. Princeton, NJ: Princeton University Press.

Daly, Ann. 1995. *Done into Dance: Isadora Duncan in America*. Bloomington: Indiana University Press.

Deligiannis, Giorgos Sioras. n.d. *Regulatory Bodies*. Facebook page. Accessed February 2, 2019. https://www.facebook.com/Regulatory-Bodies-365534213999352/.

Dendrinos, Panayis. 2008. *Contemporary Greek Male Homosexualities: Greek Gay Men's Experiences of the Family, the Military and the LGBT Movement*. Glasgow: Glasgow Thesis Service.

Dioskouridis, Stavros. 2012. "Synentefxeis / Giorgos Loukos: O Politismos tou Anti-Gklamour" Συνεντεύξεις / Γιώργος Λούκος: Ο Πολιτισμός Του Αντι-Γκλάμουρ [Interviews / Giorgos Loukos: The Culture of Anti-Glamour]." *LiFO*, April 4, 2012. Accessed September 20, 2022. https://www.lifo.gr/prosopa/synenteyjeis/giorgos-loykos-o-politismos-toy-anti-gklamoyr.

Dorf, Samuel. 2019. *Performing Antiquity: Ancient Greek Music and Dance from Paris to Delphi, 1890–1930*. Oxford: Oxford University Press.

Douzinas, Costas. 2013. *Philosophy and Resistance in the Crisis*. Malden, MA: Polity Press.

Dudziak, Johannes, and Andreas Wellnitz. 2015. *"Athen: Das neue Berlin."* [Athens: The New Berlin] September 17, 2015. Accessed April 8, 2019. https://www.zeit.de/zeit-magazin/2015/38/griechenland-athen-krise-kreativitaet-freiraeume.

Dullien, Sebastian, and Ulrike Guérot. 2012. *The Long Shadow of Ordoliberalism: Germany's Approach to the Euro Crisis*. European Council of Foreign Relations. February 22, 2012. Accessed September 10, 2022. https://ecfr.eu/publication/the_long_shadow_of_ordoliberalism_germanys_approach_to_the_euro_crisis/.

Dyer, Richard. 1997. *White*. New York: Routledge.

ELSTAT. 2017. "Deltio Typou: Erevna Ergatikou Dynamikou" Δελτίο Τύπου: Έρευνα Εργατικού Δυναμικού [Press Release: Workforce Research]. Statistics.gr. Hellenic Statistical Authority (ELSTAT). September 7, 2017. Accessed September 29, 2023. https://www.statistics.gr/documents/20181/15f5e011-039c-4fe1-ba4d-4e02299afcf6?fbclid=IwAR23lzEjp0dEQvCM5wTytNHy_YPkxVuT2gzbtc29rT3dwX8v9x5M54tUr4M.

Eurostat. 2014. "4: Labor Market." In *Eurostat Regional Yearbook 2014*, 96–116. Eurostat Statistical Books. Luxembourg: Publications Office of the European Union.

Falierou, Sofia. 2018. "Welcoming Speech at 'Dance Days Chania: Borders, Boundaries and Margins in Contemporary Dance.'" Delivered at Dance Days Chania, July 21, 2018.

Fanon, Frantz. 2008. *Black Skin, White Masks*. English translation by Richard Philcox. New York: Grove Press.

Faubion, James D. 1993. *Modern Greek Lessons: A Primer in Historical Constructivism*. Princeton, NJ: Princeton University Press.

Fensham, Rachel. 2011. "Nature, Force and Variation." In *Dancing Naturally: Nature, Neo-Classicism and Modernity in Early Twentieth-Century Dance*, edited by Rachel Fensham and Alexandra Carter, 1–15. London: Palgrave Macmillan.

Fessa-Emmanouil, Eleni. 2004. *Choros kai Theatro* Χορός και Θέατρο *[Dance and theatre]*. Athens: Efessos.

Flemming, K. E. 2010. *Greece—A Jewish History*. Princeton, NJ: Princeton University Press.

Florida, Richard. 2017. *The New Urban Crisis: How Our Cities Are Increasing Inequality, Deepening Segregation, and Failing the Middle Class—and What We Can Do About It*. New York: Basic Books.

Florida, Richard. (2002) 2012. *The Rise of the Creative Class*. New York: Basic Books.

Georgoula, Vasiliki, and Theano S. Terkenli. 2018. "Tourism Impacts of International Arts Festivals in Greece. The Cases of the Kalamata Dance Festival and Drama Short Film Festival." In *Innovative Approaches to Tourism and Leisure*, edited by V. Katsoni and K. Velander, 101–114. Springer Proceedings in Business and Economics. https://doi-org.ezproxy.library.wisc.edu/10.1007/978-3-319-67603-6_7.

Gere, David. 2004. *How to Make Dances in an Epidemic: Tracking Choreography in the Age of AIDS*. Madison: University of Wisconsin Press.

Giannou, Dimitra. 2017. "'Normalized Absence, Pathologised Presence' Understanding the Health Inequalities of LGBT People in Greece." Doctoral thesis, Durham University.

Goldman, Danielle. 2010. *I Want to Be Ready: Improvised Dance as a Practice of Freedom*. Ann Arbor: University of Michigan Press.

Gorgia, Maria. 2014. "Program notes for *On the Seesaw* [Στη Τραμπάλα]." Athens. January 2014.

Gourgouris, Stathis. 1996. *Dream Nation: Enlightenment, Colonization and the Institution of Modern Greece*. Stanford, CA: Stanford University Press.

Gourzis, Konstantinos, and Stylianos Gialis. 2017. "Gentrification in the Greek Context: Urban Transformations and Labour Markets Amid Crisis." 54th ASRDLF and 15th ERSA-GR Conference, Athens.

Greece. 2021a. 2020. Website. Accessed December 10, 2020. https://www.greece2021.gr/.

Greece. 2021b. 2020. *YouTube video*. October 21, 2020. Accessed December 18, 2020. https://www.youtube.com/watch?v=W2KUxkA9JFw&ab_channel=Greece2021.

Green Park Manifesto. 2015. Uploaded June 19, 2015. Accessed July 17, 2019. https://greenparkathens.wordpress.com/manifesto/.

Greiner, Christine. 2021. *The Body in Crisis: New Pathways and Short Circuits in Representation*. Translated by Christopher Larkosh and Grace Holleran. Ann Arbor: University of Michigan Press.

Grigoriou, Maro, and Angelos Mirayias, eds. 2004. *Choros* Χορός *[Dance]*. Athens: KOAN Books.

Halkitis, Perry N., Pamela Valera, and Maria Kantzanou. 2018. "Deterioration in Social and Economic Conditions in Greece Impact the Health of LGBT Populations: A Call to Action in the Era of Troika." *Psychology of Sexual Orientation and Gender Diversity* 5 (4): 503–507. https://doi.org/10.1037/sgd0000317.

Hamilakis, Yannis. 2009. *The Nation and Its Ruins: Antiquity, Archeology, and National Imagination in Greece*. New York: Oxford University Press.

Harding, Andrew. 2013. *"Italy Boat Sinking: Hundreds Feared Dead off Lampedusa."* Accessed January 20, 2015. www.bbc.com/news/world-europe-24380247.

Hardt, Michael, and Antonio Negri. 2012. *Declaration.* Independence, KS: Argo Navis.

Hasapoglou, Angelos, and Vasilis Spiliopoulos. 2013–2014. Με τα παντελόνια κάτω *[Pants down].* Directed by Vassilis Thomopoulos. Aired on MEGA.

Hassiotis, Anastasia. 2001a. *O Sygchronos Choros stin Ellada Epeisodio 1(*NET, *2001)* Ο Σύγχρονος Χορός στην Ελλάδα Επεισόδιο *1(*NET, *2001)* [Contemporary Dance in Greece Episode 1 (NET, 2001)] YouTube Video, 25:06. Accessed September 15, 2022. https://www.youtube.com/watch?v=CAkWyVWgYoI&t=3s.

Hassiotis, Anastasia. 2001b. *O Sygchronos Choros stin Ellada Epeisodio 6(*NET, *2001)* Ο Σύγχρονος Χορός στην Ελλάδα Επεισόδιο *6 (*NET, *2001)* [Contemporary Dance in Greece Episode 6 (NET, 2001)] YouTube Video, 26:52. Accessed September 15, 2022.

Hellenic Statistical Authority. 2021. "2021 Population-Housing Census: Press Kit." Accessed September 18, 2022. https://www.statistics.gr/en/press-kit_census_re sults_2021.

Herzfeld, Michael. 1986. *Ours Once More: Folklore, Ideology, and the Making of Modern Greece.* Austin: Austin University Press.

Herzfeld, Michael. 2002. "The Absence Presence: Discourses of Crypto-Colonialism." *The South Atlantic Quarterly* 101 (4): 899–926. https://doi.org//10 .1215/00382876-101-4-899.

Heyman, Stephen. 2017. "In Athens, an Unexpected Greek Renaissance." *Travel and Leisure,* May 4, 2017. Accessed April 8, 2019. https://www.travelandleisure.com/cul ture-design/athens-cultural-revival.

IMF (International Monetary Fund). 2021. World Economic Outlook Database: WEO Data, October 2021 Edition. Accessed December 18, 2021. https://www .imf.org/en/Publications/WEO/weo-database/2021/October.

Ioannidou, Eleftheria, and Natascha Siouzouli. 2014. "Crisis, Rupture and the Rapture of an Imperceptible Aesthetics: A Recent History of the Hellenic Festival." *Gramma: Journal of Theory and Criticism* 22 (2): 109–120.

Ioannou, Christos A. 1994. *Trade Unions in Greece: Development, Structures & Prospects.* Bonn, Germany: Electronic Ed.

Ioannou, Christos A. 1996. "Trade Unions in Greece: Change and Continuity." *Transfer: European Review of Labour and Research* 2 (3): 500–518. https://doi.or g//10.1177/102425899600020030.

Jackson, Naomi M, ed. 2004. *Right to Dance: Dancing for Rights.* Banff, Canada: Banff Center Press.

Jackson, Naomi, and Toni Shapiro-Phim. 2008. *Dance, Human Rights, and Social Justice: Dignity in Motion.* Lanham, MD: Scarecrow Press.

Jowitt, Deborah. 2001. "Beyond Description: Writing beyond the Surface." In *Moving History / Dancing Cultures: A Dance History Reader,* edited by Ann Dils and Ann Cooper Albright, 7–12. Middleton, CT: Wesleyan University Press.

Kalamata Dance Festival. 2019a. *"History & Aims: 25th International Kalamata*

Dance Festival." Accessed September 5, 2019. http://kalamatadancefestival.gr/index.php/en/the-festival/about/identity.

Kalamata Dance Festival. 2019b. "*Workshops/Lectures: 25th International Kalamata Dance Festival.*" Accessed September 5, 2019. http://kalamatadancefestival.gr/index.php/en/the-festival/past-festivals/workshops-lectures.

Kalamata Dance Festival. 2022. "Previous Editions." Accessed October 1, 2023. https://kalamatadancefestival.gr/en/previous-editions/festival-2022/.

Kalyvas, Stathis. 2015. *Modern Greece: What Everyone Needs to Know.* New York: Oxford University Press.

Kantsa, Venetia. 2014. "The Price of Marriage: Same-Sex Sexualities and Citizenship in Greece." *Sexualities* 17 (7): 818–836. https://doi.org//10.1177/13634607 1454480.

Kapetanea, Linda, and Joseph Fruček. 2015. *Europium [The end of the world will be better this year].* Performed at *Onassis Stegi, Athens.* October 30, 2015. Accessed September 2022. https://www.onassis.org/whats-on/rootlessroot.

Kapoutzidis, Giorgos. 2015. *Ethniki Ellados* Εθνική Ελλάδος *[Greek national team].* Directed by Antonis Aggelopoulos. Aired on MEGA.

Kedhar, Anusha. 2014. "Flexibility and Its Bodily Limits: Transnational South Asian Dancers in an Age of Neoliberalism." *Dance Research Journal* 46 (1): 23–40. https://doi.org//10.1017/S0149767714000163.

Kedhar, Anusha. 2020. *Flexible Bodies: British South Asian Dancers in an Age of Neoliberalism.* New York: Oxford University Press.

Khemsurov, Monica. 2010. "*REMIX; The 2.0 Report; Athens Is the New Berlin.*" *New York Times,* May 23, 2010. Accessed April 8, 2019. https://archive.nytimes.com/query.nytimes.com/gst/fullpage-980CEFD8163FF930A15756C0A9669D8B63.html.

Kitromilides, Paschalis. 2013. *Enlightenment and Revolution: The Making of Modern Greece.* Cambridge, MA: Harvard University Press.

Klein, Naomi. 2007. *The Shock Doctrine.* London: Penguin Books.

Kok, Daniel. 2015. "*PREMIERE 'PIIGS' BY DANIEL KOK / DISKODANNY.*" Accessed May 25, 2022. http://www.lifelongburning.eu/llb-13-18/projects/events/e/premiere-piigs-by-daniel-kok-diskodanny.html.

Kolokotroni, Vassiliki, and Efterpi Mitsi. 2008. *Women Writing Greece: Essays on Hellenism, Orientalism and Travel.* New York: Rodopi.

Konsola, Dora. 2006. *Politistiki Anaptyxi kai Politiki* Πολιτιστική Ανάπτυξη και Πολιτική *[Cultural Development and Policy].* Athens: Papazisis.

Kotaridis, Nikos, ed. 2007. *Rempetes kai Rempetiko Tragoudi.* Ρεμπέτες και Ρεμπέτικο Τραγούδι *[Rempetes and rempetiko songs].* Athens: Plethron.

Koundoura, Maria. 2012. *The Greek Idea: The Formation of National and Transnational Identities.* New York: Taurus Academic Studies.

Kounoupis, Georgios. 1960. *Delfiki Idea: Aggelos kai Eva Sikelianou-Eiriniki Synyparxis kai Synergasia ton Laon* Δελφική Ιδέα: Άγγελος και Εύα Σικελιανού—Ειρηνική Συνύπαρξης και Συνεργασία των Λαών *[Delphic idea: Angelos and Eva Sikelianou—Peaceful coexistence and cooperation of the peoples].* Athens: Athinae.

Krauel, Torsten. 2012. *Athen ist das neue Berlin [Athens is the new Berlin]. Die Welt*, December 1, 2012. Accessed April 8, 2019. https://www.welt.de/print/die_welt /debatte/article111739662/Athen-ist-das-neue-Berlin.html.

Kwan, SanSan. 2017. "When Is Contemporary Dance?" *Dance Research Journal* 49 (3): 38–52.

Kwon, Miwon. 2004. *One Place After Another: Site-Specific Art and Locational Identity*. Cambridge, MA: Massachusetts Institute of Technology.

Laughlin, Laurent. 2017. *Eina i Athina to Neo Verolino?* Είναι η Αθήνα το Νέο Βερολίνο; *[Is Athens the new Berlin?]*. VICE video, 21:20. Accessed February 7, 2019. https://video.vice.com/gr/video/is-athens-the-new-berlin/59b113e0298c8929 2c1a16cd.

Leontis, Artemis. 2015. "Greek Tragedy and Modern Dance: An Alternative Archaeology?" In *The Oxford Handbook of Greek Drama in the Americas*, edited by Bosher Kathryn, Fiona Macintosh, Justine McConnel, and Patrice Rankine, 204–220. New York: Oxford University Press.

Leoussi, Athena S. 1998. *Nationalism and Classicism: The Classical Body as National Symbol in Nineteenth-Century England and France*. London: St. Martin's Press.

Lepecki, André. 2006. *Exhausting Dance: Performance and the Politics of Movement*. New York: Routledge.

Lewis, Pericles, ed. 2011. *The Cambridge Companion to European Modernism*. New York: Cambridge University Press.

Loutzaki, Irene. 2001. "Folk Dance in Political Rhythms." *Yearbook for Traditional Music* 33: 127–137.

Loutzaki, Irene. 2006. "Ο χορός του Ζαλόγγου [The dance of Zaloggo]." *Archaiologia kai Technes* Αρχαιολογία και Τέχνες *[Archeology and Arts]* 100: 17–25.

Lustgarten, Anders. 2015. "*Refugees Don't Need Our Tears. They Need Us to Stop Making Them Refugees.*" *Guardian*, April 17, 2015. Accessed June 19, 2015. https://www .theguardian.com/commentisfree/2015/apr/17/refugees-eu-policy-migrants -how-many-deaths.

Macintosh, Fiona, ed. 2012. *The Ancient Dancer in the Modern World. Responses to Greek and Roman Dance*. New York: Oxford University Press.

Makrides, Vasilios N. 2009. *Hellenic Temples and Christian Churches: A Concise History of the Religious Cultures of Greece from Antiquity to Present*. New York: New York University Press.

Manou, Rallou. 1983. *O Ellinikos Choros Chthes kai Simera* Ο Ελληνικός Χορός Χθές και Σήμερα *[Greek dance yesterday and today]*. Directed by Kostas Koutsomytis. Produced by Stelios Antoniadis.

Marín, Álvaro García. 2013. "Haunted Communities: The Greek Vampire or the Uncanny at the Core of Nation Construction." In *Monstrous Manifestations: Realities and Imaginings of the Monster*, edited by Agnieszka Stasiewicz-Bienkowska and Karen Graham, 53–64. Inter-Disciplinary Press. Boston, MA: Brill. https://doi.org/10.1163/9781848882249_007.

Martin, Randy. 1998. *Critical Moves: Dance Studies in Theory and Politics*. Durham, NC: Duke University Press.

Matsas, Nestor, dir. 1969. Χοροί Και Φορεσιές Του Τόπου Μας [*Dances and regalia of our country*]. Hellenic National Audiovisual Archive. Kallithea: Greece.

Mazower, Mark. 2013. "*No Exit? Greece's Ongoing Crisis.*" *Nation*, March 13, 2013. https://www.thenation.com/article/archive/no-exit-greeces-ongoing-crisis/.

MessiniaLive. 2017. *Nikas: "Teleftaia chronia chrisimopoieitai to Kastro"* Νίκας: "Τελευταία χρονιά χρησιμοποιείται το Κάστρο" [*Nikas: "This is the last year that the Castle is used"*]. July 28, 2017. Accessed October 21, 2019. https://www.messinia live.gr/nikas-teleftaia-chronia-chrisimopoieitai-kastro/.

Most, Glenn. 2008. "Philhellenism, Cosmopolitanism, Nationalism." In *Hellenisms: Culture, Identity, and Ethnicity from Antiquity to Modernity*, edited by Katerina Zacharia, 151–167. Hampshire, UK: Ashgate Publishing.

Mylonas, Yiannis. 2019. *The "Greek Crisis" in Europe: Race, Class and Politics*. Chicago: Haymarket Books.

National Statistical Service of Greece. 2020. "*Greece Unemployment Rate.*" Accessed April 20, 2020. https://tradingeconomics.com/greece/unemployment-rate.

Nikolaidou, Afroditi. 2014. "The Performative Aesthetics of the 'Greek New Wave.'" *FILMICON: Journal of Greek Film Studies* (2). https://filmiconjournal.com/jou rnal/issue/2/2014

Nikolova, Marina. 2015. "Greek Citizenship Code-Modification of Law 4521/2014 with Law 4332/2015." European Commission. July 9, 2015. Accessed September 8, 2022. https://ec.europa.eu/migrant-integration/library-document/greek-citiz enship-code-modification-law-45212014-law-43322015_en.

Novack, Cynthia J. 1990. *Sharing the Dance: Contact Improvisation and American Culture*. Madison: University of Wisconsin Press.

Nugent, Neill. 2006. *The Government and Politics of the European Union*. New York: Palgrave Macmillan.

one small step (*ena mikro vima*; ένα μικρό βήμα). 2018. Accessed September 25, 2019. https://enamikrovima.eu/.

one small step. 2017. "one small step / 2017 / Corfu /. Workshops & Performance Projects." Vimeo Video, 1:51. Accessed September 25, 2019. https://vimeo.com /user13825699.

Orfanidou, Elpida. 2015. "Greece in 'PIIGS.'" Vimeo video, 11:57. Producer: Fu Kuen Tang. Accessed March 19, 2019. https://vimeo.com/131477007.

Osterweis, Ariel. 2013. "The Muse of Virtuosity: Desmond Richardson, Race, and Choreographic Falsetto." *Dance Research Journal* 45 (3): 53–74. https://doi.org// 10.1017/S0149767713000259.

Palmer-Sikelianos, Eva. 1993. *Upward Panic: The Autobiography of Eva Palmer-Sikelianos*. Edited by John P. Anton. Tampa: Harwood Academic Publishers.

Panagiotara, Betina. 2017. *Dance Chronicles from Athens: Artistic Practices, Structures & Discourses in a Period of Crisis*. Doctoral thesis, University of Roehampton.

Panourgia, Neni. 2009. *Dangerous Citizens: The Greek Left and the Terror of the State*. New York: Fordham University Press.

Papaeti, Anna. 2013. "Music, Torture, Testimony: Reopening the Case of the Greek Junta (1967–1974)." *The World of Music* 2 (1): 67–89.

Papaeti, Anna. 2015. "Folk Music and the Cultural Politics of the Military Junta in Greece." *Mousikos Logos* (2): 50–62.

Papaioannou, Dimitris. 2006. "2." Accessed February 3, 2020. http://www.dimitrisp apaioannou.com/en/recent/2.

Papanikolaou, Dimitris. 2018a. "Critically Queer and Haunted: Greek Identity, Crisiscapes and Doing Queer History in the Present." *Journal of Greek Media and Culture* 4 (2): 167–186. https://doi.org/10.1386/jgmc.4.2.167_1.

Papanikolaou, Dimitris. 2018b. Κάτι τρέχει με την οικογένεια: Έθνος, πόθος και συγγένεια την εποχή της κρίσης *[There is something about the family: Nation, desire and kinship at a time of crisis]*. Vol. 19. Athens: Ekdoseis Patakis.

Papanikolaou, Dimitris. 2021. *Greek Weird Wave: A Cinema of Biopolitics*. Stockport: Edinburgh University Press.

Papanikolaou, Dimitris, and Vassiliki Kolokotroni. 2018. "New Queer Greece: Performance, Politics, and Identity in Crisis." *Journal of Greek Media and Culture* 4 (2): 143–150. https://doi.org/10.1386/jgmc.4.2.143_2.

Paxton, Steve. 2003. "Drafting Interior Techniques." In *Taken by Surprise: A Dance Improvisation Reader*, edited by Ann Cooper Albright and David Gere, 175–184. Middletown, CT: Wesleyan University Press.

Pewny, Katharina. 2011. *Das Drama des Prekären: Über die Wiederkehr der Ethik in Theater und Performance [The Drama of the Precarious: About the Return of Ethics in Theater and Performance]*. Bielefeld, Germany: Transcript.

Pewny, Katharina. 2012. "The Ethics of Encounter in Contemporary Theater Performances." *Journal of Literary Theory (Berlin)* 6 (1): 271–278.

Pisimisis, Yannis. 2013. *Apantisi tis omadas Ichodrama* Απάντηση της ομάδας Ηχόδραμα *[The response of Echodrama Company]*. Published: May 21, 2013. https://www.dancetheater.gr/διευθύνσεις-σκηνών/itemlist/tag/Απάντηση %20τής%20ομάδας%20Ηχόδραμα.

Poser, Rachel. 2021. "He Wants to Save Classics from Whiteness. Can the Field Survive?" *New York Times*, February 2, 2021. https://www.nytimes.com/2021/02 /02/magazine/classics-greece-rome-whiteness.html.

Pratsika, Koula. 1991. *Erga kai Imeres* Έργα και Ημέρες *[Works and days]*. Athens: Ursa Minor.

President of the Hellenic Republic 1983. "Proedriko Diatagma 372/83: Kanonismos Organosis kai Leitourgias Anoteron Scholon Chorou" Προεδρικό Διάταγμα 372/83: Κανονισμός Οργάνωσης και Λειτουργίας Ανωτέρων Σχολών Χορού [Presidential Decree 372/83: Regulation of Organization and Operation of Higher Schools of Dance] Φ.Ε.Κ. *[Official government gazette] 131/A/23-9-83*. Accessed September 23, 2022. https://www.elinyae.gr/sites/default/files/2019 -07/131a_83.1157608215009.pdf.

Preston, Carrie J. 2011. *Modernism's Mythic Pose: Gender, Genre, Solo Performance*. New York: Oxford University Press.

Pretenderis, Kostas. 1996–1998. *Ekeines ki ego* Εκείνες κι εγώ *[They and me]*. Directed by Andreas Morfonios. Aired on ANT1.

Prickett, Stacey, and Steriani Tsintziloni. 2016. "Dancing National Ideologies: The

Athens Festival in the Cold War." *Congress on Research and Dance Conference Proceedings* 2016 (Fall 2016): 306–314. https://doi.org/10.1017/cor.2016.41.

Psaras, Marios. 2016. *The Queer Greek Weird Wave: Ethics, Politics and the Crisis of Meaning.* London: Palgrave Macmillan.

Puar, Jasbir. 2012. "Precarity Talk: A Virtual Roundtable with Lauren Berlant, Judith Butler, Bojana Cvejić, Isabell Lorey, Jasbir Puar, and Ana Vujanović." *TDR/The Drama Review* 56 (4): 163–177. https://doi.org/10.1162/DRAM_a_0 0221.

Raftis, Alkis. 1987. *The World of Greek Dance.* London: Finedawn.

R.I.C.E. on Hydra. 2013. Website. Accessed September 12, 2019. http://riceonhydra .org/.

Said, Edward. 1979. *Orientalism.* New York: Vintage Books.

Savrami, Katia. 2019. *Tracing the Landscape of Dance in Greece.* Newcastle, UK: Cambridge Scholars Publishing.

Sagris, Tasos, Schwartz, A. G., and Void Network. 2010. *We Are an Image from the Future: The Greek Revolt of December 2008.* Oakland, CA: AK Press.

Shay, Anthony. 2002. *Choreographic Politics: State Folk Dance Companies, Representation and Power.* Middletown, CT: Wesleyan Press.

Shay, Anthony. 2008. *Balkan Dance Essays on Characteristics, Performance and Teaching.* Jefferson, NC: McFarland and Co.

Shohat, Ella, and Robert Stam. 2014. *Unthinking Eurocentricism: Multiculuralism and the Media.* 2nd ed. London: Routledge.

Siebel, Walter, and Hartmut Häusserman. 1993. *Festivalisierung der Stadtpolitik: Stadtentwicklung durch große Projekte.* Vol. 13. Wiesbaden: Springer Fachmedien.

Skaperdas, Stergios. 2015. "Myths and Self-Deceptions about the Greek Debt Crisis." *Revue d'économie Politique* 125 (6): 755–785.

Smith, Helena. 2020. "Golden Dawn Guilty Verdicts Celebrated across Greece." *Guardian*, October 7, 2020. Accessed November 20, 2020. https://www.thegua rdian.com/world/2020/oct/07/golden-dawn-leader-and-ex-mps-found-guilty -in-landmark-trial.

Smith-Spark, Laura. 2016. "Mediterranean Migrant Deaths Reach Record Level in 2016." CNN, October 26, 2016. Accessed December 12, 2016. www.cnn.com/20 16/10/26/world/mediterranean-refugees-2016-record-migrant-deaths/.

Sooke, Alastair. 2017. "*Can Athens Become Europe's New Arts Capital?*" BBC, May 9, 2017. Accessed April 8, 2019. http://www.bbc.com/culture/story/20170509-can -athens-become-europes-new-arts-capital.

Stamatopoulou-Vasilakou, Chrysothemis (ed.). 2005. *Archeio Rallous Manou* Αρχείο Ραλλούς Μάνου *[Rallou Manou's archive].* Athens: Efesos.

Standing, Guy. 2011. *The Precariat: The New Dangerous Class.* London: Bloomsbury Academic.

Stavrou Karayanni, Stavros. 2004. *Dancing Fear and Desire: Race, Sexuality and Imperial Politics in Middle Eastern Dance.* Waterloo: Wilfrid Laurier University Press.

Stavrou Karayanni, Stavros. 2006. "Moving Identity: Dance in the Negotiation of

Sexuality and Ethnicity in Cyprus." *Postcolonial Studies* 9 (3): 251–266. https://doi.org//10.1080/13688790600824971.

Stein, Samuel. 2019. *Capital City: Gentrification and the Real Estate State*. Verso Books.

Stournaras, Yannis. 2019. "Lessons from the Greek Crisis: Past, Present, Future." *Atlantic Economic Journal* 47 (2): 127–135. https://doi.org//10.1007/s11293-019-09615-8.

Stratou, Dora. 1966. *Oi laikoi choroi—enas zontanos desmos me to parelthon* Οι λαϊκοί χοροί—ένας ζωντανός δεσμός με το παρελθόν *[Folk dances—Our living link with antiquity]*. Athens: Tropos Zois.

Stratou, Dora (Στράτου Δόρα). 1978. *Ellinikoi paradosiakoi choroi* Ελληνικοί παραδοσιακοί χοροί *[Greek traditional dances]*. Athens: Organismos Ekdoseos Didaktikon Vivlion.

Sutton, Barbara. 2010. *Bodies in Crisis: Culture, Violence, and Women's Resistance in Neoliberal Argentina*. Piscataway, NJ: Rutgers University Press.

Syndesmos Chorou Σύνδεσμος Χορού. N.d. *"About (en)."* Accessed February 21, 2020. Syndesmoschorou.wordpress.com/about-en.

Thornton, Sarah. 1995. *Club Cultures: Music, Media and Subcultural Capital*. Middleton, CT: Wesleyan University Press.

Tomara, Emilia. 2015. "Ena skitso . . . chilies lexeis gia ta nekrotafia tis Mesogeiou" Ένα σκίτσο . . . χίλιες λέξεις για τα νεκροταφεία της Μεσογείου *[One image . . . a thousand words for the cemeteries of the Medditeranean]*. *Kathimerini*, April 21, 2015. Accessed June 19, 2015. www.kathimerini.gr/812181/gallery/epikairothta/kosmos/ena-skitso-xilies-le3eis-gia-ta-nekrotafeia-ths-mesogeioy.

Torp, Lisbet. 1992. "Zorbas Dance: The Story of a Dance Illusion—and Its Touristic Value." *Ethnografika* 8: 207–210.

Tsaousoglou, Apostolos. 2011–2012. *Me lene Vaggeli* Με λένε Βαγγέλη *[My name is Vangelis]*. Directed by Stefanos Blatsos. Aired on MEGA.

Tsintziloni, Stergiani. 2012. "Modernizing Contemporary Dance and Greece in the Mid 1990s: Three Case Studies from SineQuaNon, Oktana Dance Theatre and Edafos Company." Doctoral Thesis, University of Roehampton.

Tsintziloni, Stergiani. 2015. "Koula Pratsika and Her Dance School: Embracing Gender, Class and the Nation in the Formative Years of Contemporary Dance Education in Greece." *Research in Dance Education* 16 (3): 276–290. https://doi.org//10.1080/14647893.2015.1036017.

Tsintziloni, Stergiani. 2018. "Mapping Ballet and Modern Dance: The Case of Athens Festival During the Cold War (1955–1966)" Dance Days Chania Conference: Borders, Boundaries and Margins in Contemporary Dance, July 21, 2018.

Tsintziloni, Stergiani. 2022. *Ypo ti Skia tou Parthenona: Choros sto Festival Athinon stin Periodo tou Psychrou Polemou (1955–1966)* Υπό τη Σκιά του Παρθενώνα: Χορός στο Φεστιβάλ Αθηνών στη Περίοδο του Ψυχρού Πολέμου *(1955–1966)* *[In the shadow of the Parthenon: Dance at the Athens Festival during the Cold War (1955–1966)]*. Athens: Kapa.

Tsintziloni, Stergiani, and Betina Panagiotara. 2015. "A Shifting Landscape: Contemporary Greek Dance and Conditions of Crisis." *The Journal of Greek Media & Culture* 1 (1): 29–45. https://doi.org/10.1386/jgmc.1.1.29_1.

Tzartzani, Ioanna. 2014. "Embodying the Crisis: The Body as a Site of Resistance in Post-Bailout Greece." *Choros International Journal* 3 (Spring): 40–49.

Tziovas, Dimitris. 1997. *Greek Modernism and Beyond*. Lanham, MD: Rowman & Littlefield.

UN (United Nations) Department of Technical Cooperation for Development. 1988. *Fifth United Nations Conference on the Standardization of the Geographical Names, Montréal, 18–31 August 1987. Vol. 1, Report for the Conference.* E/CONF.79/5.

Van Assche, Annelies. 2020. *Labor and Aesthetics in European Contemporary Dance: Dancing Precarity.* Cham, Switzerland: Palgrave Macmillan.

Varvitsioti, Eleni. 2019. "To 48oro pou odigise sta capital controls" Το 48ωρο που οδήγησε στα capital controls [The 48 hours that led to capital controls].*Kathimerini*, September 1, 2019. Accessed February 2022. https://www.kathimerini.gr/econo my/local/1040652/to-48oro-poy-odigise-sta-capital-controls/.

Voulgaris, Yannis. 2008. *I Ellada tis Metapolitefsis, 1974–1990: Statheri Dimokratia Simademeni apo tin Metapolemiki Istoria.* Η Ελλάδα της Μεταπολίτευσης, *1974–1990: Σταθερή Δημοκρατία Σημαδεμένη από τη Μεταπολεμική Ιστορία [Greece in the Metapolitefsi, 1974–1990: Stable Democracy Marked by Postwar History].* Athens: Themelio.

Wickstrom, Maurya. 2012. *Performance in the Blockades of Neoliberalism: Thinking the Political Anew.* London: Palgrave Macmillam.

Wilder, Charly. 2018. *"Athens, Rising." New York Times,* June 18, 2018. Accessed April 8, 2019. https://www.nytimes.com/2018/06/18/travel/athens-after-the-econo mic-crisis.html.

Woodward, Jill. 2018. *"bodies of resilience* (2015)." YouTube video, 9:01. December 14, 2018. Accessed September 19, 2022. https://www.youtube.com/watch?v=WD9v o2eW7G0.

Xafa, Miranda. 2013. "Life after Debt." *World Economics* 14 (1): 81–102.

Xydakis, Nikos. 2013. "Epichorigisi me Erotimatiko apo to ESPA pros Chorotheatriki Omada" Επιχορήγηση με Ερωτηματικά απο το ΕΣΠΑ προς Χοροθεατρική Ομάδα [An ESIF subsidy with question marks for a Tanztheater ensemble]. *Dance-theater*, May 19, 2013. Accessed September 01, 2020. https://www.dancetheater .gr/νέα/item/4607-επιχορήγηση-με-ερωτηματικά-από-το-εσπ.

Yalouri, Eleana. 2001. *The Acropolis: Global Fame, Local Claim.* Oxford: Berg Publishers.

Yardley, Jim, and Elisabetta Povoledo. 2013. *"Migrants Die as Burning Boat Capsizes Off Italy." New York Times,* October 3. Accessed January 20, 2015. www.nytimes .com/2013/10/04/world/europe/scores-die-in-shipwreck-off-sicily.html?_r=1.

Zacharia, Katerina, ed. 2008. *Hellenisms: Culture, Identity, and Ethnicity from Antiquity to Modernity.* London: Routledge.

Zervas, Theodore. 2012. *The Making of a Modern Greek Identity: Education, Nationalism, and the Teaching of a Greek National Past. East European Monographs.* New York: Columbia University Press.

Zervas, Theodore. 2017. *Formal and Informal Education During the Rise of Greek Nationalism: Learning to be Greek*. Chicago: Palgrave Macmillan.

Zervou, Natalie. 2017a. "Fragments of the European Refugee Crisis: Performing Displacement and the Re-Shaping of Greek Identity." *TDR: The Drama Review* 61 (2): 32–47. https://doi.org/10.1162/DRAM_a_00646.

Zervou, Natalie. 2017b. "Rethinking Fragile Landscapes during the Greek Crisis: Precarious Aesthetics and Methodologies in Athenian Dance Performances." *Research in Drama Education: The Journal of Applied Theatre and Performance* 22 (1): 104–115. https://doi.org/10.1080/13569783.2016.1263555.

Zervou, Natalie. 2019. "Emerging Frameworks for Engaging Precarity and 'Otherness' in Greek Contemporary Dance Performances." *Dance Research Journal* 51 (1): 20–32. https://doi.org/10.1017/S0149767719000020.

Zervou, Natalie. (2014) 2019. "Appropriations of Hellenism: A Reconsideration of Early Twentieth-Century American Physical Culture Practices." In *Dancing Dialogues: A Collection of Articles from Choros Intenational Dance Journal (2012–2018)*, edited by Katia Savrami. Vol. 1. Athens: Dian Publishers.

Zervou, Natalie. 2020. "Walking Backward: Choreographing the Greek Crisis." In *Futures of Dance Studies*, by Janice Ross, Rebecca Schneider, and Susan Manning, 397–412. Madison: University of Wisconsin Press.

Zestanakis, Panagiotis. 2017. "Gender and Sexuality in Three Late-1980s Greek Lifestyle Magazines: Playboy, Status and Click." *Journal of Greek Media and Culture* 3 (1): 95–115. https://doi.org/10.1386/jgmc.3.1.95_1.

Zestanakis, Panagiotis. 2020. "From Media Idiom to Political Argument: Uses of 'Lifestyle' in the Early Years of the Greek Crisis, 2009–2015." *Journal of Modern Greek Studies* 38 (1): 209–238. https://doi.org//10.1353/mgs.2020.0010.

Zorba, Myrsini. 2009. "Conceptualizing Greek Cultural Policy: The Non-Democratization of Public Culture." *International Journal of Cultural Policy* 15 (3): 245–259. https://doi.org//10.1080/10286630802621522.

Choreographic Works

Andreou, Katerina. 2016. *A Kind of Fierce*. Performed at at Peiraios 260 during the Athens and Epidaurus Festival. July 31, 2016.

Andronikidis, Panagiotis, and Despina Stamos. 2013. *PASStresPASS*. Performed at Irene Olympic Stadium during the Anti-racist Festival, Athens. June 30, 2013.

Andronikidis, Panagiotis, Teti Nikolopoulou, and Niki Stergiou. 2015. *Rizes [Ρίζες; Roots]*. Performed at Art63, Athens. November 21, 2015.

Argyriou, Tzeni. 2012. *Memoria Obscura / Αφανής Μνήμη*. Performed at Regional Theatre of Grevena. October 5, 2012.

Argyriou, Tzeni, and Vassilis Gerodimou. 2014. *Memorandum—Enas Michanismos Enthymisis Memorandum: Ένας Μηχανισμός Ενθύμησης [Memorandum—A mechanism of reminder]*. Performed by Miguel Pereira, Soledad Zarka and Simon Rummel at Building E. Athens and Epidaurus Festival. June 19, 2014.

Gorgia, Maria. 2012. *Krymmeni stous Elaiones Κρυμμένη στους Ελαιώνες Κρυμμένη* στους Ελαιώνες *[Hidden in the olive groves]*. Performed by Rania Glymitsa at the Athens and Epidaurus Festival. June 27, 2012.

Gorgia, Maria. 2012. *To Stroma* Το Στρώμα *[The mattress]*. Performed by Stavros Apostolatos at Six d.o.g.s., Athens. March 4, 2012.

Gorgia, Maria. 2014. *Sti Trampala* Στη Τραμπάλα *[On the seesaw]*. Performed by Sania Strimbakou and Stavros Apostolatos at Rabbithole Theater, Athens. January 25, 2014.

Gorgia, Maria. 2015. *Stin Akri tou Vatira* Στην Άκρη του Βατήρα *[At the edge of the springboard]*. Performed by Sania Strimbakou and Timos Zechas at Bangladesh, Athens. May 6, 2015.

Goro, Ermira. 2014. *A Quiet Voice*. Performed at Peiraios 260 during the Athens and Epidaurus Festival, Athens. July 7, 2014.

Kallimani, Panagiota. 2014. *Contreplongées*. Performed at Onassis Stegi: Upper Stage, Athens. February 6, 2014.

Kanellopoulou, Athanasia. 2013. *lo(e)verland*. Performed at Akropoditi Dance Center. April 6, 2013.

Kanellopoulou, Athanasia. 2018. *99 corners of a possible self*. Performed by Kanellopoulou Athanasia. Kalamata Dance Festival, Kalamata. July 17, 2018.

Karounis, Yannis, and Malkotsis Ermis. 2010. *Atafoi Nekroi* Άταφοι Νεκροί [Unburied Dead]. Performed at Booze Cooperative during the Athens Video Dance Festival October 1-30, 2010.

Kok, Daniel. 2015. *PIIGS*. Performed by Jorge Conçalves, Sheena McGrandles, Luigi Coppola, Elpida Orfanidou, Diego Agulló at Maxim Gorki Theater, Berlin. March 5, 2015.

Lampiri, Artemis. 2014. *META*. Performed by Flora Kalomiri, Candy Karra, Artemis Lampiri and Ioanna Heitzanoglou at Thiseion Theatre. May 16–25, 2014.

Liatziviry, Chrysiis. 2014. *Efthrafsto Tipota* Εύθραυστο Τίποτα *[Fragile nothing]*. Performed by Sofia Kyriazidou, Yannis Polyzos, Eleni Lagadinou and Christina Sagou at Χώρος Τέχνης 14η Μέρα, Athens. March 3, 2014.

Limnaios, Toula. 2018. *tempus fugit*. Performed by Daniel Afonso, Leonard D'Aquino, Alba de Miguel, Priscilla Fiuza, Alessio Scandale, Hironori Sugata and Karolina Wyrwal at Eastern Moat Theater, Chania. July 22, 2018.

Louzioti, Dafne, Thais Mennsitieri, and Noora Baker. 2015. *Obey, Deceive, Devour*. Performed by CACTUS performance. art. collective at National Gardens, Athens. June 19, 2015.

Michos, Konstantinos. 2010–2011. *Audition* Βάκχες *[Audition Bacchae]*. Performed by Lathos Kinisi. Site specific Euripides Street, Athens.

Michos, Konstantinos, and Antonis Stavrinos. 2014. *Mono* Μόνο *[Only]*. Performed at EMPROS Theatre, Athens. May 31, 2014.

Orfanidou, Elpida. 2015b. *One Is Almost Never*. Performed by Elpida Orfanidou at Michael Cacoyannis Foundation, Athens. June 5, 2015.

RootlessRoot. 2015. *Europium [The end of the world will be better this year]*. Performed by Paul Blackman, Linda Kapetanea, Jacob Ingram-Dodd, Konstantinas Efthymiadou, and Manuel Ronda at Onassis Stegi, Athens. October 30, 2015.

Interviews

Andronikidis, Panagiotis. April 9, 2014.

Antypa, Freda. October 5, 2015.

Dimitrakopoulou, Stella. December 20, 2018.

Falierou, Sofia. October 3, 2018.

Gorgia, Maria. May 2, 2014.

Goro, Ermira. August 27, 2014.

Kerasopoulou, Ioanna. October 14, 2018.

Koliopoulou, Maria. December 12, 2019.

Liatziviry, Chrysiis. March 5, 2014.

Mertzani, Christina, and Evangelos Poulinas. May 28, 2019.

Michos, Konstantinos. March 5, 2014.

Mitsos, Yannis. October 10, 2018.

Mylona, Eleni. October 10, 2018.

Novakovits, Elena. November 22, 2018.

Orfanidou, Elpida. July 10, 2018.

Paraskevopoulou, Ioanna. March 1, 2019.

Pasakopoulou, Martha. December 10. 2018.

Psychogiopoulou, Ariadni, and Angeliki Sigourou. January 16, 2020.

Savrami, Katia. January 9, 2014.

Stamos, Despina, and Jill Woodward. July 5, 2014.

Tsintziloni, Stergiani. January 20, 2014.

Vomvolou, Rodia. November 13, 2018.

Index